# Censorship in Romania

# Censorship in Romania

## Lidia Vianu

Central European University Press
Budapest

Central European University Press
Október 6. utca 12
H-1051 Budapest
Hungary

ISBN 963 9116 09 2 Paperback

Designed and composed by Judit Mihala
in Bodoni 11pt
and printed and bound by
Gyomai Kner Nyomda Rt., Hungary

# Contents

# Preface

Between the two world wars, Romania was part of Europe, considering herself in many ways France's little sister. French was the best-known foreign language, everybody started school by learning it, and many middle- and upper-class families spoke French as their first language. When history turned against them, the intellectuals always took refuge in France, and after the advent of communism many remained there, as did Ionesco, Brâncuşi, Enesco, and Cioran. Many Romanians attended French universities. Our language itself had a French aroma. All our neologisms flew straight from Paris. Today, however, English is foreign language number one in Romania, and most eyes are turned to America.

Until the beginning of World War II, life in Romania was largely what it is trying to become now—closer to Western Europe; with free economy, an abundance of books from all over the world, a freedom to travel if one had the means, a thorough system of education, and a literature of our own. Romania was not an advanced capitalist state; there was much poverty at many levels, but Romania was holding her own. People born in the first two or three decades of this century can easily attest to that.

World War II and the Russian invasion fell like an axe. They distorted and ruined what was in the bud. Starting the war as Germany's ally, we turned against Germany on August 23, 1944, whereupon the Russians marched in. History sometimes plays dirty tricks on people. We were sacrificed, pushed to the outskirts of Europe, and swallowed by mouths hidden behind the iron curtain.

Nobody wanted Romania to turn communist. Although it was later said that a large-scale illegal communist movement had existed in Romania before 1947, that was not true. Soviet Russia took hold of us, and Europe forsook Romania. Since 1947, we have been on our own.

The first elections after the war, free only in name, brought to power a so-called democratic government, the Russian Trojan horse. Once pushed into Romania, it soon led to the forced abdication of King Michael on December 30, 1947, and Romania became a people's republic.

The first president of the People's Republic of Romania was Gheorghe Gheorghiu-Dej. He carried out horrifying tasks, all imposed by Soviet Russia. Stalin was still alive, though not for long. The Romanians set about demolishing everything that reminded the current activists of the former regime. Capitalism was a sentence, no longer a word. It could easily send anyone to prison, and it did. There was some open resistance to communism in the mountains, and covert rejection existed all over the country. Those detected—and most of them were—were ruthlessly imprisoned. Romania had political prisoners who had fought against the Russians (at the beginning of the war), owned large factories or much land, or had taken part in the Iron Guard, a fascist organization. Crowds of people were imprisoned for their past or their present: for having relatives abroad, for uttering a word or a joke against communism, perhaps for being under suspicion of reactionary activities. Double-speak became an indispensable survival tool. Thoughts may still have been free, but uttering them aloud could lead to hell—a hell which, as the regime claimed, was paved with good intentions.When Gheorghiu-Dej died in 1965, capitalism had been totally eradicated in Romania.

The second (and last) communist president was the much-hated Nicolae Ceauşescu. He pushed human endurance to its limits. Under his leadership, Romania largely became a concentration camp. Ceauşescu's initial days were promising, a period of political thaw. For a very brief time, Romania seemed to open to the West, publishing more daring books and welcoming foreigners. Many Romanians were taken in by Ceauşescu's inflammatory speech when the Russians invaded Czechoslovakia in 1968. People started to hope that positive change was imminent. Those who had not sensed the danger were soon awakened to reality by the July Theses, a Communist Party booklet published in 1970, which forbade Romanians everything but the right to breathe.

Ceauşescu devised all possible ways to kill whatever we had. He flattened our public language itself, requiring everyone to use the stilted phrases of meaningless propaganda. He destroyed individual privacy, keeping people busy with work and desperate hunts for food, clothing, and all the other basic necessities. Later he deprived Romanians of heat, electricity, and water. Orwell's narratives seem naive compared to what Romania endured. Worst of all, the specter that rose to stifle all hope, was Ceauşescu's cherished Securitate. It forced us to become deaf and dumb. It crushed us below the level of animals. And yet it also bred an antidote.

We have survived, we are catching up, we are not dead. Seeds flying in the wind, always find soil on which to grow. Romania is in limbo now, making sure that the earlier hell is completely purged. The best mirrors of that process are the writers' minds—which brings us to the reason this book came into being: We all need to see ourselves in perspective, especially after a struggle with death.

For writers, the censorship imposed by communist standards presented a fundamental dilemma. Either they agreed to be silent or their work would not be published. And yet, slowly but surely, creative minds found ways to outwit censorship. It required unusual energy, acquaintances in the right places, and *savoir faire*. A strong bond between writer and reader came into being, and the writer was eager to express what he was not allowed to say. The reader avidly waited for the least hint about how to read between the lines, an art perfected under communist censorship. Censored writers joined hands with censored readers in a dance of bitter frustration.

What was censorship? In simple terms, it meant an enormous "NO." Unless you praised communism, the "new man," and the two Ceauşescus and the bright future of their eternal order, you could not publish. Words, images, ideas, a list of the most unimaginable offenses—all were banned. When a work reached the censor, the writer actually felt that a vital artery had been opened, and he was signing a pact with the devil.

Self-censorship tried to disarm the censor. It was a slow death of the spirit, yet most writers managed to survive. In 1990, when the time came for them to speak freely, after the fall of communism, many experienced a strange writer's block. Some unburdened their souls into journalism. Others waited. Seven years later, a new literature began to emerge. Not all wounds have healed; some writers will never publish again. But others—who preserved their mental freedom or were too young to be affected by censorship or who chose not to publish at all and are only now publishing what they wrote in secret—keep literature alive.

* * *

This book presents the testimonies of writers chronologically, between 1947 and 1990, to show how the three groups reacted to censorship and its aftermath.

The first group consists of writers educated before World War II, who had to learn how to pretend later in life. They learned it well, but kept their innermost freedom. Some still speak the wooden language of imposed silence. For them, our interviews were rather awkward. I enjoyed watching them, and some showed courage in emerging from the Orwellian world unscarred. But this group is small.

The second group includes writers who may have had the privilege of a number of school years under an earlier regime, but who had to start—if possible, to continue—publishing under the communists. They adapted, fell silent for decades, even went to prison or defected. Each choice was hell. This generation most bitterly experienced censorship in Romania. What they say now about the maiming of their speech and their efforts to preserve their sanity is tragic. For those who adapted very well and actually managed to fool—or cooperate with—the censors, one must read between the lines. Compromise is hard to remember and the humiliation of communism should not be prolonged. I am sure that for these writers, our interview was a nightmare in which they expressed themselves as gracefully as they could.

The third group was born under communism. I chose only the rebels, rather than those who could not discover on their own where the truth lay and act accordingly. In our case, this was neither lie nor die, but survive at all bitter costs. Some published a lot and used the famous "lizards"—truths in disguise, which fooled the vigilant eye of the Party. Others became cryptic, and many wrote for the drawer, as the saying goes. They had been so frustrated that the chance at an interview on censorship made them jump with joy and excitement. Freedom was a new, exhilarating experience to them, and they embraced it avidly.

Romanian writers had lived in a concentration camp of the mind, and they have been rushing out of it, amazingly self-assured, as if they had been free forever.

Censorship brought one good thing to literature: as Paul Valéry used to say, any obstacle in front of creation is a true sun. Not being able to say what you think was an excellent school of poetic indirectness, creating its devious writers and its eager readers who were always ready to probe between the lines. The conspiracy of writer-reader was a marvel of obliqueness and dissent at the same time. Literature and politics strolled hand in hand for fifty years.

Read the interviews, read the literature that accompanies them, all published under the rule of censorship, and try not to pass judgment. There may have been mistakes—*Errare humanum est*—when they lied, but their free minds never died. This book is here to prove it.

\* \* \*

I want to thank the Fulbright Program for my fellowship at SUNY Binghamton in 1991–92, which prompted and afforded me the time to write this book. I must also thank Dr. John Hicks, who edited some of the interviews while he was still studying under Professor Marilyn Gaddis Rose; Professor Rose's friendship and support meant a great deal to me.

**Lidia Vianu**

Berkeley, California
Fall 1997

\* \* \*

Publisher's note: all interviews, poems, and short stories were translated from the original Romanian by the author.

# George Macovescu

**born 1913**

*Diplomat, writer, professor: general secretary of the Ministry of Information, 1945–1947; Romanian chargé d'affaires in London, 1947–1949; magistrate of the Ministry of Foreign Affairs, Bucharest, 1949–1952; chief magistrate of the Romanian cinematography, Bucharest, 1955–1959; envoy extraordinary, minister plenipotentiary in the United States, 1959–1961; deputy minister of foreign affairs of Romania, Bucharest, 1961–1967; first deputy minister, 1967–1972; minister, 1972–1978; head of the Writers' Union for many years before the fall of communism; professor in the Department of Romanian Language and Literature, Bucharest, 1949–81*

## The Odyssey of a Volume

These are old entries in my diary that describe the publication of the book, *Walt Whitman—Carl Sandburg—Poems.*

*April 9, 1986.* I have finished translating the collection of poems I selected from the works of Whitman and Sandburg. In the very short preface for the book, which contains one hundred poems, I wrote, "In the following pages, you will not find Walt Whitman as you know him from his famous poems. I searched for him in *Leaves of Grass*. I looked for the poet of spring and flowers, of the prairie and the sea, of the rain song and the ocean howl, of love and friendship, of peace and vital questions, of life and the sadness of leaving it. I looked for him in the depths of his lyricism.

"Carl Sandburg's poems, with two exceptions, were chosen from the cycle *Smoke and Steel*, published in 1920, the song which brought fame to the American poet from the Mid-West."

I have finished the translation, but I have a long way to go until the collection is published.

*June 3, 1986.* The book is already typed. The manager of Eminescu Publishing House promises me that he will do his best to speed up the publishing process. But V.R. is not the only one to decide in this matter. The major obstacles are only beginning to appear.

*June 6, 1986.* The typed manuscript was sent to the publishing house today. I am jotting this down so that I will remember how long it takes for my book to be published.

*June 10, 1986.* In spite of the innumerable promises made on the phone, the publishing house will tell me nothing about the fate of my book. I am beginning to understand this silence. The first "obstacles" from above have begun to appear. I am preparing my soul to be very patient.

*October 6, 1986.* When I called, the head of the publishing house, who was obviously embarrassed, told me that my book of Whitman and Sandburg translations was included in the plan for 1987. I knew that it had been meant for 1986. I must wait. I am patient.

The other day, when a writer told me that his book would soon be out, I retorted, "Don't say that your book has been published until it has been sold!" Sometimes all the copies of a book are withdrawn from bookstores.

I am patient. But it is not the patience of one who accepts humiliation, insult, persecution. It is a patience which stares at the future.

*May 22, 1987.* Considering some incidents that happened to me during the last few years—they offered no explanation when they rejected my film-manuscript *I Can't Love You,* and they give no reason for postponing the publication of my translation—I have the feeling that unless something unusual happens I am writing for later times, for a time after my death. But I am not affected much by this feeling. I would have liked to see my books published, but, faced with ignorance, stubbornness, hatred, vengeance, I forfeit all pleasure and continue to write. Confronted with the written page, I am the only master.

*June 2, 1987.* As a first step related to the fact that my translation has not yet been published—I still have not been given any explanation for that—I have decided to withdraw my manuscript and try some other way.

*June 6, 1987.* One year has passed since I submitted my manuscript to the publisher. So I have sent V.R., its head, the following letter:

> On June 6, 1986, I submitted my manuscript for the book, *Poems by Walt Whitman and Carl Sandburg,* which I selected and translated myself to your publishing house. On June 10, 1986 (I must say, quite soon thereafter. A credit to your organization!), I received the editor's comments for my manuscript and took care of the matter. On June 15,

1986, I returned the manuscript to your offices, and no changes have been suggested to me since then, which means that, as far as the editor is concerned, the book was accepted.

Now, an entire year has elapsed, and my book has not been published. I do not know why. I am an upstanding citizen of this country and a member of the Writers' Union. I also know my rights, which include the right to write and publish.

One does not beg for one's rights; one wins them. Consequently, as a first step, I hereby withdraw my manuscript. Please take the necessary measures to return to me the copy I submitted on June 6, 1986, as soon as possible. It was kept in the drawer for an entire year. That should be enough, even allowing for abuses of power.

Sincerely,

**George Macovescu**

P.S. I will not object to you showing this letter to other people, if you feel it necessary.

N.B. The odyssey of my manuscript will not, in any way, change the personal relationship between the two of us, which has lasted for so long and is based on my respect for you.

**G. M.**

*June 13, 1987.* They called from Eminescu publishing house to say that they will begin printing the book which they had kept for more than a year. But I won't believe it until I see it in bookstores. Experience has taught me to be skeptical. It has also taught me that . . . one cannot beg for one's rights; one must win them.

*June 18, 1987.* When the posthumous exhibition of the painter H. Catargi was opened, I saw V.R., the manager of the publishing house. I said nothing, but he told me that "by the end of the year, my translation will be in the bookstores". I answered, "I won't believe it until I see the last copy sold." I told him that I would not become part of the insidious game played by those who had the power to decide and that I maintained my position as shown in my letter of June 6.

*September 11, 1987.* Today I discussed the technical specifications for my book. I gave my suggestions (size, type face, illustrations, covers, etc.), but nothing was accepted because "orders from high above" require drastic cuts. For most books, the covers are made of the worst cardboard; the paper is yellow; the characters are unclear. No color, of course. The poor technicians are not really allowed to do their jobs as they know how. One ugly book is released after the next, and they will be destroyed so easily. I can hardly believe my memories of excellent printing in this country!

*November 27, 1987.* At last, almost 17 months after submitting my manuscript to the publishing house, I saw the first proofs today.

*November 28, 1987.* I have proofread and corrected the translation. There were not too many mistakes. I re-read the poems by Whitman and Sandburg with the pleasure of having accomplished something, something that could enrich Romanian culture.

*February 26, 1988.* The publishing house has sent me the first copy, which lay in its drawers for such a long time without any serious official reasons. It is not the fault of the publishing house; the "cabinets" and the "kulturniks" are to blame. They are trying to take revenge on me in this way for things I did or would not do. But it won't work.

The small odyssey of a book of translations has come to an end. I wonder if another is to follow.

(Released to me in 1991)

# Maria Banuş

born 1914

*Poet, author: she has published volumes of poetry, along with several works of fiction, and drama; she fought against fascism between 1939–1944 and has translated and anthologized world literature; her poems have been translated into many languages*

## No Ideal in the World Could Justify It

**Lidia Vianu:** Mrs. Maria Banuş, I should like to begin by asking you how you made your debut as a poet, because you are an important poet for Romanian literature, and maybe not enough known to present Romanian critics. Can you help decipher the mystery Maria Banuş?

**Maria Banuş:** It may be too much to say "the mystery, Maria Banuş." It may be too much to say that I am not well known, too. I have been known and widely accepted. But discreetly. If you want to call it a mystery, it can be explained also by the fact that during the so-called obsessive decade, in the '50s, I was too officially accepted. I believed in Marxism and socialism at the time. I was convinced that would bring the happiness of Romania and of all peoples, when we had overcome the fight between classes, the suffering—inherent to the erection of the society we were dreaming of, devoid of exploited and exploitation.

But I gradually learnt the revelations coming from the Soviet Union (the Khrushchev report, etc.). I experienced a long, agonizing emotional and intellectual process. I had become a "good believer." The brainwashing, the stifling of the spirit, manipulation, as it is called now, had taken effect on me.

The process of clearing up, of coming out of the "trance," was slow, agonizing, accompanied by guilt and doubt, by returns to the dogma, the axiom of historical necessity.

**L. V.** What did you feel, when you switched from the way you wrote before the war, to what was written in the Popular Republic of Romania? How did you adapt? You were a writer before 1945. What did you experience when you were compelled to adapt to a new ideology and the necessity to write in a particular way, for a particular level of intelligence?

**M. B.** I will not look upon myself as a victim. I may be a victim of my own genetic inheritance and biographical fate. My contemporaries, intellectuals all over the world, went the same way, only it took them a shorter time to understand that distortion, the abysmal discrepancy between theory and practice, which shatter the theoretical basis of the doctrine.

**L. V.** I suspect the belief in communism was your own choice. You were not compelled to do it?

**M. B.** As I told you before, I do not want to appear as a victim, but I am not guilty of anything, either. The starting point was ethical. I am not ashamed of my youthful revolt, suffering, and indignation, when faced with the social inequality of the world I lived in.

"Crush the cruel, unjust order": this flame of revolt has existed since ancient times to our days, and has been food for religions, faiths, social doctrines, more or less utopian or scientific. My soul found warmth at the same flame of revolt.

I was young. The Second World War was drawing near. Many intellectuals in Romania were lured by the fascist mermaid song. By my ethnic origin, and by education, I could not possibly join the extreme right. Yet I was looking for *absolution*. Mine, of the country, of the world. I was ripe for radical, antifascist, Marxism socialism. I read, I studied Hegel, a little of Marx (too difficult!), Engels, Lenin . . . .

Yes, I felt I had to join in and help as much as I could to find the good days, to abolish human exploitation. Today we can easily see the vulnerable, naive imaginings, in the "end of history," as foretold by Fukuyama. The pink horizon ("give everybody what they need . . .") looked far away then, but we could make it come closer. We did not back up from anything in view of this extraordinary end. Now, decades later, I am forced to simplify things. The complex process of sacrificing lots of aesthetic values on the altar of ideology was not easy. I wrote: "My soul is yours, comrades,/ Yet forgets you/ Alone, in the poem, it climbs down again,/ Under hot leafy tombstones . . . ."

I myself find it hard to understand how that spiritual process actually took place, combining rationalistic Cartesianism—tradition of the Western culture I had grown in— with utopian messianism, garbed in scientific armour.

But the need for *absolution* was the strongest impulse of all. It swallowed, it encompassed incongruities, sophisms, in dogmatic submission *avant la lettre*, even before it was imposed on us from the outside, by the communist power.

**L. V.** Do you consider this to be only your fault, or was it the fault of the public you were writing for, people who had been brainwashed—or, at least you imagined they should have been brainwashed? Was it also the fault of censorship, which did not allow you to publish anything else? Did censorship actually prevent you from publishing anything else? Did you try to publish anything different?

**M. B.** After Stalin's death, after the horrifying revelations of Khrushchev's report, it would have been *logical, natural* for this fog to clear off my brain. But I had become a very good *believer.*

**L. V.** Then, you did believe out of your own, free will.

**M. B.** I was shattered. How can I put this to you? Imagine a good Catholic in sixteenth-century Spain. Travellers coming from the New World tell him about abominable crimes, about the extermination of natives, all in the name of true faith.

Our man is shattered, scared by what he hears. He tells himself: the traveller distorts, exaggerates, turns isolated, inevitable excesses into a general rule.

Christianism can by no means be contradicted by the crimes perpetrated by immoral individuals in the name of faith.

I know my comparison is not perfect. No comparison ever is. I only meant to help you understand. I am also trying to explain to myself what happened to me and other honest people, devoted to the Cause. They only talk now about opportunists, "collaborationists," they say there were no honest adherents to the socialist doctrine, the communist movement in Romania . . . . We were not many, indeed. But we existed. We must not forget that during the years before the Second World War, as well as during the war itself, the opposition to chauvinistic and criminal fascism was closely connected to the communist movement. Most antifascists and communists appeared to many people to be fighting together.

**L. V.** But you also coexisted, afterwards, with the horrors of the gulag.

**M. B.** They were more remote from me than Columbus's America to the Christian in sixteenth-century Spain. My knowledge was abstract, little, insufficient. There is a huge distance between indirect knowledge and concrete, personal experience. I am a townswoman. I always had my small circle of intellectuals, especially leftists.

I wonder: if my father had been a peasant and had been imprisoned by communists for refusing to join a collective farm, what would I have thought? What would I have felt? How would I have reacted?

From within the party, whose old adept I was, I reacted in a totally different way to the ideological pressure I experienced. Now I can say one thing, which would have seemed indecent to me if uttered during the years of dictatorship. During the war, I was part of the group of antifascist fighters, who risked their lives for their beliefs. I did not go to prison only by chance, owing to the courage of some people with whom I had been politically connected, and who, under arrest, though tortured, gave no names. . . . I must confess that the endless, torturing meetings which I took part in during the '60s, and during which I often was violently criticized, since the party leadership required that, poisoned my life, haunted my sleepless nights.

I could not understand. That was the worst torture of all. I did not suspect I was part of a dirty policy, meant to annihilate all intellectual opposition. By all means. Among others, by finding scapegoats within the communist party.

They, I mean we, were supposed to be a clear warning to the outsiders. The separation between subjective and objective— "subjectively, you meant well, but objectively you are against the party and the revolution"—had to be accepted, mentally and emotionally encompassed. Otherwise one could become as mad as a hatter, drowning in the absurd.

This was my concrete, daily experience, which wrung my nerves, marked my existence, as a woman, as a writer. Where was my lucidity? Had I ever had it? I had lost it on the way, anyway. The Soviet Union was the fortress of peace. We belonged to the side of the "righteous."

**L. V.** Was it also the side of the privileged?

**M. B.** I was obsessed with the nightmare of a third world war. I wrote long, enthusiastic, romantic, rhetorical poems, which called for friendship among peoples, for peace and love ("America, I Am Talking to You," "At the Gates of Heaven").

In the '70s, the revelations of the communist genocide became more and more numerous and frightening. It was an agonizing time for me. I left my old beliefs, and found another way of viewing history, the place and use of poetry, social and aesthetic problems.

**L. V.** I understand it was not that simple.

**M. B.** Alongside with this prolonged ethical, social, aesthetic torment, existential themes penetrated into my poetry, the "eternal" themes of life and death, of fate. . . . I did not hide anything essential. I went as far as one could speak and write under dictatorship, during the last three decades, before December 1989.

My experiences, the changes in my thinking and emotions, were obvious in my interviews, articles, and in my poems, especially. The volume *I Was Just Leaving the Arena*, 1967, was the crucial moment of my departure from what had been, the poet's return to the eternal uses of poetry. By use I also mean usage, language. I talked, I wrote about my obsessions, but during the long, agonizing, agitated meetings and debates at the Writers' Union, I was "quiet as a swan." Any criticism seemed to me—was I right? was I wrong?—useless fretting. The law came from "above," and the abuses could not be stopped.

**L. V.** What about your privileges? Did they stop? Were they affected by self-censorship?

**M. B.** Like any genuine Romanian writer, I did fight censorship. It was not an easy fight. But it became even harder when they decreed that censorship had been abolished. The heads of the dragon multiplied. The monster grew out of all proportion, diffuse, hard to detect.

Previously, when censorship was official, openly there, you found on the manuscript the signs for what could not be printed. The editor of the book told you, too. He would say, "Look, this can't be published, for this or that reason." Sometimes, very seldom, the supreme censor himself would see you. You tried to convince him that your intentions, your ideas were different from the meaning the small censor, his inferior, attributed to them. Rarely, of course, you happened to win. But, at least, it was pretty clear: this is O.K., that is not. You made a compromise, he made another. . . . You gave up a line. He allowed the poem to pass.

The moment censorship was abolished, the first huge obstacle was the editor of the book. The publishing house was his living. If you persisted, he could be left without a job.

I had inserted a few articles about Eugène Ionesco in my prose volume *The Chimera*. Only, a short time before that, he had made I don't know what political assertions. For the time being, he was *persona non grata*. The volume could not be published if the horrendous name was not taken out.

I tried to reason with several levels of censorship, which was supposed to have disappeared, by the way. Nothing doing. While the book was being printed, praising articles about Eugène Ionesco were published again by our press. Within a few months, he had become persona *grata* again. This is just one example, out of thousands.

**L. V.** Was self-censorship worse than before?

**M. B.** It existed, to a certain extent. It was part of us. It was a victory over yourself when you could ignore it. When you could write freely, without compulsion or tricks, what in the depth of your conscience you felt had to be brought to light.

Here is an example out of the many possible instances, a poem, a short dialogue, *Encounter, Afterwards:*

> "What's on your hands, my little girl?"
>
> "Blood, father. I have played.
>
> They killed me. I have killed."
>
> "The ugly game."

Any reader understands that I, the author, have not killed anyone, in fact. That in the huge historical tragedy I felt responsible, because I had considered myself to belong to the side of the "righteous," when, as a matter of fact, ideology, changed into state power, had made millions of victims in all socialist countries.

It was my self-criticism, if you want. I had lived in a tower. Not the ivory tower. A tower soiled with innocent blood. We are back again to the question of abstract and direct knowledge; the relationship between means and aim. No matter how much dialectics I may have studied, from Socrates to Hegel, I was wondering anxiously: how large or solid could the pedestal of crimes and suffering be, the pedestal on which (according to dialectical materialism) the monument of the sublime aim would be erected? "The Ideal City." What was taking place was unacceptable. No ideal in the world could justify it.

My conscience, educated in the spirit of European, Judeo-Christian ethics, could no longer bear a discipline, a militant's duty, which had not been correctly understood, in fact. I had to sever my ties. Like the four million Romanian citizens, I also became the owner of a party identity card which meant nothing any more. Member fees were written in there, no more. Alongside with most Romanian writers, I chose to oppose the political pressure we were subjected to by means of my works. It was natural that a poem like *Encounter, Afterwards* should not have pleased censorship.

But, the same as inside the Securitate, censorship was divided, and sometimes we benefitted from that. This is my explanation that such poems could however be printed in my volumes or other poets' books, during the last two decades of Ceauşescu's dictatorship.

**L. V.** So, you broke your ties, and thus your work gave up this ideology. Did you turn into a dissident? Do you still believe in communism? Maybe it was not well put into practice? At least, this is what your fellow poet, Nina Cassian, states.

**M. B.** I hate the labels so often used under the communist dictatorship. I do not write visceral poems. Yet, I believe that, in my poetry, at all its stages, spontaneity and genuineness have been most important.

When I write, I do not debate with myself on an intellectual, aesthetic or political level, whether my poetry is modern, modernist, postmodernist. . . . Whether I confess or I am interested in social matters. I do have ties with the movement of ideas and the contemporary currents. I have crossed so many currents! Not in vain, though. They all enriched my poetry. I am sure I have used much of what the avant-garde brought new— surrealism, for instance— but I did not really subscribe to any current. I am a lonely bird. Yes, something of the kind . . . .

I am a whole, made up of my existence, my social views, my aesthetic views. This self sometimes becomes poetry. Moods, ideas, images, metaphors, parables. The parable was more often used during the years of dictatorship. But, after all, poetry does not name things like speech. Consequently, it has an easier fate than fiction under dictatorship, because fiction is more direct. Except oneiric prose, which is the sister of poetry.

**L. V.** There came a time, then, when you stopped believing in communism.

**M. B.** I was against it, of course. I shall never claim I was a dissident in what I wrote. You know the joke about those who wanted to benefit from what they had done of old, during the dictatorship. They were supposed to have been illegalists, more or less. The joke said: "We were so few, and so many of us are left." *À rebours*, this is what happens now to the former dissenters of communism. Many people want to profit by past "merits." I have never wanted a position, now, at my age, even less than ever. I do not boast about it, though. It is not a quality, maybe. It might be a defect, in fact. The same as my shyness in social connections. In the literary world, friendships are important for a poet's creation.

I am thinking of Nichita Stănescu. His friendship with Matei Călinescu, until the latter left the country, was certainly good for his philosophical and poetic education.

I have lived like a snail in its shell and it has not been good for me. I am proud, though, as a poet, and I suffer when I am forgotten. Surrounded by silence, indifference or hostility, I feel . . . you can imagine how I feel . . . I feel I am stifled. I am experiencing this again, now. I should like to believe this is because of this period of transition, because I am afraid of developing a persecution mania . . . .

I suffered a lot when literary critics in the '70s and early '80s received my first volumes after the "clearing up" of my poetic sky with coldness, or total unwillingness to understand. I could understand their displeasure when faced with a poet who had largely been published and appreciated officially in the '60s. I was happy when their attitude changed, and I mean especially the most important personalities of Romanian criticism: Nicolae Manolescu, Eugen Simion, Ovid S. Crohmălniceanu, Lucian Raicu, Dumitru Micu. Then there were Georges Emmanuel Clancier, Alain Bosquet in France. It is a great incentive to write if you know you still exist in the conscience of critics and poetry lovers.

**L. V.** What are you writing now?

**M. B.** I am experiencing a hard, confusing time. Not only for me, of course. I am part of a large group of poets, here and in all ex-communist countries. It may also be a poetic stasis for me. I have never been very productive as a poet, or very disciplined in the act of writing. . . . Silence, feeling of aridity. Experiences accumulate in the meanwhile, and become poetic. The time of eruption in the poem comes then . . . .

I should like to hope—it may be wishful thinking—that at my age of 80, which is almost here, it will be the same again.

**L. V.** Retrospectively, as a poet, do you feel that your historical fate, the history you have crossed, has helped you, or do you feel it was a tragedy, which maimed your poetical power?

**M. B.** It is not easy to become aware of one's limits, of one's power of resistance to spiritual drugs. But it is a necessary thing to do, in order to regain lost lucidity.

As I was telling you, healing was not sudden. In fear and humility, I realized that for a quarter of a century I had only been an atom in the ocean of the *social imagination.*

The perverse, very well orchestrated technique of putting minds to sleep, and making them believe the most incredible lies—such as the well-known trials (Political trials, in which intellectuals were accused because of their beliefs and most often imprisoned. After 1945, they were organized by the communists.) in 1938, till those in the '60s—worked on me, too. I really believed. I forced myself to believe, lest I should betray the Revolution.

Beginning with the early '70s, their drugs lost effect. I returned to *dubito ergo sum,* and I found my lost poetic self.

**L. V.** An abandoned creed and a reborn poetry?

**M. B.** Speaking from a human point of view, at a certain time (especially in the '50s) I had an ethical advantage. I could not separate my fate from that of my fellow human beings. I wanted a better fate for everyone. I overcame my fear of prison, torture, death. From this point of view, I lived more beautifully, less selfishly . . . .

Aesthetically speaking, of course I was maimed. A large part of my vitality and poetic strength were wasted. But does that matter, if we consider now all the victims of the communist system? What darkens the end of my life is not that I took part in my youth in the greatest utopia of our century. What embitters me is what this utopia has become in reality.

**L. V.** This would be a very effective end for our interview, but I have come here devoured by the curiosity to see how the poet Maria Banuş whom, in my childhood, I did not read, because I hated patriotic poems, coexists with the same poet after 1970. I have been told how the stages followed each other. You told me very honestly how you adapted and re-adapted. Allow me one last question, if you will answer it: do you consider you are only Romanian? Is there another range of problems in your soul, which, I must say, I found expressed in some of your poems?

**M. B.** Undoubtedly. I am a Romanian Jew. Poems like *Pogrom,* or *My Ancestors,* quite well known, translated in many volumes of mine, very impressive for the readers, testify to this.

We Jews, whether Romanian, Czech, Polish, Russian, or whatever else, are divided, schizoid, schizothyme natures. . . . It is an uncomfortable situation: being both inside and outside a community. But, with a French word, the position is also *enrichissante*. In your inner world, you feel enriched by a complex, very special experience.

It is enough to wonder: "Can the person who's talking to me so kindly although he or she doesn't know me, be aware that I am a Jew? If he were, would he behave in the same way?" It is enough to experience this, and such incidents are repeated many times during one's lifetime, to make you feel Jewish all over and convey this to your descendants, genetically.

My parents are what is known as assimilated Jews. My grandmother still made the prayer on Friday night. I can see her even now, a veil on her head, in front of the lit candles. My mother fasted once a year, on Yom Kippur. In the courtyard of the prayer house, I stayed with the children, inhaling the sweet smell of quinces and nutmeg . . . .

I learnt religion and history of religions from my nice high school teacher, an Orthodox priest, from the Bible, which I reread over and over again, or from Mircea Eliade and other histories of religions and mythologies. In the early 40's, I was a student at the Bucharest University. I had nice fellows, we were all friends. I sat in the same desk with one of them. I told him, "I am a Jew," and he moved a few desks farther away.

It is true, they did not beat me. Boys were beaten. When my debut volume, *The Girls' Country*, came out, it was very well received. But venomous voices criticized it, here and there, and mocked at my Jewish origin.

When you are young and hypersensitive, discrimination, injustice hurt a lot and stigmatize forever. Humility and pride grow together. You learn how to live with your inner contradictions. You are an intro- and an extrovert. Humour and tragedy. Sarcasm and sympathy.

My education is Romanian and cosmopolitan, mainly Western. My religion is cosmic and poetic ecstasy, the privileged moments when you are immersed in the unique, infinite whole. Is this agnosticism?

Great God, I do not know you, I cannot encompass you, my mind is too small. You are endless . . . I am alone, weak, lost in confusion. I need a father, a warm, kind breast, where I can lay my head in despair or suffering. I say, like all the others: "God help me." When I am hurt or am afraid, I utter in my mind, "Our Father, who art in Heaven, hallowed be Thy name, Thy kingdom come, Thy will be done, on Earth as in Heaven. . . ."

My mother taught me this prayer . . . I knelt next to my bed and said it at night, before going to sleep. Is it Jewish? Is it Christian? Judeo-Christian, like the whole spiritual world wherein we were born. This is my own imagination, too, the only effective peace maker.

November 1992

# Poetry

### The Cycle

After I have learned everything very well:
figures, beings, objects,
I stop.
I am left like the village idiot,
watching the smoke.
I have forgotten everything.
There is a cave ahead.
If I step down.
I find a meadow.
I graze. I am a horse, a lamb,
and I discover the blade of grass.
I step down again,
I stretch my tree roots
inside sticky clay.
I step down again.
I wait. I wait inside  myself.
A stone.
Light trembles around.
I  am beginning to understand from the other side.

### It Will Be Nice, After All

It will be nice, after all,
we shall have ever whiter, more numerous and newer hospitals,
better and better equipped,
for ever more numerous, more interesting patients,
all many coloured,
and we will have more and more TV sets
for more and more convalescents,
so that they may enjoy themselves,
because we shall have more and more pastimes
for those who are bored,
and we will have more and more reasons to be bored
for those who enjoy themselves,
and we will have more and more noise
for those ill with too much quiet,
and enough quiet for those who—
and we will have more and more sex
and more and more cache-sex,

and we will have more and  more soul
and more and more cache-soul,
and it will be nice, after all.

## Clothes

Clothes, give me clothes
for SOMETHING,
old beautiful clothes, to cover
SOMETHING, the much feared void.
Take out of the wardrobe,
out of the drawers of childhood,
or the storehouse of the big theatre,
angel clothes.
Remember, the one who comes in April,
holding a willow branch,
growing from his large, floating sleeve
which covers the much feared void.

## Procession

We shall lift this huge stone
and take it
and it will be our child
our old man
and we shall rock it
and it will be our home
and we shall carry it
and it will be God
and we shall carry him
with his grave
with his cradle
we shall lift this huge stone
and carry it.

## He Tells Us Nothing

He tells us nothing,
lest he should scare the child inside us,
who plays the game of life,
and splashes with his palms,
he likes the sound of splashing,
and laughs face towards sundown.
Whatever I ask, he answers

blankly, "Play!"
And hides behind common words,
behind bars of cloud.

## One of the Games

Sea games.
A group of untanned tourists
ordered about by their guide
play the following game:
six couples volunteer
six paper rolls are brought,
the six young men
start wrapping
from head to foot
the six young women
using the six paper rolls.
"Faster, gentlemen", the guide shouts,
"he who finishes the MUMMY is the winner."

The six mummies are perfect at last,
stiff, well wrapped,
and so fast, that you can't tell who the winner is,
but the illusion is unbelievable.

## We Shall Get Well

We shall get well, we shall
we shall hear and see again
how the water drips from the eaves,
the greenish metal cock will shine,
as our first totem shone.
We shall get better soon,
get rid of the yellow, worn out bandages,
and smell again,
and taste tears and salty water.

Thus I lie to my old, trusting soul,
I promise it a transparent day, in Eastern blue,
and it kneels down and believes the lie
and however strange it may seem,
a young, hesitating animal
shakes its mane, it is born.

## I Must Say

I must say
how the rooms bloomed, unseen;
how white and fresh the street was,
like the parting in the hair of a loved one;
and how the kid frisked and quivered;
how it is all gone.

When, heavily, like a bear,
life climbed down from a black den,
she embraced it, and pressed it, pressed it.
The shell broke. Night went out.
And the soul of the moon, its secret yolk
sadly, how sadly dripped down.

## Song to End

I am tired. I am with myself.
They hanged me in the darkness, as if I were an ear ring.
Somebody said: you, colt,
then: you, rose...
I am tired of myself like an ear ring,
and I am afraid of everything, of the years
with thick bee humming.
What is the blood saying now, what?
"Sleep, Maria, sleep well."

## Darkness Fell

Darkness and truth fell.
Bees are coming back.
We come back burdened,
from wherever we went.

Ashes and weeping are in the air:
pity us, who come back!
We come back with honey, but where are now
the sweet hives we worked for?

A scream scatters our savings:
no more entrance in the hive!
We are denied the huge body,
we were torn from. . .

## Tide

Sing the tide, Maria,
sing it now, when it overwhelms,

call it now, when it falls,
sing the wave falling.

Tremble, blade, be happy;
the rain will start pouring,
the sky is dark with water
restless water.

Fear, body, fear!
You know what comes after the quake.
You slide blind inside the house,
as in a forest.

Tremble, blade, and obey.
How much fretting can there be?
The dark arms will rescue, drop you,
down, in the depths.

# Ion Negoiţescu

1921–1992

*Literary critic: defected to Germany in the mid-1970s and continued writing there until his death*

## The Freedom of Expression is the Salt of Culture

**Lidia Vianu:** What do censorship and self-censorship mean to a literary critic?

**Ion Negoiţescu:** Just like Henry de Montherlant during the war, I believe that censorship can sharpen the writer's/critic's mind by making him strive to cheat it. With an allusive style, you can sometimes make the public see it. You can "expose" it, while winning the approval of the readers who know what it is all about. Anyway, it is much better without censorship, because the writing process is free to pursue any train of thought. The freedom of expression is the salt of culture.

Self-censorship is even more dangerous than censorship itself, because it can struggle free from the writer's critical mind and act subconsciously, falsifying the message. For example, under the pressure of censorship you avoid treating certain topics, certain authors, while being positive (no hypocrisy implied) that these topics and authors are of no interest to you, when, in fact, you are afraid of censorship and try to avoid facing it. In this way, even if it is correct, the critical act, though very honest, diverges from its natural path and, because of that, the critic's creative power is diminished.

When faced with communist censorship, I never wrote—nor was I forced to write—the opposite of what I thought. Those who did so, did it at their own expense. I have never been a Marxist; I have never used the words "Marx" and "Marxism." Some use them only to hide non-Marxist ideas behind these words. But, on the other hand, I was forced to express my opinions somewhat discreetly, or even to keep silent regarding certain topics; but I have always been careful to keep my true thoughts unaltered, though confined to the area allowed to us.

**LV.** Did you feel the effects of censorship on your own texts? In what way?

**I. N.** Censorship was, generally speaking, "ideological," but it could be very subjective, such as when the censor's personal reputation was at stake: he liked some authors, disliked critics, was a sadist and was also loyal to the terror of the system. There were also censors who were too conscientious because they themselves were afraid. The encounter with the censor could also become a deal: "I'll change or give up this statement, but leave that one unchanged." A clumsy, often awkward game, a true battle, between giving in and holding one's own. Some of my texts were rejected entirely, or first published as they were, and then when I wanted to reprint them in a collection, I was required to change them. A collection of critical texts previously published in various reviews (*Aladdin's Lamp*) was destroyed as soon as it had been printed, and my collection of translations from Lichtenberg's *Aphorisms* was withdrawn from bookstores and public libraries because the author was considered "reactionary." (Was it ignorance? The author was a representative of the Aufklärung [Enlightenment])

After I had defected ("forgotten to return home," as we used to say), all the books I had published were, of course, withdrawn; my name was forbidden.

**L. V.** Did censorship alter your sphere of interests and your desire to write?

**I. N.** During the period of acute socialist realism (1948-1955), I willingly did not publish anything. Between 1958 and 1964, after I had been "exposed" as anti-Marxist in *The Spark,* I was arrested and jailed. In the late seventies, freedom of creation seemed to be returning within the communist system. (It was relative, but true.) Poetry, fiction, aesthetic criticism (using the new methods known in the West) had come back to life. I wrote and published a number of books and was always present in the literary press, either with my own texts, or with reviews of my own books.

As long as the acute, or even the milder socialist realism had lasted, my interest in writing was considerably weaker; this interest was, paradoxically, reborn while in prison, where I had no pen or paper. It may have been because I felt I had to fill the time that passed unspeakably slowly, somehow give it substance. In prison I "wrote" poems in my memory and conceived the structure of a *History of Romanian Literature.* When I was released, I hurried to write down everything I had written in my mind, with an enormous and systematic effort of memory. The poems and the "plan" were soon printed, but nobody was to know that they were the product of my years in prison.

Here, I must distinguish between the various stages of censorship and their consequences. During the first stage, the period of acute Socialist Realism, when I gave up writing, I read only those books which would be useful to my future activity. There was always the hope that the reign of the absurd would some day cease. I read more, mainly philosophy and theology. Yet I made plans: I planned a monthly literary journal and tried to work on it with some friends. Then I compiled an anthology of "classical" Romanian poetry, including poetry from its beginning until 1945. It still, to this day, has not been published; it may have been lost. Finally I started writing again. I wrote the essay "Eminescu's Poetry," which was published in 1968. I typed ten copies and spread them around (aesthetical samizdat!). At my trial in 1961, where I was sentenced to five years in prison and all my "belongings" (manuscripts, books) were confiscated, a copy of this essay was used as evidence.

**L. V.** Did censorship ever discourage you or prevent you from writing? Could it have made you give up writing altogether?

**I. N.** I experienced moments of deep depression and was very discouraged. I even attempted suicide after the July Theses of the Party, in 1970, when I was subjected to interdictions and public persecution again.* Those persecutions found me in full critical activity and seemed to be worse than the interdictions during the period of Socialist Realism when I willingly withdrew from the field of publication, but I hoped (vainly, perhaps) that things would change soon. This return to severe censorship destroyed all my hope because I had learned from my experience under communism that one can never be too sure that alternating terror ("turning the switch" on and off) is not part of the perverse "logic" of the system, its sadistic and firm logic. Suicide meant, in fact, the extreme and fatal decision of giving up writing. When I left prison I had the feeling that I would no longer be able to adjust to freedom, that I would not be able to write again. Later, I simply did not want to write. But, because of the effects my suicide attempt had on public opinion, the officials were alarmed and allowed me to publish a few books which they had rejected before. Resurrection after three months of hospitalization did not produce a renewed desire to write. I started writing well again only after a few years of exile, at last finishing, though far from home, my old project of a *History of Romanian Literature*.

**L. V.** How did you manage to publish and what were the chances for an unknown author? What was one supposed to do to see oneself in print?

**I. N.** When I was a teenager, still in high school, during the bourgeois regime, I made my debut as a poet in local magazines. I was helped by editors or people who published in Cluj, Transylvania, where I lived. During my last year in high school, I published some essays in a weekly newspaper which was run by my philosophy teacher. My first book, a surrealist "novel," was published in 1941, at my own expense, when I was a college student. In 1947, I was awarded the prize for "young writers" by the Royal Foundation publishing house, for a volume of criticism which was to be published the following year. But it never was

---

*The 1970 July Theses of the Romanian Communist Party was a booklet of principles and norms that were meant to perfect the process of brain washing of the whole population. They claimed to help the formation of the New Human Being (the perfect communist)—L. V.

published because Romania became a communist state and the Royal Foundation disappeared. It was not until 1966 that I was able to publish another, a quarter of a century later.

**L. V.** What are your memories of the corruption which ruled the publication of books during the totalitarian system?

**I. N.** I never found myself in the position of bribing editors or heads of publishing houses, but I understand that bribing was common.

**L. V.** How would you characterize your reaction to the falsification of culture by the totalitarian system?

**I. N.** By one word. Horror.

**L. V.** Can you ever forget the hatred for the lies and slogans you experienced as a pupil or student, when you were least prepared to defend yourself against indoctrination?

**I. N.** Because I graduated during the bourgeois regime, during the regime of the freedom of thought, I was spared this.

**L. V.** What tricks did you use to cheat the censors?

**I. N.** Speaking of the censors from the so-called Press Direction, I did know two persons who valued good books; they had been educated in the bourgeois society. I do not remember having too many difficulties because of the Press Direction, which was in fact official censorship. I did get in trouble with the Council of Culture, though. They hated me because of my nonconformism, and they tried to find fault with everything in order to delay or prevent the publication of my books. There, I was taught lessons of righteousness and false advice. A few heads of publishing houses liked me; others rejected me. One of them even did both, depending on the "ideological breeze" coming from the Council of Culture. All of these point to the complexity of communist censorship, known for its shrewd hierarchy. During the war, under military dictatorship, there was just one censorship, with very permissive local centres. I could, for instance, talk in favour of Jewish writers.

**L. V.** Is censorship one of the reasons why you left the country?

**I. N.** It is, of course, the main reason, next to the general atmosphere, in which cowardice and basic private interests supported the injustices of the communist system.

**L. V.** Do you think that Romanian culture is democratic today? Has the literary taste, the public, had enough time to forget communist rules?

**I. N.** In culture, in the world of cultural creators, the results of democracy are seen today. Writing is free: anything can be said. But this new, free culture was created by those who oppose the communists who still rule the country. Now, the officials censor them economically. Selling books and papers in the country has become very difficult. The enormous increase in the price of paper is downright prohibitive.

**L. V.** How do you view the future of Romanian culture? What will be printed? What will be read? How will we live in the near future? Do you trust the young people to have the power to change the horrible habits of the generations of activists?

**I. N.** The near future is fairly uncertain, vague. The fact that, in the past, there was no ample, organized, widespread opposition is followed today by the political confusion and moral disarray of Romanian society. Confused, young intellectuals prefer to emigrate, rather than fight to establish a new atmosphere. The writers who, during the communist dictatorship, thought that the most efficient way of opposing the communist regime was to retreat into the ivory tower of literary creation, far removed from any political unrest, today run the risk of losing their audience and means of creative renewal. I think that Romania appears to lack a respectable identity to most of its citizens. In the chaos and poverty prevailing now in my country, society finds it hard to get its bearings, without which there can be no progress. In Romania we can observe a fatal chasm between creative intellectuals and the rest of the population. And for the time being, I see no way of bridging this chasm, especially if we take into consideration that within this framework there is room enough for radical nationalism.

**L. V.** To what culture do you think that you belong now?

**I. N.** I feel that I belong to that Romanian culture which was created by writers who lived abroad for a long time, such as Titu Maiorescu and Lucian Blaga. Throughout all their works, Maiorescu and Blaga strove to view Romanian realities with Western eyes and not to interpret the West in Romanian terms.

**L. V.** What was your reaction when you switched from repressing truth in Romania to the Western freedom of expression?

**I. N.** My hopes were too high, and bitter disappointments inevitably followed.

**L. V.** Is all literature which was written in Romania during censorship bad?

**I. N.** Romanians are gifted enough. Consequently, when Socialist Realism weakened in the late '70s, Romanian literature returned to life in a spectacular way. Many enduring works were written, especially poetry and criticism. I even witnessed interesting new modalities, which continued the good literature written between the two world wars. However hard it may have been for them, Romanian writers have kept in touch with the modern West, as is clearly seen in the works of fiction and criticism produced by the younger generations. Even during the last years of Ceauşescu's terror, some remarkable books came out, totally alien to the mentality of the regime.

**L. V.** What do you think of the authors who made compromises with the system in order to be able to publish? Could one publish without compromising?

**I. N.** The writers who enjoyed social and material advantages because they supported the communist regime have been punished by the aesthetic faults which undermine their works. One could publish without compromising if one accepted that one would be pushed to the margins of society and fight censorship if one took risks for the sake of culture.

**L. V.** Do you think that it is correct to consider that literature should not have anything to do with politics, as many people do?

**I. N.** No, I do not. By "literature" we must understand writers as citizens, not their works. Political opposition, which is manifested in the press or the opposition parties, can help Romanian society heal. Consequently, the works can go their way, following criteria other than those of day-to-day life, but, as citizens, writers must do their duty to immediate reality.

November 1991

# Vera Călin

**born 1921**

*Essayist, translator, professor of comparative literature: she has lived in Los Angeles since the 1970s*

## Romania Is Not Yet Out of Chaos

**Lidia Vianu:** How did censorship affect authors and texts?

**Vera Călin:** In communist Romania, censorship affected authors and texts in a variety of ways. It prevented the publication of anything that was not considered "useful" to the regime. It eliminated anything which could have been interpreted as hostile or alien to communism and Marxist ideology, and especially anything which could have been taken as irreverent to the person of the dictator. Furthermore it affected authors and texts by adding a word here and there or a sentence intended to neutralize something that might have sounded ambiguous or could have been interpreted "the wrong way," or to emphasize something that did not sound explicit enough. The obsession with "the correct line"—be it political, national, aesthetic—was a reality every writer had to live with.

**L. V.** How would you explain self-censorship?

**V. C.** Self-censorship, which I consider far more devastating for a writer's creative process than censorship, is, ultimately, an induced mechanism of self-protection. The fear of seeing one's text mutilated or rejected would make a writer unconsciously use a more cautious or, for that matter, more explicit expression; he would avoid anything which might strike the censor as inappropriate. It all begins with the writer's satisfaction at smuggling a few heterodox ideas into his text, in a way which makes them look inoffensive, or at altering the subtext so that it might escape the censor. Eventually, self-censorship distorts not only the process of writing, but also the process of artistic thinking as well. It becomes an intellectual and emotional brake, automatically functioning in the psyche of a preconditioned individual.

**L. V.** Did you ever see communism as a rescue from fascism?

**V. C.** During the war and the Nazi dictatorship, many people—especially Jews—faced two alternatives: Nazism or Communism. For some representatives of the intelligentsia—Gentiles and Jews alike—the precedent represented by many avant-garde movements, which were mostly politically left-oriented, was also important. Ignoring the horrors of Stalinism—the purges, the gulag, the exposing trials—became a process of self-delusion which was necessary for survival. Or as a Jew pragmatically put it, "Stalin killed indiscriminately, so there was a chance for a Jew to escape. Hitler singled out all Jews for extermination."

**L. V.** Did you experience any animosity because of your Jewish nationality?

**V. C.** As far as I am concerned, I think that the answer to all the questions concerning my Jewishness might be a paraphrase of Sartre's statement, "Being Jewish, just like being old, does not necessarily depend on what one feels, but on what others decide."

**L. V.** Could you place the censorship you experienced in Romania in the context of similar phenomena in world literature?

**V. C.** The censorship I experienced in Romania was not fundamentally different from that functioning under any other dictatorship: Nazism, Italian or Spanish fascism, etc.

**L. V.** What do you think of the writers who thought that it was better to compromise and publish than to be silent and in prison?

**V. C.** The question of the moral superiority of the writers who kept silent over the others sounds somewhat simplistic to me and cannot be answered globally. There were areas of culture which almost escaped censorship. That is why Preda's *Moromeții*, Nichita Stănescu's poems, Călinescu's *Bietul Ioanide*, etc., could be published. Of course, it all depended on whether it was a period of freeze or one of thaw. As far as criticism is concerned, writing about Elizabethan drama or, for that matter, French neoclassicism, was almost safe. Besides, being silent would not mean imprisonment for a writer. Many writers chose to be silent or made a living translating the classics. Ion Vinea, for instance.

**L. V.** Do you agree with the idea that literature should no longer have anything to do with politics?

**V. C.** In my opinion, Romanian writers should now feel free to write about whatever appeals to them.

**L. V.** Do you keep up to date with Romanian literature? Was all of it bad before? Is all of it good now?

**V. C.** I have remained in touch with Romanian literature ever since I left Romania. It was not hopelessly and globally bad before the "revolution," as I tried to demonstrate before. As for the present, Romania is not yet out of chaos. There is a severe shortage of paper over there. The publishing houses, which have mushroomed recently, are commercial enterprises; they are interested in satisfying the requirements of very questionable taste. It is too early to pass judgement on Romanian postcommunist literature.

**L. V.** Was censorship one of the reasons you left Romania?

**V. C.** Censorship was only one factor in a very complex sequence of circumstances which made me leave Romania.

**L. V.** Which culture do you feel that you now belong to?

**V. C.** America is a multicultural land. It is the country of pluralism, par excellence. I cannot unhesitatingly say that I feel integrated in a specifically American culture. Things might have been different if I had settled on the east coast. I prefer to say that, after fifteen years of American life within the framework of American cultural pluralism, I am still culturally European.

November 1991

# Ştefan Augustin Doinaş

**born 1922**

*Poet, essayist, translator, editor: he has published sixteen volumes of poetry, five books of criticism, and thirty major translations; he served as editor in chief of the literary review titled* The 20th Century *and as director of the foundation by the same name.*

## Censorship Distorted Consciences

**Lidia Vianu:** What do you understand by censorship in Romania?

**Ştefan Augustin Doinaş:** In my opinion, censorship means falsifying or forbidding the free expression of thoughts and feelings. It was exercised in Romania during the entire period of Bolshevik totalitarianism in two ways. First, it was a state institution, with clerks who read the texts and decided what was acceptable to the Communist Party or what lay outside the party line. Whatever lay outside the line was removed from the text. Sometimes there were administrative consequences, or even social and political ones. The author could be fired or put on trial. He could even be sent to prison. Official state censorship, enforced by employees, became increasingly more organized during the forty years of communist dictatorship.

Escape from this dictatorship was possible at first, when it was more strongly rejected than later, because people were used to expressing their thoughts freely in the previous regime, and they felt as a personal offense any attempt at reducing their personal freedom.

This censorship was exerted on the texts. That means that, on the one hand, it affected all publications. On the other hand, it affected all books that were published. Consequently, it functioned on the ministry level, censoring publications, and on the level of the publishing houses, censoring the publishing houses themselves. Of course as far as the recent years are concerned, editorial censorship began and functioned on three levels. The editor who read the text was required to be the first censor of the text in question. The director of the publishing house, or some other high-ranking person in the hierarchy of the publishing house, had the responsibility of censoring the text a second time. And, finally, the third censor was the official censor, who, as I said, was paid for that purpose. In special cases, it sometimes happened that an adjunct of the Minister himself, such as the sinister Mihai Dulea (formerly a very powerfu censor), would ask to read and work on certain manuscripts himself.

The second kind of censorship, which, in my opinion, became a very insidious, shrewd way of violating people's thoughts and reducing their freedom, is self- or inner censorship. Under the pressure of outside forces, menaces, extremely varied risks— whose variety depended on particular day, age, or person—the author found out that he was afraid of saying certain things. Being afraid, he censored himself. He forbade himself to say things which he knew would be objectionable to the censor.

In my opinion, this was a very serious matter. It was part of the brain-washing required by the process of creating a new class consciousness, for forming what we used to call the new type of human being—the goal of all utopias, but especially that of the communist utopia, which set about doing just that with very adequate and refined instruments. I had a colleague who exposed this reality to Ceauşescu himself in 1973, if I am not mistaken. His name was Bakonski. During a meeting at the Palace of the Republic, as it was called—previously named the throne hall—he said, "I have nothing against the state institution called censorship. It is an honorable institution, so to say, like all other state institutions. It is not my right to define its use. But I strongly object to everything connected with what we call the institution of inner censorship. When the censor takes root in my conscience, it has become very serious." Of course he was silenced at once, rudely enough, but in a tone and manner that Ceauşescu had at the time, namely reassuring all of us that no administrative measures would be taken against my colleague. Indeed, that did not happen.

**L. V.** What were the concrete results of this double censorship which was exerted upon everything written in Romania during those years?

**Ş. A. D.** As long as only external censorship was exerted, by the state institutions, we experienced what was called the dictatorship of socialist realism, when we can say that Romanian literature was almost strangled. Few valuable works appeared during this time. To say nothing of the fact that even our great writers from the past were censored and forbidden. When Gheorghe Gheorghiu-Dej fell, and Ceauşescu succeeded him around 1968, the year of the greatest freedom our genial leader was able to bestow upon us, things changed for the better. There was almost no censorship at all.

During a meeting with the Head of State, at a conference of the Writers' Union, when, among others, I also objected to censorship, Ceauşescu went so far as to announce the dismantling of censorship. In fact, he had merely changed the name of this institution. But he could not abolish the inner censor, which lived quite comfortably inside our very brains. I remember that during that meeting, due to some of my colleagues' indiscretion, I did the following thing in order to plead against censorship: in my speech, I referred only to poets. I quoted excerpts from books of poems by some five or six persons which had been issued at that time. Those poets gave me those books with their blessings, and for all their poems they restored the lines which had been removed, or changed back what the censors had made them modify. I read the true versions of those poems aloud, and the audience was terribly amused, though there was much bitterness in their joy, of course. What came to light was ridiculous, grotesque. The changes required by the censors were really horrifying. It was a kind of terror exerted on thoughts, especially on clear and articulate thoughts, which expressed ideas that could be dangerous. They tried to destroy those vital knots of imagination where power stems from. Images, metaphors were censored. Why? Well, they knew what they were doing. It is well known that lyrical expression, more than anything else, is an ambiguous mode of communication. An image which seems to represent a part of reality always says more than that. So many theories have demonstrated beyond doubt that poetry is and states only what we mean it does say when we read it. It was natural that the censor would be as cautious as possible and try to leave in the poem only one, unambiguous meaning. The censor sought a language which would communicate only one thing at a time, the same thing, in fact, over and over again, and even with determination, if possible. Plurisemantic language was changed into an obvious one, which was meant to obey and serve as propaganda. Of course all poets and fiction writers understood the mechanism. All creators understood their pledge very well. Consequently, our literature began to flourish the moment it discovered the so-called aesopic language.

**L. V.** Was that a literary code? Do you mean the so-called lizards?

**Ş. A. D.** Prose writers began creating extremely significant pieces of fiction, perfectly applicable to our situation, but they took precautions, so that they could always argue, "Well, I did not mean our present situation. I just wrote about this or that ancient myth which says there is a plague in Thebes. I do not mean that there is a plague in another city or society." They prepared demonstrations of justification such as that in their minds. This was especially true for poetry, I would say. It is true that those few years of freedom made our contact with Western poetry and other parts of the world easier.

Consequently, the propagandistic poetry of the 1950s was radically different. It changed when new generations of poets appeared. I am a member of this generation; I belong to the generation of 1945, but I did not start publishing until after 1962. My first book was published in 1964, although I had published poems ever since 1939. So, the language of poetry became aesopic. After renewed contact with Western poetry, our poetry became more and more difficult, more cryptic. This was very difficult for the censors as well because they found it increasingly difficult to make a pronouncement about this text or that one. First of all, they did not understand the texts. In fact it was not really a matter of understanding. One does not understand poetry; one has a certain type of sensibility which can devour poetry. But the censors, of course, did not possess that. Many poets wrote in this manner, and I think that this mode of expression was mostly used in poetry.

Something else happened also. In the meantime, it was realized that a series of writers had become celebrities due to their works. Public conscience was somehow marked by the fact that communism could not be achieved without the aid of writers. The writer was a public figure; he appeared on radio and TV and acquired social prestige, so to say. When this happened, censors began discriminating. Certain writers were very severely censored, while others were allowed to do whatever they wanted. I must confess that I often benefited from this discrimination, finding myself on the favored side. The censors were unable to censor my poems.

**L. V.** What about the young poets?

**Ş. A. D.** They were the real victims. That is why a time came, during the last years of Ceauşescu's reign, when young literature was simply strangled. Especially poetry. That meant that no more young writers were accepted into the Writers' Union. The decision seemed to have originated with the horrible Elena, and many of our fellow writers in the Union very rigorously enforced her wishes. I found it incredible that anyone would have been willing to do so.

Despite all that, I would say that, except for the decade of the '50s, which were the years of horror, Romanian culture could not be strangled by censorship. On the other hand, we can say that the saddest of all things happened: inner censorship appeared. Because of this, a lot of extremely gifted writers, whose names I will not mention, failed to express their thoughts. Not so much because they were forbidden, but because they did not have the least amount of courage to be sincere, did not have the courage to be honest about their own substance, what was more valuable inside of them, what had to be expressed if they wanted to be what they were entitled to be.

On the other hand poetic language became more refined because of the same kind of censorship. I know that this subject has been discussed ever since the czars in Russia. Back then, people used to say that the goal of censorship was to teach the writer to become more intelligent and refined. So that the censor would not have to change a word of what he had written. It is not very different from what happened here. Lyrical poetry became occult, hidden, as it was trying to avoid the murdering eye of censorship which was watching. I really do not know if that was a real and great advantage for our poetry, but I do know that the aesopic language was good, because it brought us all closer to the essence of poetry, which is plurisemantic language. Each of us found his or her own way of expressing thoughts without being detected. It is also true that many of us had to take risks. The main risk was that, in my mind, I was positive that I had said what I had meant to say, but objectively, the text did not convey those things. I had squeezed them into a kind of understatement. When the reader approached my text, he could not go back on my tracks, nor could he reach the same conclusions I thought I had expressed, because, as a matter of fact, they were not there. In fact, my text did not attempt to hide anything. I had and still have friends who are literary critics and who are intelligent enough to be able to talk about this openly with me. We talked about this aspect many times. Could this or that text be accepted by the censors? It very often happened that my friends would say, "This text is perfectly acceptable. It contains nothing that might be dangerous." It did not contain what I had thought it did, then.

Such was the risk taken by a person who wanted to be obscure in his writings, to be difficult, who wanted to offer texts which would have to be decoded. Those writers thought their inner reality was automatically transferred into verbal expression. Well, language is a forbidding medium, which has to be fought fiercely, and whose results are, more often than not, uncertain. Secondly, language is a living body itself. It speaks for itself, expresses itself, and we cannot always master it. Quite often, it is language which masters us. Because of this, a lot of things could remain alive which inner censorship could have killed, because language often independently expresses some things that we are afraid to say.

Of course, today, when we read these texts after a while, lots of texts from that period may lose the meaning they had then, *illo tempore*, and no longer be incentive, or at least insinuating, as they seemed to be at that time. The reverse may happen as well: texts which did not seem to be the least bit subversive back then, may appear so now. This is all very natural. There exists an unwilling expressivity, noticed by a reader coming from a long time during which expectancies and tastes have changed, and this makes the reader read the text in a different frame of mind than at the time when it was written. It can happen the same way to a text written in the '50s or '60s, which is read in a completely different way in the '90s. In general, I think that communist censorship did not succeed in strangling Romanian culture, except for the last few years. But it did manage to falsify a number of works and writers to some extent. As far as the writers are concerned, this is a much more serious question. Very gifted writers were trapped by power, so to say. It happened either for the sake of some official jobs which they coveted, or because of their weak natures, when they became something they had not wanted to become, but could not stop the course of events, so they kept being promoted, step by step, towards power. You know, from a certain point down, anyone who has some personal power is turned into a slave of the highest power.

That is why, today, we can name some—though not too many— great creators whose works are tarnished and whose personalities are often doubted, whose force of character and behavior during that entire period is debatable. With the exception of some very shrewd, wicked years, when they made it a point not to let anyone go untarnished, when everyone was supposed to be involved in something that would prove loyalty to the party—except for those years when the official power tried to tarnish all of us, the process I have already mentioned took place. That is, one was more or less ignored once one reached a certain level of cultural authority. He was asked to participate, but even the least pretext was enough to discourage them. This is the reason why I think we must blame our colleagues who held high offices or enjoyed some prestige and agreed to praise Ceauşescu. It was not really obligatory to do that.

**L. V.** Was there no real pressure?

**Ş. A. D.** Security agents could call your home to require what they wanted you to do, but they could do nothing to you if you said, "No." There was pressure and blackmail. But, in fact, nothing happened if you simply refused. You were not fired. You were not tried or imprisoned. Your tires were not slashed at night.

**L. V.** What was the most evil effect of censorship?

**Ş. A. D.** The most obnoxious effect of censorship was that it ruined one's conscience. It mutilated the creative spirit of some very gifted people, the main damage to Romanian culture. Those who still possessed some courage could publish their works almost, if not exactly, as they had been conceived. There were also people who knew that a price had to be paid; after writing a very conformist book, they published one which expressed their true feelings. I think these people had a true awareness of their value, and a certain force of character, though a bit elastic and wavering. But they did what they felt they could at that moment.

Until open dissidence came into play, this is how things worked.

**L. V.** Do we have a way back now? What is left after censorship? Which way should we go?

**Ş. A. D.** I was affected by self-censorship: I compromised. In the '60s, I could publish only if I paid the price. In 1957, I was imprisoned, and after my release I was exiled from cultural life for five years. From social life, too. I could not publish. This lasted until I wrote a certain kind of poems. I was lucky because culture found a greater degree of freedom soon afterwards, so I could stop writing like that. I could escape from what I had been compelled to accept.

**L. V.** How many years were you in prison?

**Ş. A. D.** Just one, 1957. But to return to what is taking place now, we live in an age of more than freedom. "Libertinage" is what I would call it. Everyone does what they want, but no great work of art has appeared yet. This freedom is not as good for us as it seems. We spend our energy on insignificant things. We get involved in politics, perhaps because we were forced, and in fact forbidden, to do that, to do it properly, I mean, according to our convictions and conscience. This may be the reason we find it so hard to sit down and write. Everyday life weighs on us. At the same time, we must also lead a cultural battle, at the level of book-writing, a battle I would term the unfair competition of a certain type of literature, which is not at all stimulating. Our literary market has been invaded by the literature produced between the two world wars: sensational, idyllic, licentious, pornographic . . .

**L. V.** Do you also take into consideration here the uneducated audience?

**Ş. A. D.** Yes. Obviously our audience is uneducated. Some readers have chosen this literature for which it had longed. The audience which was faithful to the rest of us has been changed by the present conditions all of us now experience. No one is interested in our literature now. People look for those things which mirror historical events: memoirs, diaries of ideas, of the war or of prison years. These things were forbidden here before the revolution. Communism did not let us know anything. This new kind of book bars our prospect a little. In order to survive, our newborn publishing houses have agreed to this and hastened in that direction. I think this will take some time. The pessimists say that we will witness the strangling of culture. The first decades of the next century will be almost devoid of culture. Culture is on its way out. Unless it finds some shape which we can not foresee, specific to the time we are in. All these things are uttered by people who dare predict the future. The death of culture has often been foretold by philosophers. If Hegel really had been right, we would have been at the bottom of the pit by now. Consequently, I am a well-tempered optimist. I believe that culture will survive anyway, of course after having survived a serious crisis. It will survive because man is a complex being and part of him is eager for values. Man will always need the values of culture.

July 1991

# Poetry

## Within a Poem

    it is however a noise which is promoted to the rank of language
by the noises which survive with the gag in their mouths:
    things which, by means of the meaning bestowed upon them now,
will reach victoriously a presence and an appearance
    beings which, living in air, water and fire, announce
simultaneously the splendour of these elements to which they belong
    woods with crooked arms in the wind, which show people how to
shatter their handcuffs
    people who confess to the gods how alien they feel on this daily
offended planet
    this is the drum patter made by the soft feet of the lines as they
climb the dumb customs

## The Making-Up Lesson

allow me to make you up
beloved face
dear aunt Hope!

first
a thick
*fond de teint*
after the fashion of the century which is coming to an end

when did these lively eyes
go blind?

two dark eye circles
will make them petulant again
on one cheek
the same inherited beauty spot
constantly erased by a few Fathers Superior

You know
today the weary face is in fashion
the red cheekbones

a hair pin at the corner of the mouth—
and the question: how will you smile?
is solved

the too austere cut of the face
will be softened
by cotton balls

like a smoke and shade cloud
we also
soften the stubborn chin

here you are—
now climb up to the rostrum
with a cheerful air
see—the crowd acclaims you
frantically and makes waves
like the grass

come on, aunt! hurry up:
before your beard
grows

## The Icy Psalm

fists as big as jugs
I beat my chest
I strike
as if at the butcher's gates
and I scream:

the wall of tears is daily
erected, isn't it?

this country was the
promised land
once, wasn't it?

me, praise?!

yes—
this is my share
indeed
keep your lips sealed!

with the wheelbarrow of humiliation
carry
to the threshold of your senile
god
this first and last
disgusted
psalm of mine!

## Dig On, Dig On

a cloud comes from the direction of the sea and passes in vain
the chalk in the eye the sand in the throat
                                        barren
age of prayers trains us to wait
daily invented adders amuse us
with their whistle
                    ashes fall down on bells
look—the sublime poured in the glass is dry
film stars cut out of books embellish the windshields

so dig on at peace: a common grave is
always useful
                    don't lose it—take care!
like a gag too early stuck in its mouth
                                        History
oho! is ruthless with such carelessness
another cloud is coming from the direction of the sea
and passing in vain

## Adrift

sour sea—sea like urea
greedy sea:
as if Korea were welcoming us!
has time spat us out into space?

mad day—day of a long seige
day when we row on galleys:
as if the Middle Ages were engulfing us!
has space lost us among its ages?

terrible night—starless night
night when fears grow fat:
up on top of the mountains the back of my country
has accumulated exhaustion in a hump

my God—if we knew a place and moment
no matter how small, but full of pride!
my mouth spits out gall—with horror
the bones are shouting in their coffins

# Nina Cassian

**born 1924**

*Poet, prose writer: defected in 1985 and now lives in New York; she has written forty books of poetry and two of prose*

## I Dream of Belonging to the Global Culture

**Lidia Vianu:** How much did censorship and self-censorship affect you? Do you still believe communism is a good philosophy? Did you ever give in to totalitarianism without realizing how bad it was? Would you say you were a victim of your belief, which in turn came as a consequence of your being a Jew and fighting or fearing fascism? Do you agree that, now, after 1989, Romanian literature should no longer have anything to do with politics? Did you write anything political under communism (for or against it) and in the United States? Do you consider yourself a fighting poet? Were you ever the target of anti-Semitism? What culture do you think you belong to now?

**Nina Cassian:** Your questions are so closely connected that I cannot answer each in turn. I will refer to them globally, running the risk of lacking a certain consistency.

I will begin with an autobiographical sketch. As the preface to my book of selected poems, *Life Sentence*, released in 1990 by Norton & Company, points out, I joined the illegal communist youth movement in 1940, when I was sixteen.

It was war time. Fascism was strong. But I must honestly say that my being a persecuted Jew, deprived of all rights, menaced by pogrom and deportation, was not the main reason for my choice. What appealed to me was the wide scope of the "Charter" of communism, which included the gradual abolition of all bloodshed and antagonisms in the world. Antagonism between the sexes and among races, peoples, nations, classes, etc. They were all sources of massacres, oppression, and inequality. I thought it possible that wars, states, money might disappear in a humane society. This would ensure the harmonious evolution of the individual: free from discrimination, ruled by fundamental moral and cultural values. It is well known that other minds who were more mature than a teenager such as myself embraced such generous ideals. Much wiser and more experienced minds such as Koestler, Brecht and Sartre, to name just a few, fell into this orbit. First rank creative sensibilities such as Eluard, Esenin, Eisenstein, Maiakovski, Lorca, Picasso, Ristos, the surrealist leftists from Breton to Buñuel, and many others, from all over the world, devoted their energy to this . . . utopia? . . . aspiration? . . . hope? . . . humanist theory? . . . faith? . . . or whatever other name may be attributed to it.

Of those whom I have mentioned or omitted, the majority has seen its spiritual edifices crumble as the oppressive systems began to act concretely, starting with the one in the Soviet Union, spreading through the countries of Eastern Europe. Some committed suicide. Others denied their former beliefs. And still others kept their faith inactive, hoping that history would rehabilitate itself . . . .

Early in my childhood, during the war and the first two or three years after it, I considered myself part of the avant-garde, that is, a "revolutionary in both life and art!"

My poetry was modern, iconoclastic, somewhat explosive, enjoying complete freedom of imagination.

Between 1945 and 1947, we witnessed surrealistic exhibitions in Romania. Surrealistic poems and books were published, and it indeed seemed that a happy era was starting. Yet, in 1948, the Iron Curtain fell not only on the political and social structure of the country, but on the cultural field as well.

I will mainly concentrate on my own experience.

My debut book, *Scale 1/1,* published at the end of 1947, was literally executed in three consecutive articles published by the main Party paper, *The Spark.* I was accused of elitist expression (which implicitly meant "despising the people"), of modernism (which was related to bourgeois decadence), of evasionism (basically of refuting "new realities").

The tone of those articles was brutal, menacing. The book was cremated, and its author, though not murdered, not even arrested, was morally persecuted for over a decade.

No matter what I wrote, I was still accused. I tried in good faith to change my style, to reduce the field of my imagination and vocabulary in order to be "understood by the people" (which in fact implied a subtle disdain for the people, but then I was not aware of that at that time, when I believed that the Party always had to be right). I had not yet struggled free from the rotten influence of Western art, that could be felt in my writings in spite of all my striving, my bourgeois education, etc.

All that was written at that time was considered *political.* Therefore, everything was either friendly or hostile to the Party. Censorship was exerted not only on the themes which were in fact few in number: the fight for peace and against imperialism, work contests, praise of the Soviet Union and especially

Stalin, of course, odes to the Party, etc. It was also exerted on "style." Love poems were forbidden. Love was a private matter, not a general concern. Metaphors had been banished since they were frivolous ornaments. Assonance was not "favorably regarded," nor was free verse or anything that differed from the official, stereotyped formula whose tone was declamatory, pompous, or merely flat and simplistic.

My beliefs were dealt blow after blow. I found it impossible to understand how free verse could be incompatible with the Party's policy, or how metaphors could endanger the future of mankind. Gradually, I became aware of the essential perversity of the devices they used. They attempted to crush our personalities (and art itself, as a manifestation of personality) in order to create an amorphous, easily handled mass.

My mood became more and more conflictual as I noticed that, in the midst of the golden ideas I had once cherished and the surrounding reality, the Party had interfered as a sinister force: it fraudulently called itself "communist." By all means possible, from demagogy to terror, it had become the absolute ruler of an important part of the human planet.

Of course the process entailed much more than that. It included the whole society, not only the minority of art-creators, but I could only generalize from my own experience.

My system of reference, my criteria, the ideals of my conscience got sick with doubt, indignation, stupor, and fear. They were deeply menaced by the totalitarian lies, by the physical and mental cruelty that dominated our lives.

Around 1953, my "milk source" dried up. For about two years I could no longer write; during this time I composed music.

Around 1956, a kind of timid thaw began. Again, its roots were in the Soviet Union. In Romania we said, "Love was set free," which meant that it started to be accepted. After completing some musical pieces, whose language was mysterious—if not impossible for the censors to decode—I returned to the literary scene. I did not resume the inspiration of my debut. Who knows what my poetry would have been if it had developed "normally"? It might have had a certain genuineness and freshness about which we could not have even dreamed during the previous years.

Censorship continued to operate with varying degrees of intensity. I had got into the habit of comparing it to Brâncuşi's Infinite Column, a repetition of tensed and flexed segments. During "milder" periods, true literature began to breathe freely. Important young poets appeared. They were born in a more favorable age with a destiny less tortured than mine. As if after long, exhausting forced labor, the supremacy of politics was at least amended—if not abolished—and often avoided without the danger of possible consequences.

We must, however, state that the political dimension has at all times been attached to the work of many great poets, among them Horace, Dante, Shakespeare. I do not condemn this political dimension; I only react to the abusive demand that it should replace all the other categories and be turned into clamorous propaganda and forgery.

During the demagogical years when Ceauşescu's reign was just beginning, a certain relative freedom of creation was apparent, and it seemed impossible that we would ever return to the previous aberrations. Yet in the early '80s, Ceauşescu showed his true colors, by trying to bring back the creation of works which were devoid of artistic value, works which were conventional, falsely patriotic, imbued until suffocation with praise of the leader and his wife. But the mechanism of freed creation could no longer be stopped. A kind of parallel literature arose. On the one hand, there were the official, ridiculous and shameless books. On the other, the creation to which "nothing human was alien," even showing more or less obvious rebellion against the regime, religious feeling, the fantastic side and other directions, which had formerly been unthinkable.

This paradoxical situation implied also a kind of manipulation. Writers accepted that they had to co-exist peacefully with the rulers, wanting to create without having major changes imposed upon their works, although they did not hesitate to object publicly to the increasing decay of the economy, of thought, morals and behavior on many occasions.

No wonder, then, that writers were persecuted. Fewer and fewer books were published, and those that were published were published in smaller and smaller numbers of copies. Authors received poor royalties. No additional printings were allowed—even for bestsellers. Photos of authors were not allowed on book covers. And the like.

In this polluted atmosphere where chauvinism and anti-Semitism, cold and darkness, in addition to material poverty were accompanied by the daily ration of absurdities, the result of the leading couple's paranoia, I can safely say that at least between 1966 and 1985, when I left the country, I take responsibility for all the books I published and for my civic attitude.

Now that there is freedom of speech, what will happen in Romania after decades of oppression, perversity, and exasperation? Some privileges will inevitably be lost because of the radical social changes. The market economy is coming into play. But I could hardly predict how the writers' creative potential will react. For the time being, most of them are frantically involved in politics.

I do not consider myself a fighting poet like Byron, but, undoubtedly, I have fought for my ideas and my ethical beliefs in my works. And I will continue doing just that. In Romania or America, wherever I may be, I dream of belonging to the global culture, not just to one small part of it. This is not arrogance; it comes from the fact that I was fed on it and owe everything I know to it.

I apologize for the brevity of these notes, which have neither the seriousness of an essay nor the charm of a more biographical narrative.

As far as my own future is concerned, I do not want too much. I would just want to be like Kleist's hero, who "except for the sadness caused by the general misery of the world, felt well."

December 1991

## Poetry

IF I TAKE TWO STEPS, I AROUSE A TURMOIL OF INSECTS.
They lie buried deep down, in the entrails of grass,
sucking summer's juices, moving short lines—their bodies,
the candid insects and the predatory ones;
I take a step and the ground is moist with insects,
and I take one more step and I am clothed in insects
from sole to thigh and waist,
I wall myself in their stable, enduring flight,
in their hard work, to help them change me
into a statue of insects, a humming pillar
in memory of summer...


LOOK, BITTER IS THE WATER,
the fish swell and burst
and float, ugly and gloomy,
like the bowels of a fabulous
animal which has burst.
Bitterness, next to our lips.
Disgust, next to our bodies.
Our present, ever more remote.


Nobody Cares
about the need of the fish to drink pure water
and about our need
to feed the world with seven fish.
This is the day when it stinks
of corpse, in water, over the land
—a sign that our carefree age is over.


EVERY DAY THE SAME DECISION: FROM NOW ON . . .
And "on" keeps moving on this side
and "now"—has already been.
The shadow of the orange rose

is the same colour as the shadow of the white rose
against the whitewashed wall, which, at the end of some day,
accepts them.
The sun sets,
and I decide: from now on . . .


THE RABBIT WHICH INVENTED THAT SCREAM
to stir the hunter's pity—
but neither the hunter, nor his dog
ever gave up snatching
its body, like a fur glove,
still warm after having been worn—

the rabbit, which invented no more than a scream
stronger than its frame,
to enter death with it,
the rabbit, which has no other image
about solemnity, except its rending,
ridiculous scream...


WITH A THIN PLATINUM PENCIL,
the moon underlines the horizon.

But I lied.
The moon's daughter is a liar.
When it is cold in the world,
a streak of light is not enough
to underline our existence.


NOT ABOUT LOVE.
I will not find refuge
in the cowardly syllable: you,
I will remain among species
rare and odd,
sentenced to slow death
because of inertia.

## Innocent

You need not be guilty
in order to be punished.
Look what happened to the flower:
it had hardly bloomed, pink among leaves,
and the huge animal came
and blew an insult over it.

## The Dagger

I can't understand why that man
follows me with his hatred
I have not harmed him.
Our children have never fought.
We never had a lovers' quarrel
or one caused by wealth.
And yet whenever I go down the street,
that man points at me
and shouts: "Kill her!"

That man scours towns and villages
and says he can't live
because of me.
"You will see", he says, "how she will pull down
the house I mean to put up
and will kill my cattle
and will dirty my manger".

I have never harmed him.
But once, long ago,
that man tried to kill me
and, although it was night, I saw
his horrible face
and a long, sharp leaf,
glittering in his hand.

## Idyll

It is strange how charmingly
death approaches me:
it anoints me inside and out
with sweet disgust for life
with tender lassitude

it takes me farther away from myself carefully
separates me from my skeleton
spreads my flesh all over
so tenderly

that I feel like weeping.

## If I Had Died in an Earthquake

Whom do you want to hold in your arms?
I was a little girl, I was a little boy.
I grew up out of childhood
too tall by a head,
I entered youth with a shoulder that was too small.

And when I reached the golden proportion,
a movement came
a lead movement
—what can I say . . .
The poet would say: I am a beautiful memory.

## Dedication

If the flesh is disappointed
(rather crushed, hacked)
the spirit stays, the green alcohol
of the fruit I was.

Read my book and get drunk
on the fragrance of my flesh.

## Morning Gymnastics

I wake up and tell myself: I am lost.
It is my first thought at dawn.
I start my day beautifully
with this murdering thought.

God have pity on me
—that's my second thought, and then
I get out of bed
and live as if
nothing had happened.

## Horizon

There must, however, be
an area of salvation.
Sad are the countries
which do not touch the sea.
Gloomy the people
who do not touch what is outside them
to flow into immensity.

## Thrillers

The cylindrical, the spherical witness,
and it is enough for everything to fall into the dark,
for the jurors to forget their lucid opinions
and nobody knows any more
who killed whom,
who will kill whom
and the sentence is postponed *sine die*,
in eternal confusion.

Only the victim and the murderer know for sure
whose part is which, from the first to the last act.

## Fable

They cut one of the angel's wings.
However, try to fly, God said,
however, try to fly,
even if you are not graceful,
the aesthetic point of view does not matter here
what matters is only your ability to master your unbalance.
It is an experiment of mine with angels.

Well, then.
The angel fell
through light and bitter  cold.
With burnt feathers,
his only wing
hung powerless.
Still burning with speed,
much later, he alighted
on the roof of a house.
His feet, hand, face
were all blood.

People looked up and said:
"Here's a stork".

## Poetry

A graphite path starts from this pencil
and a letter, like a dog, treads down it,
and here is a word, like an inhabited town
where I may arrive tomorrow.

# Petre Ghelmez

born 1932

*Poet, editor, journalist: he has written eight books of poetry and seven books of children's literature*

## Censorship Is a Tension

**Lidia Vianu:** How would you define the writer's attitude toward censorship?

**Petre Ghelmez:** Censorship has always existed and will not disappear. It is a tension of various degrees, hidden or open, but constant.

**L. V.** Do you mean that a work of art cannot exist without censorship?

**P. G.** Oh, yes, it can. The work exists outside censorship. But censorship tries to shape it somehow. There is a censorship of habit, for example. Considered in connection with our habits (and our everyday life consists of innumerable habits!), the work of art is a kind of anti-habit, something totally new, an exception, completely original in thinking and feeling. The banal punishes the work at once! For example, I do not know how cave men reacted when standing in front of the paintings at Altamira, Vieja, or Lascaux 3,000 years ago. But I can guess that some, if not all, were opposed to them. And I wonder whether the tribal "chief" or his "magus" would have been happy to find himself painted on the walls of the cave, as supreme hunters of the largest bison! The middle class of the cave might have wanted to be there also. . . . Every middle class wants that!

**L. V.** Is that a joke?

**P. G.** Not at all. . . . Centuries have passed, but habits have remained the same. They have even got worse . . .

**L. V.** Such as?

**P. G.** Well, let's consider something more recent. In the sixth century A.D., if one was named Procopius of Cesarea and wanted to write a history of the wars of the Byzantine empire under Justinian and Theodora, one realized that one could not tell the whole truth about the two emperors because one's life would be in danger. So one wrote secretly, for posterity, a biting addition to the wars, which one actually entitled "Secret History."

**L. V.** So, when the pressure of censorship is felt, writers write for the drawer, right?

**P. G.** Sometimes, but that is only partially true, because the writer is a living organ of communication. He needs to communicate with his reader. Otherwise he cannot breathe.

**L. V.** Censorship stifles him?

**P. G.** If it can. . . . But fortunately, when confronted with great artists, censorship has always been powerless.

**L. V.** Has it?

**P. G.** Yes, it has. If, for instance, you lived in France in the eighteenth century and wanted to criticize French society, you could not. The eighteenth century had its own kind of censorship. Each century has had it. But if you wanted to criticize French society, and your name was Montesquieu, that's a totally different matter. Then you write *Persian Letters* and have the two Persians, Rica and Usbek, express your thoughts as violently as possible, and you get away with it. In the same way, if you lived in eighteenth century England and wanted to mock English society, censorship prevented you. But, if your name was Jonathan Swift, you could write *Gulliver's Travels* and your goal was reached. If you were Cervantes in Spain, you could write *Don Quixote*. If you were Gogol in Russia, you could write *Dead Souls*, and so on . . . .

**L. V.** What about Romania, during Ceauşescu's censorship?

**P. G.** You mean Romania during totalitarian censorship, after World War II, right?

**L. V.** Right.

**P. G.** Then, if your name was Nicolae Labiş (1935–1956), you wrote a book of poems symbolically entitled *Fight Inertia* while everyone else was writing dogmatic, proletcultist poetry. You went through a lot of trouble before you saw it in print—you even died in the meantime—because the censors kept asking you what you meant by "inertia," what you were hinting at. You might answer, or those who came after you might say, that you meant "the principle of inertia" in general. Of course the censors mistrusted you. But you, or those who came after you, keep saying that the very essence of the "new age," which was supposed to fight inertia, suggested that title to you. Finally the book is published. And the readers understand that this inertia characterizes their "new age" itself! Thus, communication, the major goal of the act of writing, has taken place.

If your name was Marin Preda, and you were extraordinarily gifted and wrote a long, dense novel entitled *The Most Beloved on Earth*, and in it you showed the atrocities of a former "obsessive" decade (as we call the '50s) in Romania's history, it was unbelievably successful because absolutely everyone felt that the evil in the book, and the suffering there, were, in fact, their own. They are very much present.

Metaphor, this wonderful vehicle of the human spirit, carrying deep and multiple meanings, is the secret, unvanquishable weapon of the writer. During these years, I have seen fantastic shows on Bucharest's stages, in which Shakespeare, Molière, Gogol, and Caragiale mocked monstrous realities in other places and other times, which every onlooker felt was his very own. We must admit that this was sometimes possible because of the censors' complicity . . . the censors are human, too, after all . . . .

**L. V.** Now, tell me what you can do when your name is Petre Ghelmez, and you want to publish poems in the 1950s.

**P. G.** It is hard to say, just like that. It's easier to know what others did or should have done. . . . It's much harder to know what you did or should have done under certain circumstances . . . .

**L. V.** But you spoke about a certain tension that has always existed between writer and censorship. Did you experience it?

**P. G.** Yes, I did, from the start. I published my first poem in a magazine in 1955, and then I waited until 1967 for my first book. Why so long, you may ask. Because I wanted to avoid the ideological themes imposed so vehemently in the '50s. I waited for twelve years . . . but I do not regret the wait. My debut book appeared in the collection *The Morning Star*, which had published other important poets of the new generation such as Nichita Stănescu, Cezar Baltag, Ana Blandiana. I did not have to compromise, either in style or theme. Some of the writers who published at that time no longer want to admit that they wrote what they did under the "demands of the time." Thank God, waiting for twelve years, I was able to avoid that . . . .

**L. V.** What happened later?

**P. G.** My first book had an air of mystery, of awe vis-à-vis the miracles of the universe. The third one, from 1972, was already an appeal to wakefulness vis-à-vis danger. Dangers inside and outside ourselves. There was danger everywhere.

**L. V.** Was it difficult to publish?

**P. G.** No. I used metaphors.

**L. V.** Things have become very tough lately. Was your poetry influenced in any way?

**P. G.** The final stage, the ten years before December 1989, was the one during which Romanian society was officially presented as perfect, while, in reality, it was more and more degraded, both socially and materially. Poetry is the most sensitive amoeba in the universe. It could not fail to react to what was happening around it. For nine years I worked on a book of poems which I entitled *The Atomic Paradise*. A paradise which contradicts itself! An oxymoron. A paradise in which everything is upside down. Impossible tensions are ready to burst. The only hope left is love for mankind. This volume was published at the beginning of 1989. You know what happened then . . . I read the book afterwards and I was horrified. It had been more than a premonition! One of the mysteries of poetry . . . .

**L. V.** So the book was published shortly before the end of 1989?

**P. G.** Precisely. And without any changes. My great surprise was that, at the very end of the year when people would think of everything but poetry, when history came to life in the streets, the book vanished from bookstores almost immediately.

**L. V.** Has the tension of censorship finally disappeared?

**P. G.** Has it really? Ideological censorship no longer exists. But we have economic, commercial censorship now . . . and the censorship of bad taste. The new publishers, eager to make money, no longer want good literature; they want "sexy." Adventure sells more easily. Porno, too. Poetry has always found it very, very difficult to survive!

**L. V.** What about the writing process? Has anything changed there?

**P. G.** Not for the real writer. His ultimate censor is Eternity. The universe is eternal; the poet is transitory. The tension will never be resolved.

July 1991

# Poetry

### Legend in the Computer

A legend,
A very old Asian legend tells us:
"When thrown in the Daemon Cave
A sinner
Prayed to Buddha so fervently,
That the latter had mercy
And sent him a way,
Only one way towards rescue, at last:
A spider thread!
Desperately catching
At the hanging, sticky silk,
So fragile,
The unfortunate man felt dragged through the black tunnel
Up, towards the stars,
From among the blind rocks,
By the strong rope.
Rather dead than alive,
He reached the edge of the abyss,
And catching sight of light, wondered:
Suppose the thread broke!

And the thread broke!"

Here I am, on the plastic lawn,
Examining the legends of the world in a minicomputer,
Formulating questions:

Suppose the sinner was not even a sinner?
Suppose he refused to pray to anyone, in fact?

Suppose Buddha was meditating and could not
Or would not hear him?

Suppose once he had touched
The edge of the abyss,
There was no trace of light to see?

Suppose that, frightened,
He avoided the question on purpose?

Suppose he wondered, though, but
That thing, like a hair thread, did not break?

Suppose he felt he was leaving the depth
And meant to go back into it?

Suppose myself—I asked Buddha
For a way,
Just one way out, at last,
And Buddha,
Smiling *serenissim,*
Sent it to me at once!

Suppose suppose!

## The Screams

"Why the butterfly, too? Why the butterfly, too?"—I asked.
The syllables
Spread all over, like the dice of perfect gamblers
And nobody heard.

"Why the fish, too? Why the fish, too?"—I asked.
The mouth of fire
Gulped the wrinkled skin of the sea,
Out of the salt whirlpool
No flame came.

"Why the grass, too? Why the grass, too?"—I asked.
The word,
Like a head cut off,
Fell in the fountains of the clouds,
The spring was not born.

"Why the star, too? Why the star, too?"—I asked.
The echo
Jumped from mountain to mountain,
No thought, no bridge turned up
Under its body.

"Why me too? Why me too?"—I asked.
The screams
Reached the bottom of the sky,
The blind mole underground
Came and told me at last why was why.

## Hamlet

I envy you, prince of melancholy,
Painful knight of the dilemma.

Yorick's skull,
Which you hold in your left hand,
The palm crossed by the heartbeats,
Answered your question long ago.

When Yorick's skull
Is not your own,
The answer is easier
And even immortal.

But the skull which I hold in my hand
Is mine!
Living urn,
With the bright serpents of thought,
When you carry it in your hand,
You can at least utter the question!

Alone in the whole Universe,
Holding my own skull, dripping with blood...

Pity me, prince!

## The Perfect City

I turned my head and looked
Once, just once,
At that perfect city,
With its perfect streets,
With its perfect trees,
With its perfect waters
Nailed along the edges of the lake
Like perfect shrouds
Over the generals' coffins.

"What did you see?"—you asked me. "What did you see?"
"Nothing! Oh, nothing!"—I replied.
"No, no, no, that's not true! You did see something!
You caught sight of it!
Otherwise your hair, your face,
Would not have grown white in a moment".
"Oh, I can swear, I saw nothing,
I felt no pain...
It didn't even seem to!

One can grow white because of what one can't see, too!"

## Preserves

It has been estimated: it is much more convenient
To have the song of the crickets
Without the crickets being alive.

The song goes beyond space and time.
The crickets,
With their slanting gait,
Always remind us of some lost battle.

Many wear wooden artificial limbs
Where the wings grow.

The preserves of cricket song
Are much more convenient!
You can mix them yourself,
With however much salt and pepper you wish.

Whatever they may say,
We must keep a strict
Digestive diet of emotions!

Very important:
When you have finished the song,
Do not throw empty cans
Into the fire!

Or into the grass...
There is a real danger
That crickets might be reborn
Out of oxygen flames,

Or vegetal flames,
Like a Phoenix!

## The Bridge

Everybody would go out of town
And look beyond the bridge.

The lovers
Counted the cyclists in coloured T shirts
Vanishing at the other end
Of the bridge.

Old people
Told the brave deeds of their ancestors,
Which had taken place
At the foot of the bridge
Floating in mist.

Children
Sent their buzzing kites
Beyond the beyond side of the bridge.

Grown up women and men
Talked about fields,
Orchards and herds with much milk,
At the unseen end of the bridge.

A traveller, reaching the town at sunset,
Told them
It was not true,
There was no bridge beyond the barrier,
And no water,
He himself had come on foot,
His boots were full of dust,
He was hungry and thirsty,
He was dead tired,
And he would like to lie down in a bed.

That traveller
Was chased away with stones
By the inhabitants of the town.

# Eugen Simion

born 1933

*Literary critic, professor of Romanian literature: vice president of the Romanian Academy*

## The Romanian Literary Critic Still Cherishes Utopias

**Lidia Vianu:** What does censorship mean to a literary critic?

**Eugen Simion:** It means living with a claw piercing the nape of your neck. When you start writing, you can feel it sticking into your flesh, numbing your critical sense and diminishing the courage of saying the whole truth about a piece of literature or a cultural event. Or rather: censorship can be seen as ideological and, obviously, moral taboos—yes, this will do, but no, that will not work. This is *inner censorship* (let us agree to call it that) and it takes shape in time. First an interdiction, later a suspicion, then a yellow or a red sign (I am using traffic signs as connotations), and in this way, willingly or unwillingly, the literary critic (or anyone who writes) finds himself besieged by a space of alarm within the spirit: it says, careful, dangerous area! . . . Any writer who lived in a totalitarian regime knows this kind of censorship, the toughest and the most dangerous, as it involves a complicity of each individual conscience. Even if at first the conscience rejects this censorship, even if it vehemently opposes political implications in literature, the writer can only choose between writing nothing (and his conscience can be very clean then) and writing (publishing, too), in which case he accepts a set of limitations. In time, the spirit devises its own system of censorship. This is what I called inner censorship; it saves you from real dangers but it also numbs, to a certain degree, your critical spirit.

Besides that, there is *outer censorship* (official), which became an institution during the totalitarian regime: it is represented by the general director with the rank of a minister, deputy director, the hierarchy of censors. They read your article or your book and pronounce *feu vert* for publication or reject what you have written. It is a complete rejection, or, as it often happens, certain excerpts or only one sentence, a mere word. There is a third censorship, as well: that which follows the publication of the book or study. I shall call it *voluntary censorship*. Somebody, an ideologist, a conscientious activist, a retired professor, a wary fellow writer reads your book and reveals ideological trespassing. . . . He mentions it to the right persons or he writes about it himself, in a newspaper. . . . We have to do here with enmities, envy, hidden interests. An opponent wants to stab you in the back so he uses this incident and does just that. As the age in question called it, he "creates a problem," and the problem may easily lead to the book being withdrawn from bookshops. It happened to me too, in 1976. It is a situation in which the writer who is menaced goes to his friends, acquaintances, relatives, writes official statements, requests to be seen officially, explains, justifies, refutes the accusations and sometimes succeeds in saving his book . . . .

In short: there are at least three kinds of censorship, three barriers imposed on the critical text in a totalitarian regime. The only weapons the literary critic can use in order to save his book are his agility and compromise. I am talking about the literary critic who is an author. His other role, as critic (interpreter of a literary work) is not an easy one, either. The critic can become a hideous censor, underlining the ideological "errors" of the work, or a nimble interpreter who avoids the difficult points of the work: he pretends he has overlooked them. A . . . positive complicity. This is what genuine Romanian literary criticism has been doing for fifty years . . . .

**L. V.** In what way did censorship affect your work before 1990?

**E. S.** The effect derives from my previous explanation. I could not deal with certain aspects of the literary work and I could not judge correctly *official literature*. I preferred to keep silent instead of tampering with the truth or mystifying it. I am aware that *silence* in bad times is debatable, as moral attitude, I mean, but it seemed to me more important to be able to talk about genuine literature than not to be able to speak at all. . . . My books were never spared by all kinds of censorship. I fought hard for each and every page. Take this out, replace that sentence or that word. It was a kind of harassment in which both parties were hardened and experienced. I came to know all the tricks of censorship and we had all become experts in avoiding it. I remember that our great prose writer Marin Preda had a very efficient, peasant strategy versus censorship: he planted a "tough" scene on purpose (a scene that was certain to be unacceptable to censorship), knowing that the censors' discontent would focus on that. Upon further argument, he eliminated it, thus saving others, much more important from a literary point of view. It was rigorous planning. Preda could thus fool the aggressive censor . . . .

**L. V.** What was your relationship with contemporary literature, knowing that censorship never spared it at all?

**E. S.** It varied. I have published four volumes (about 2,500 pages) about post-war Romanian literature. I could not write about the diaspora and, as I have already mentioned, I systematically avoided writing about the fake writers, the official ones. Silence is a weapon of criticism. Together with other critics, I brought back to life the idea of the autonomy of the aesthetic and made use of it as much as was possible. Paradoxically, after 1960 there was a very strong literature in Romania. Take poetry, for instance. A generation of important poets wrote (Nichita Stănescu, Marin Sorescu, Leonid Dimov . . . ). These and many others, are, to some extent, the "creation" of literary criticism.

**L. V.** You have never written about those writers who were known to cooperate with the regime and you have not accepted the communist ideology in what you wrote. How did you survive, how did you go on publishing?

**E. S.** As I said before: I programmatically ignored the fake or compromising writers, I promoted the genuine ones, who made small concessions in order to survive. It was a secret and fertile complicity between literary criticism and literature proper. It was not easy, but it could be done.

**L. V.** You have published many volumes about contemporary Romanian literature, you wrote about authors in exile (Eugène Ionesco, Eliade, Cioran) at a time when their work was forbidden in our country. How did you manage to do that?

**E. S.** This is a long and complicated story. Political "thaw" helped me write about Eliade, Cioran, Eugène Ionesco. . . . Then they became suddenly strict and those names were forbidden. There came another thaw, and I was like Sisyphus with the huge stone . . . .These were the cruelties of history and the patience, the agility of the critic! What can I say, we do not choose history, the same as we can hardly choose our parents.

**L. V.** You are a professor, you teach contemporary Romanian literature. You must have had a constant silent agreement with your students. How would you define this liaison dangereuse, which you must have had with those who read your weekly articles in *Literary Romania?*

**E. S.** My strategy in front of my students was the same: *exclusion by omission.* I ignored fake literature. The students understood and shared my game. We managed. I do not boast with this, I am only trying to explain what I did to be able to continue. To be able to support literature. There were sacrifices, of course. I only became a professor in 1990. I never held any position anywhere. I was a kind of impoverished nobleman, partly free within a system of interdictions.

**L. V.** Literary criticism was published a lot more easily and books were purchased more easily before. Between political and economic censorship, which is worse? What do you expect from the future?

**E. S.** That is quite right. Economic censorship is terrifying. I have not found out tricks to outsmart it yet. I feel confused. I still enjoy writing even if today literary criticism has lost its former importance. A TV advertisement means more to a writer than an article written by me or another literary critic. Sad but true. Yet, I mean to finish my project concerning contemporary literature. I am preparing the fifth volume of the work titled *Contemporary Romanian Writers*, where I write about the diaspora, and I mean to publish the 3,000 pages or so in two volumes. As you can see, although pushed aside, poor as he is, the Romanian literary critic still cherishes utopias.

July 1997

# Matei Călinescu

born 1934

*Literary critic: he left Romania in 1973; served as professor of comparative litera-
ture at the University of Indiana, Bloomington; and has written three volumes of
poetry, one novel, and six books of criticism, he has published in Romania and
the United States*

## The Intellectual Scar

**Lidia Vianu:** Is censorship one of the reasons why you are not in Romania
now?

**Matei Călinescu:** Yes, but only one. Censorship—I mean formal, institutional
censorship—is in fact only one, and perhaps not even the most important
means by which a totalitarian regime exerts control over the mind. With regard
to mind control, I would distinguish three aspects or stages, which I shall call:
(1) "pre-censorship," (2) censorship proper, and (3) "post-censorship." My clas-
sification, it goes without saying, is a reflection of my personal experience—as
will be seen presently—but it also attempts to give a broader view of censorship
in totalitarian societies.

Precensorship is by far the most important element in my triad.
Precensorship should not be confused with self-censorship, although self-censorship is part of it. By precensorship I mean all the repressive means by which
the totalitarian power achieves a general atmosphere of ideological or ideology-
related terror. This terror is often physical and is felt—in different degrees—by
all members of society. Its main consequence is the appearance of what I call
"hostage mentality." Let me briefly explain this notion by evoking a personal
memory. As a high-school student in Bucharest, between 1946 and 1952, I
developed an interest in writing—I wrote, like most adolescents, poetry. I also
wrote aphorisms and embarrassingly naive cogitations. At the same time, I also
started a personal diary. The country, in the meantime, was being Russified
along the lines of Stalin's model of socialism (people were terrorized into being

happy). Many were arrested and interned, with or without trial, in forced labor camps, the most notorious of which was the pharaonic Danube–Black Sea Canal. I myself came from a "bourgeois" family (my father was an engineer who had studied in France, and my mother came from a land-owning family, whose possessions had been nationalized), and I was very much aware of belonging to a persecuted group. Among those arrested at the time were many "bourgeois" intellectuals and all sorts of stories circulated about the reasons for their arrests. I remember the case of one of them, Alice Voinescu, the author of several books (one of them on Montaigne), who was rumored to have corresponded with André Gide, and who, like Gide, had kept a journal for many years. When she was arrested, so the story went—and this was no doubt a true story—that journal was confiscated by the Securitate, and many other people whose names were mentioned in it were interrogated and arrested. What did all this mean to a young writer and fledgling diarist like myself? Even though I did not think of publication—I and my friends at Titu Maiorescu Lycée, among whom was the future dissident psychiatrist Ion Vianu, profoundly despised the official writers who obeyed the rules of socialist realism—the general atmosphere of intellectual terror could not help but influence me. And here I come back to the issue of hostage mentality. My personal diary from that time, which is lost, did not contain the names of friends or other people, for fear that if something happened to me, they might also be incriminated. And something could happen to me—or someone with my social background—virtually at any time. The result was that my personal diary was all along, and quite paradoxically, very impersonal and abstract. The most specific things in it were my reading impressions, including names of authors and titles of books. Would you describe the situation that I have just referred to as a case of censorship, or self-censorship, or would you agree with me that we must invent something like the awkward category of precensorship in order to account for it?

**L. V.** It certainly is a case of censorship before censorship was actually exerted, a pre-effect—precensorship being therefore the best name you could give it. Did it prevent you from wanting to write or actually writing? And if it did not, how did you overcome it in your mind? How did you live with the burden of knowing that you were not free to write, before even thinking that you would not be free to publish?

**M. C.** Precensorship did not prevent me from continuing to write but it certainly had an impact on what I was writing and, more subtly, on my style. I think that a certain vagueness, a certain evasiveness in my writing in Romania for years to come had its origin in that situation. To portray the pervasiveness of the ideological terror, I would like to add that what I have called precensorship affected not only what one wrote, but also what one read. People were imprisoned then—and as late as 1958 or 1960, I think—and were scared by the mere fact of having read it, of having internalized its words and heretical ideas, of having participated, although invisibly, in an ideological crime. Precensorship was perhaps the main strategy of making people—people who did not believe in communism or anything like that—feel guilty of ideological "sins," of what Orwell called "thought-crimes."

Let me repeat that, at the time, and also during my years as a student (1952–1957), I never thought of publishing, I was writing exclusively for myself and some friends. As for my journal, you may also note that the genre is, by its constitutive rule, intended to have only one reader, its author. This is so, even though many modern writers have conceived of their journals for partial or total publication even during their lifetimes (André Gide, Julien Green, et al.). The fact that my view of the journal as a secret genre is correct can be verified very simply by the absence of the rhetorical convention of the "dear reader" from any diary, published or unpublished. But my diary at the time was really, I mean not only rhetorically, a form of secret writing. We know, of course, that secrecy of any kind is anathema to any totalitarian state or institution. Precensorship and the hostage mentality brought about by it were designed to create a totally transparent society. A transparent society, a society without secrecy or privacy—that may be one of the best definitions of the totalitarian ideal, whether on the left or the right. Democracy is always nontransparent, opaque.

**L. V.** When did you come into contact with the second phase of your triad, namely real censorship?

**M. C.** My first steady job after graduating from the university was that of a proofreader for *Gazeta literară*, which I got in the fall of 1958. One of my best friends at the time, Nichita Stănescu, who was a part-time poetry editor for *Gazeta literară*, had managed to persuade Paul Georgescu, the editor in chief, to hire me. That was a very interesting period. I had as colleagues in the proofreading room of the printing house where I worked ("a printing house in hell," to quote William Blake jokingly) the future literary critic Gabriel Dimisianu, the future essayist and art historian Modest Morariu, and the translator in verse of Boileau's *Art Poétique*, Ionel Marinescu. That was the time when I first became acquainted with the reality of censorship. As I noticed then, there were at least three kinds of censorship, among which the institutional one, called euphemistically *Direcţia presei* (the Press Directorate) was probably the least important. The most feared was the control over the magazine by the ideological section of the Central Committee of the party. Its apparatchiks always scrutinized the page proofs in the final stages and could eliminate anything without any explanation. The mere fact that something was expunged by the ideological section spelled great potential trouble: it pointed to the danger of heresy and to the possibility of Party inquisition and exorcism. Another kind of censorship was that exerted by the staff of the magazine and the editor in chief. Finally, there was the Press Directorate, which might delete certain phrases or words (at that time all words having to do with religion, God, angels, etc. were forbidden, even in poetic metaphors. It was considered a sign of good augury when in 1959, Nichita Stănescu managed to publish a poem in which he mentioned an angel's wing).

It was at that time that I started publishing. First poems and then short reviews. I was part of a group of young writers, among whom I would mention here: Nichita Stănescu, Mircea Ivănescu, Petre Stoica, Cezar Baltag. We were all what I would call secret modernists and were obliquely and sometimes almost schizophrenically encouraged by Paul Georgescu, who was, if one can conceive of this, at once a Stalinist, a Trotskyite, and an admirer of Arthur Koestler, André Gide, André Malraux, and George Orwell. Paul Georgescu was a total fanatic and a total cynic at the same time, and he was certainly endowed with superior intelligence and great literary flair. As I was beginning to publish, I was conscious that I had entered a new kind of game, with its unwritten rules, protocols, ruses, etc. The literary situation I was entering into was, morally speaking, one of duplicity, unless the writer had managed to practise effective self-persuasion to the point that he came to believe sincerely the propagandistic idiocies of socialist realism (I knew quite a few who had managed to do precisely that). Working within the constraints of censorship (in all three senses pointed out above) was the equivalent of signing a pact with the devil in the hope of eventually being able to fool him. My problem, and the problem of my friends and colleagues as well, was basically that of the secret sharers of a forbidden creed or heresy, trying to communicate deviously their innermost convictions to a larger public.

**L. V.** How devious could you afford to be? How far could you go without being afraid that you might lose your audience? That communication might actually disappear?

**M. C.** Your question brings up the great dilemma of oblique communication under conditions of totalitarian censorship and, more broadly, mind control. One hopes to trick the devil, but one often ends up fooling oneself. The mere fact of accepting the game on the censorship's terms leads to concessions and compromises that can only become a burden on one's conscience. To relieve oneself of this burden, one often finishes by justifying the (bad) means in the name of the (good) end. Our illusion at the time was that the system—in this case, the system of literary communication—could be changed from within. This was a fallacy. On the other hand, my friends and I were, later on, and in a certain sense, lucky: the Romanian communist regime went through a period of quasiliberalization between 1964 and 1971. What this meant was that precensorship became generally less .oppressive (although it was extremely oppressive when it was focused on specific dissidents or potential dissidents), censorship proper was relaxed, and what I have called postcensorship also became more tolerable.

**L. V.** What do you mean by postcensorship? What harm did it do, after the major harm done by precensorship and censorship proper? So many potentially good writers were nipped in the bud by the first two that, in order to reach the third level of the inferno, you had to have something really devilish in your mind. How much did the pact with the devil—even when the devil *was* fooled—affect the mind of the writer who went on writing and made more and more blood-signed pacts?

**M. C.** By postcensorship I mean a purely mental thing, namely, what happens in the mind of the writer who has seen his book published, and what happens in the mind of the reader as he assesses the book. Let me clarify myself. Postcensorship is not an institution or anything externally identifiable; it is a state of mind. It comprises a variety of possible feelings, going from the satisfaction of having evaded the censor or of having been able to express part of the truth (one can never hope to tell the whole truth within a system of political censorship) to a sense of futility, shame, weariness. Once the complex struggle of writing a worthwhile book and getting it through censorship with all the kinds of self-censorship involved is over, writers behave differently. Some are proud, even (by way of psychological compensation) immensely proud—hence the widespread attitudes of egotism and megalomania among the literary intelligentsia in totalitarian countries. Seen from outside, this megalomania may look somewhat exotic and even picturesque. Seen from the inside, it may become maddening. (Jokingly, one of my reasons for leaving Romania in 1973, was the fact that there I was surrounded by too many geniuses: since the late '60s, I have become increasingly allergic to the physical presence of a literary genius.) Other writers are, on the contrary, inclined to self-criticism and self-doubt. They use the following kind of logic: since my book has been published, there must be something wrong with it.

**L. V.** You have published an immensely successful book, even by today's standards. You published it while you were in Romania. Did you ever think that there was something wrong with it? Were you frustrated or discouraged from writing at some point in your literary life in Romania? How do you see the past, present and future fate of other writers like you, who are still there, struggling with what is now called freedom?

**M. C.** The book was a short novel of sorts, centering around an unlikely character, a quixotic Jewish prophet in the Balkan city of Bucharest. I wrote it "for the drawer" in the early 1960s (the first edition appeared in 1969). But when I submitted the manuscript (in 1968) the quasi-liberalization of which I spoke earlier had reached its highest point; censorship was still very much in place. Precensorship was less oppressive, but the hostage mentality still existed and the rare dissidents were its first victims. They were ostracized by their colleagues for the benefit of the profession, of the Writers' Union, for the welfare of the literary intelligentsia as a category, whose interests might otherwise be harmed. Institutional censorship was more tolerant, and postcensorship more bearable. Still, I had to take certain precautions in submitting my manuscript. I had to make it clear, for instance, that the character of my book lived in the 1920s and 1930s, which took away or at least limited the contemporary meaning of the book. There were other changes or omissions I did myself or accepted at the suggestion of a very friendly editor. The book was a success, but over the years, particularly since 1973, my feelings about it have changed. To be quite frank, for some time, I have been afraid of re-reading it. Perhaps less than to re-read other things I wrote in Romania, particularly between 1958 and 1964, but still. A couple of years ago, a friend of mine, a former student of mine at the University of Bucharest who now lives in Athens, Greece, wrote me suggesting a translation of the book into Greek. I said, "No. Let's wait." Perhaps one day I will have the courage to re-read the book, and then I might consider a new Romanian edition with a long autobiographical preface. Perhaps that preface will save the book, at least in my eyes. Of course it would be wrong to blame only the censors. When one does not succeed in fooling the devil, one must blame oneself in the first place. To conclude, I would say that postcensorship is the consciousness of an intellectual scar—and this scar remains for the rest of one's life, whether that life is spent under totalitarianism or outside it.

May 1992

# Ion Vianu

**born 1934**

*Essayist, psychiatrist: he was the first Romanian psychiatrist to condemn the use of psychiatry for political purposes; he left Romania in 1977 and settled in Switzerland, where he still resides*

## The Trap of History

**Lidia Vianu:**\* What do you know about the pressure of totalitarianism on culture in Romania? Is there any connection between the iron heel of censorship and the reason why you left the country and culture you belong to, as much as your father, the literary critic Tudor Vianu?

**Ion Vianu:** I understand from the questions you are asking that we shall deal with three topics. First: why did I leave Romania? Second, I shall tell you why, when it became possible, I returned there, although I had thought I should never see it again. And third, I must try to define what became of me after the ordeals I have experienced. In other words, I must state my present identity.

First I ought to try and remember what I had become during the years that preceded my exile, the early '70s. It is not easy to talk about it, not because I might have forgotten what happened then, because I have not forgotten that in the least. Nor because, for one reason or another, I might feel embarrassed to do it. My only reason is that I am in the process of writing my memoirs, and it may seem paradoxical that, at this very moment, I find it hard to remember. I feel a kind of inner pressure within myself, in view of this very effort to retrace my steps towards my lost time. Consequently, whenever I try to set this tension free, I feel a kind of anxiety, as if I were betraying my supreme effort. But I shall try, nevertheless.

I do not mean to recall too many details, but I must say one thing, which seems to me to be important, even essential, maybe. In the early '70s, I had a very good position in Romania, I was a pretty well known doctor, even very well

\* The name of the interviewer and the interviewee happen to be the same by pure coincidence—L. V.

known, I should say; I had started to write essays of psychiatry and literary essays as well. They must now be forgotten, of course, after such a long time when my name was only associated with aspects of the political and social life. I was a well connected man, I knew lots of people, owing to the fact that I was part and parcel of the whole of Romanian life. First there were my family connections, then the schools I had attended, and where I had met so many people, then my connections with the medical world, which was so complete and deep in itself. In this respect, I remember that Alexandru Rossetti, a friend of my father's, had noticed I knew the medical world so well that he never went to see a doctor without asking me first who the best specialist was, whose advice he should seek. I had started saying jokingly that my profession should be that of medical adviser.

When I "dissented"—I think this verb will have to be included in our vocabulary—, that is, when I decided to escape drastically from Romanian society at the time, and emigrate, I happened to meet an elderly friend, a very well known doctor, whom I saw again when I came back, doctor Constantin Bălăceanu Stolnici. He made then a remark which was very much to the point. He told me: "You dealt them a heavy blow, and they won't forgive you, as you are part of the establishment, and they can't forgive those who belong to the establishment and deal such blows." I was amazed and asked him: "What do you mean, that I belong to the establishment? I am not a member of the Communist Party, I am no official person, do not have a special position in this world, I am a completely independent individual. How can you say I belong to the establishment?" He retorted: "Yes, you do, because they have tried to allure you, they were under the impression they had managed to seduce you, and now they are losing you." I was shocked by Bălăceanu's remark, it was food for thought for a long while, and at last I realized he had been right.

We must distinguish between what you feel, your own image of yourself, and the way the others perceive you. Those who are very close to you, have one image, totally different from those who are relatively farther away, and a third image belongs to those who know very little about you, vaguely and from very far away. In a subjective way, I have always felt very remote from "those." I place "those" between inverted commas, because I have a whole theory of communism as historical stage, during which the power belongs to "those," meaning the people who are essentially hostile and unfamiliar. Although I had never adhered to their faith, their system of values, their aspirations and wishes, I had however, objectively, come close to them, by means of my social position and especially the way "those" people viewed me.

Later on, when I was the object of fairly thorough investigations of the Securitate, and when, in principle, they had allowed me and my family to leave the country, a Securitate colonel told me one day—and I told the story to Eugène Ionesco, who mentioned it in a short essay, entitled *Doctor Vianu Arrives in Paris*. The colonel told me: "How can a man like you, Doctor Vianu, who is so well educated, join the tramps and bums? You could have told us in a civilized, agreeable way, that you wished to leave the country, and we would have been favorably inclined to grant you your wish." There was some truth in this, I admit: I had surprised them and had had to overcome certain inner obstacles in order to do it.

I shall go back a few years before that, to 1971, when I visited Paris for three months, with a fellowship offered by the World Health Organization, in order to help me study psychotherapy. I saw all kinds of interesting institutions, I became acquainted with various methods that could be used in our country as well, and I also met a lot of people, a lot of Romanians. Some of them were very close to my family and had already been there for a long time. It was a time when all Romanians abroad were trying hard to persuade those inside the country, those whom they loved more or less, to defect, too. One of them did that to me, to the very last moment, when I was packing to come back to my country. Faced with my flat refusal, he stared me in the eye silently, then told me: "You are a fool."

His remark, far from tender, haunted me when I had returned. I kept wondering: "Have you really been a fool, to come back?" I soon discovered that, provided you are true to yourself and aware of it, you just can't do anything until you are ripe for it, have grown up to do that particular act. During that year, 1971, the year of Ceaușescu's cultural revolution, I was not ripe to defect. I felt I had to go back. Something in my fate had not been carried out.

**L. V.** In your opinion, in what way did communism, in its Romanian variant, affect the thoughts of common people and of intellectuals? How much pressure was put on everyday and on cultural life?

**I. V.** For years I kept saying afterwards that I had not drunk up the bitterness in my cup. It may look like a paradox, but what pushed me farther away and broke all my ties with society was that the latter had somehow gone beyond the state of a crisis and headed towards a kind of organization. As a teenager, I had experienced Stalinism. Then Stalin had died, but nothing really changed for the better in Romania. The Hungarian revolution of 1956 took place. We were young and we all had a short glimpse of hope, which did not last more than a few days. It was followed by a terrifying counterrevolution, during which many were again sacrificed. Yet, later, easier years followed, years of hope, years when, among my contemporaries, a generation of poets, of writers, came to light. For a while, we were under the impression that we would be able to start again what our parents had lost, that we could, in our turn, be a generation that could build something in Romania.

These were the years of Nichita Stănescu's first poems, the years when my friend of a lifetime, Matei Călinescu, published *The Life and Opinions of Zacharias Lichter*, years when, though hard and with many obstacles, we began to travel abroad, and we witnessed a relative prosperity.

Yet, very soon we had to realize that we had reached a kind of flat height, that progress could not continue, because these were at the same time the years when a new class began to emerge and gather strength, and the name of a "new class" was used by Milovan Djilas, a theoretician of communism, whom I read very carefully at the time. I mean, this was the period when a new class, above all others, emerged, and we had no affinity with it. They were snobbish enough to wish to seduce us. Frankly speaking, in a certain way, they would have liked a truce with us. But, subjectively speaking, it was then that I felt I had severed my ties, because I had nothing in common with these people, and, in order to rescue my own identity, I had to differentiate myself from them. On the other hand, Romania had fallen prey to a general corruption, which deeply disgusted me. It was the empire of bribery.

The word we used—baksheesh—is in fact of Turkish origin. It actually means, if I am not wrong, the gift of pity made in the Islamic code, in the Prophet's commandments, I think, the generous gift required by God, from the rich to the poor. . . . But the baksheesh in this meaning of the word did not exist, either in Romania, or in the rest of the communist world. This meaning of the word was a very unimportant side of Romanian life. In the first place, it was the poor who had to pay those richer than themselves, in order to obtain certain advantages. It was absolutely unbearable. With each new day, each new year, I realized I was sinking ever more deeply in this marsh, and I would not be able to survive unless I severed all my ties at one blow.

I began to realize that this new, selfish, rapacious, and fundamentally stupid class had a one and only wish: to prevent those who were not privileged to climb higher up. The situation could not get better and was not going to get better in Romania, anyway, because these people, whom I hated from the depth of my heart, did not want prosperity for anyone else. Dire poverty had to be kept alive, and I think this is essential, since the communists were certain, to the very end, to their cruel and final end, that their power was safe only if surrounded by misery. With their cynicism, which I should call purely Leninist, they had found out that as soon as man had a respite, as soon as he could make a good living, he became emancipated, dared too much, and discovered a principle that could ruin his society.

They did not know, and had no way of knowing that this strategy would lead them to their doom, in the long run, and thought they would end by dominating the world till the end of times. The same Lenin I mentioned once said that a power which is determined to be absolute really has absolute power, and can never be deprived of it. In time, during Brezhnevism, and in Romania during Ceauşism, this principle evolved. The doctrine was that whoever managed to perpetrate misery had the power, and could keep it indefinitely long.

**L. V.** What were the new criteria of normality?

**I. V.** This was the genesis of my revolt. I did experience a mood of revolt. It can only be explained in this way, as a deep rejection, which is inherent in certain features of my nature, a specific configuration which can also be proved astrologically, in my astral theme.

During the years that preceded the exile, I became stronger inside. I felt more and more in control of myself. I thought, and reality showed I was right, I could make my fate, and I tried to put this conviction into practice. I was extremely lucid, and I knew that, by leaving my country, I would become, at least at first, not a stronger, but a weaker man. It was natural to expect that, and I never thought any other way. I knew that, away from my roots, I ran the risk of losing that strength which helped me keep myself under control, and gave me a certain power over the world. This inner force which I felt was meant to lead me to the moment of crisis, of the decision to sever my ties, thus fulfilling my particular fate.

I remember the day I went to the passport department of the "militia" in order to write my first application to leave the country. At that time, first of all, before actually applying to leave, you had to kind of denounce yourself, to take what was called the "small forms," which were in fact a mere sheet of paper, without the value of an official application. They merely announced that you intended to leave. I took my place in a line, beside all kinds of people, who only had one thing in common—they all declared the fact that they belonged to a community with which they did not want to have anything to do any more.

It was then that I became one of the tramps. I was a respectable bourgeois who announced he did not want to belong to his world any more. The militia man who was distributing the forms was amazed to see a gentleman like myself on the point of making such an extraordinary statement. I was determined to break with *them* for ever.

I remember that, in the early '70s, together with the same Matei Călinescu I talked about before, I had found out and enthusiastically practised the Zen philosophy. We had even written together a few Zen poems. It was a discipline of the void. We tried to get close to nothingness. In my first act of exile, which took place in the absence of my friend Matei, who had emigrated before, I did something quite close to Zen Buddhism. I tried to follow my fate by an act of denial. I rejected a corrupt society, a society with which I felt nothing in common any more. I rejected Romanian society, overwhelmed, as it was, by the stigma of communism.

That was the time when I approached Paul Goma, a man who seems to me to be an extraordinary being from all points of view. I went to Goma with Ion Negoițescu, and we met there the "tramps," the marginal beings. We went there in order to sign his protest, which at once deprived us of our respectability, that despicable respectability, which I reject. I denounced the political abuses of psychiatry. After Goma had been arrested, I saw a whole world of humiliated, simple, crushed people gathering around us, which honored me unspeakably. I had at last escaped from that honorable world of communism. After all these, I had to leave the country at a moment when I think I did not feel like it, because I felt so good, so much at peace with myself, and when I had reached the stage of rejecting the surrounding corrupt world.

**L. V.** What did you feel when you escaped from the falsifying restrictions of communist propaganda? Was freedom (the opposite pole of life in Romania, but not of your inner life, as you say) an intellectual or emotional shock?

**I. V.** What I told you before made my departure even more tragic, because I was parting with a country wherein I had finally found my place, with a society I agreed to, precisely because I had dared reject it, at last.

I remember the day I left Romania. It was July 28, 1977, at 7 o'clock in the morning. I arrived at the Otopeni Airport, in order to take the plane for Paris. I had been there the day before, when I had registered the few suitcases I was allowed to take along. The day before, there had been no one at Otopeni, it was a deserted airport, maybe the most Asian airport in Europe. Suddenly, surprise: the next day, the day I had to leave, the airport was unbearably crowded. It did not fit into any of my previous images of the airport. All the people moved a lot, but nobody spoke. They only made signs. I imagined I might have an attack of paranoia, but I remembered, at last, that at that time the deaf and dumb had had their Olympic games in Bucharest. The games were over, and on that day, the deaf and dumb were leaving for some other place in Europe, in the world, which explained the crowd, and their mysterious gestures of communication. It also explained the silence.

So, this is how I left, together with the deaf and dumb, a country to which I no longer belonged, in fact. I was leaving *those* behind, meaning those who had stolen my country from me. But I was also leaving behind many other people, whom I should not have wished to leave, and whom I was sacrificing, in a way. I was leaving behind me the memory of my parents and of their joyful circle of friends, who had educated me, and had filled my childhood with stories and jokes. I was leaving behind so many wonderful people, who had formed me.

An extraordinary incident suddenly occurs to me. I was sixteen. It was in 1950. My father, who must have wanted to see me grow up, had urged me to go on a trip around the country. This is how, one summer night, on the first Sunday after the Romanian day of Saint Elijah, I arrived at the foot of Mount Găina (the hen). For centuries, a "girl fair" had been held there. It did not exist any more, it was no longer a place where young men found a wife. It was just a fair, held on that peak in the Apuseni mountains. That place is an orographic center, which means it is a peak from which several mountain lines spring, like rays of rock. I consequently arrived there in the evening. Together with a huge crowd, I was to reach the peak in the morning, when the fair opened. I started climbing, with one group. I could hardly be seen in the dark. All of a sudden, it started raining. It was raining heavily. I was drenched and cold. My thin coat was all wet pretty soon, and I felt drenched to the bone.

It so happened that I was walking side by side with a peasant, a man who seemed to be very old to me. But, when you are sixteen, even a man of forty can seem old to you. He saw me shivering, lost, alone, and he took off his coat. It was a coat of home made wool, still impregnated with sheep fat, and it was wonderful protection against the rain. He compelled me to put it on. He was left with only his shirt on. I tried to refuse, and told him: "You'll get drenched now, why should you give me your coat?" He said: "Oh, don't worry. You are young and used to the town. I am well used to all this." So I climbed, with his coat on, while he, with a peasant's stoicism, walked in the rain. It was morning when we arrived at the peak. We found women who sold warm milk. I drank a glass, the sun came out, my man took his coat, said good-bye, and I have never seen him again.

These were the people I was leaving behind, and many others whom I knew. But my closest friends had left several years before. My circle of friends existed no more, and I was to meet them there, even if they were thousands of miles away. We were together in another world, while the country I was leaving stayed beyond, more and more seemingly untrue.

More than once in my life, I was under the impression that good providence, unless this is a pleonasm, protected me. When I arrived in the West, with my wife and two children, we were four people who had lost everything. All we had left was our health and freedom, which, of course, is a lot. The unknown was awaiting us.

We arrived in Paris on a Thursday. On Friday, a possible job occurred, as vice-manager of a psychiatry clinic at Nyon, in Switzerland. On Saturday I called the manager, who gave me an appointment for a week later. I actually met him nine days after my arrival, and he hired me. I had only left Romania two weeks before, and I was already starting work. That is the reason why I felt protected by an enormous force, who would not abandon me to chance, but would give me self-confidence instead. Soon, I settled down in a dreamland, a place even a millionaire would have envied me. Our apartment was part of a villa on the shore of the Leman lake. I had to climb down a meadow in order to reach the water. It was paradise.

But, like many other heavenly places, it was only apparently so. I had had a particular autonomy as a doctor in Romania. In that very small clinic, I suddenly found myself at the mercy of a manager who was an autocrat, and medically quite absurd. The patients were mostly rich, very demanding. And, besides, during those months I began to feel the burden of solitude. I had left such a dense social atmosphere, even though it was infernally so at times, and found myself surrounded by a handful of people, in a totally different world, which was rigid and hopeless. I had foreseen all that, but it was difficult, nonetheless.

Fortunately, there was more to my life than that. Running many risks, I had denounced the abusive use of psychiatry to political purposes. It was natural, then, that I should become a member of the Swiss association against the use of psychiatry to political purposes. From the very first moment, I met extremely generous people, extremely warm and intelligent, very kind to me, too, and, although I was the most recent member, I felt happy and equal among them. Although I was in Switzerland, somewhere between Geneva and Lausanne, I was in touch with very close and very good friends from Paris. I had known some of them for a very long time. Such was Marie France Ionesco. I met others only then, and among them there were Mihnea Berindei and his wife, Catherine. I associated with them in order to found, during that year, the League for Human Rights in Romania. That gave us an aim and a connection with our homeland. It was the connection with the country we had lost. We seemed to find our country again, in that way. We found especially the humiliated, crushed country where lies were the only truth, where opportunism reigned, yet where people had the courage to speak, nevertheless. While I had been there, I had had that courage myself.

At that time, we did not have high hopes of fundamental changes. There were there free but tortured consciences, tortured souls and tortured bodies, too. We meant to help them survive and continue telling the truth. A few years later, my good friend Gelu Ionescu managed to leave the country as well, and became an editor for Radio Free Europe. On that occasion, I started contributing more systematically to that "spoken paper of Romanians everywhere." My voice was heard in the country again, more general and not very substantial, at first, maybe, but growing into a firm, authoritative tone.

However, I had to make a living. I only had a temporary status at the Métairie clinic, where I worked. It was hard for me to cope with my submission there, and there was no possibility of promotion, actually. So, I decided to take all my medical exams, which I passed between the ages of forty-six and forty-seven. I soon became a doctor for the second time, this time at Geneva University. In 1981, I opened my own psychiatry ward, in a charming town between Geneva and Lausanne, closer to Lausanne, in fact. That town was Morges, where I have been working and living ever since.

There are small successes which can delight you more than glory. It was my case when I managed to do this. At the same time, for the first time in my life, I was a free man, not only in my intention and subjectivity, but also in reality, and as far as my position in the world was concerned.

In order to fill in the picture of those years of my exile, I ought to talk about what the experience of travelling meant to me. I started travelling farther and farther away, and my trips enlarged like a series of concentric circles. I went back to Paris, of course, knowing it better and better. Although I was not living in Paris, it had become my second native town, I might say. It also was the place in the world where I had the largest number of friends: Marie France, Mihnea, my old friend Jean Cantacuzène, whom I had found again, and many others, about whom I shall talk in detail some other time.

There were other places, too. The French provinces, with delightful land-scapes, with admirable monuments, such as the Romance cathedrals of Burgundy, then there was Britannia, with its view of that huge lung of the world, the Atlantic Ocean. The Mediterranean shores, Toscana, Florence and Sienna, towns endowed with so many geniuses. Sicily, with its vestiges of ancient civi-lization, from Greeks to the French, crossing the Norman and Gothic ages. Greece revealed antiquity to me in another way than what I had learnt as a philology student. It also revealed the Christian tradition. For instance, I remember my visit to the Isle of Patmos, where, from under tombstones, voices foretold the apocalypse of Saint John the Theologian, and sent it to the scribe of Prohoros. Egypt followed, then Israel, and, at last, the States, where I partook of liberty more than anywhere else. There I met Monica, my mother's sister, and her children. I had not seen her since 1948.

The years passed by. I experienced a lot. First of all, I fought for human rights and more dignity. I came to know Europe and that remote part of Europe and the West which is America. A new conscience was born in me: the European conscience.

As a nucleus, it had existed in me since childhood, when I had lived in my parents' home, in that atmosphere impregnated by Western culture, by means of books, stories, and the short trips between 1946–1947. Now I had become an inhabitant of that Western world myself. Constantly thinking of my near past, of what I had experienced in Romania, I was aware of something monstrous going on in the country I had left behind. This country had become the home of all my thoughts and dreams. A kind of plot was taking place there. We had to oppose it by all means. They wanted to take our country out of Europe, of European tradi-tion, and to make it plunge again into the fatality that had always ambushed it, and menaced it now more than ever—the return to Asia.

**L. V.** I suppose you stay in touch with what is going on in Romania now. What do you think is the direction of Romanian culture and society today (not tomor-row; tomorrow is much too far away, in the present hot climate) ?

**I. V.** I find the meaning of my leaving Romania very obvious now. It did not amount to abandoning it, but to preserving it, by means of a very fragile umbili-cal cord, within that Europe out of which obscure and monstrous forces were trying to pluck it. During the late '70s and the early '80s, I certainly had no hope whatever of returning to Romania. I kept telling myself, "I must do some-thing. We who are here must do something, lest the ever thinner and more men-aced cord that connected Romania to Europe should break completely." We had to keep up the hopes of those who kept on resisting inside the country, under such very hard circumstances. We had to show them that something could still be done in order to keep alive the hope of revival. We had to keep aflame the spark that would kindle the fire again. After 1985, when the first signs of weakness and decay of the socialist systems began to appear, I started seeing things in a different light. Although remote, the prospect of a change did not appear impossible any more. The effort was even more worth trying. Encouraging news reached us from inside the country. More and more people dared speak out. For instance, in the autumn of 1989, over 100 people stated openly and publicly that they opposed Ceauşescu. This opposition, not very numerous, maybe, but extremely significant, was slow in taking shape, and was an echo of the opposition in the West.

In mid-1989, I had an exciting experience. For the first time, I was heading East. Things had changed in Hungary. The communists were still in power, but the regime was irreversibly dying. On June 16, 1989, the solemn ceremony of Imre Nagy's second burial took place. He had been Prime Minister during the 1956 counterrevolution, and had been executed by his own party comrades, after a long captivity in Romania.

I took part in this ceremony together with a number of friends in the Paris League for Human Rights in Romania, and the Romanians' Democratic Union in Germany. Then we met members of the Hungarian Democratic Forum. We reached a solemn common statement, which, in my opinion, is highly important historically, since it is the first of its kind, after 1945. The statement focussed on the absolute necessity of an agreement between Romanians and Hungarians. Our statement was followed by strong protests, coming from the Western extreme right, and from Romanian officialities, who saw treason in this gesture of peace and reconcilement. I was not in the least astonished that during the following years, after the revolution, the official circles reiterated the same accusations. In doing this, they merely revealed their organic ties with those who had accused us before, in June 1989.

Yet, we were happy to see that our initiative was approved of by almost all democratic intellectuals in the West, by King Michael I, too. King Michael's presiding presence was, during all these years of exile, the most important support for us. He gave us self-confidence. Encouraging voices came from the country, too. Such was that of Doina Cornea (dissident whose messages were broadcast by Radio Free Europe), whose opposition had all our admiration.

The fall of 1989 brought that long line of spectacular events: the disappearance of the border between the two Germanies, directly or mediated by Hungary and Austria, the Velvet Revolution in Prague, Honecker's resignation, the fall of the Berlin wall soon afterwards, Bulgarian president Feodor Jivkov's resignation in Bulgaria, and, at last, as a pearl in the crown, the Romanian revolution and the execution of the infamous tyrants, who had defied a whole country for a quarter of a century.

I wonder if anyone can ever describe the utmost excitement, the sharp attention with which those of us who were abroad watched what was going on in Romania then. We had no more nights, we did not leave our radio sets for a minute, and our eyes were riveted to the TV screens, which showed us the revolution directly. On December 21, together with those in our town and those in Geneva, who were as exuberant as we were, I celebrated the fall of dictatorship, in a town square. We witnessed from afar the formation of the first unified council of the National Salvation Front. During the following days, we witnessed the neocommunist turn of events inside that newly formed council. It was sanctioned by the first resignations from the newly formed government, that of Doina Cornea and Ana Blandiana, then some others. Very soon afterwards, in January, a very important piece of news arrived: the Romanian Association of Free Psychiatrists was founded. It denounced the use of psychiatry to political purposes. That was the moment I understood I had to go there.

**L. V.** Did you have direct clashes with the official power, as a doctor, before you left? Did your profession compel you to do things you disapproved of?

**I. V.** Unfortunately, the field of psychiatry had been extremely tarnished by the cooperation with the Securitate. At the same time, it was a test for the ability of Romanian society to break with the past, and I felt I had a specific mission to promote a radical turn of events towards democracy. I was soon to find out the task was no trifling matter. There was a persistent opposition on the part of what could be called the psychiatric nomenklatura, meaning those who had been our leaders for decades, and who had exerted a very strong influence on psychiatry in general.

During a number of travels to Romania, together with important representatives of international psychiatry, in 1990, 1991, 1992, we demonstrated beyond any reasonable doubt that during Ceauşescu's time there existed political abuses in psychiatry. People who were either mentally sane, or a little deranged, had been hospitalized and treated by psychiatrists only in order to prevent them from objecting to the regime. This abnormal behavior for a doctor, this abusive collaboration of some psychiatrists, was implicitly acknowledged by the officials, if we consider that many victims of psychiatry were rehabilitated by committees all over the country, which investigated abuses. Many victims were morally rehabilitated and material amends were made to them.

In spite of all that, the government and the leading psychiatrists never admitted explicitly and officially these abuses had existed in the past. At best, it was admitted that there had been abuses—but "unsystematical." We had offered them the chance to come out in the open and say that mistakes had been committed and they could now be left behind. Very few psychiatrists accepted to do this. Some admitted privately that abuses had been made, but most of those who had been implicated—I must make it clear that their number was small, compared to the total number of psychiatrists in the country—did not even admit to abuses at all, thus denying reality, or refusing to see it, in spite of the recognition *de facto*, which was brought by rehabilitations and material amends.

**L. V.** How would you describe the communist organization of the human brain? What came first for intellectuals' minds, especially those minds which were determined not to allow themselves to be crushed?

**I. V.** I had the bitter experience, though it was no surprise to me, of seeing a press and TV campaign start against psychiatrist Valeriu Țuculescu, Romila and me. It was highly violent, obviously base. We were accused of lies and treason of the homeland. The typically communist reflex, that any criticism concerning the past or the present was a denial of one's country, came into being again. It was as if the country were supposed to send a radiant, perfect image abroad, in accordance with the old communist principles.

But I found more than this ambiguity in the country. I found good things, too. I could notice that the moral backbone was still there. I found people who had opposed the past in a wonderful way, in speech and brave deeds, as well as in their intellectual essence, which always surprised foreigners who visited Romania. They were clear-minded, pure, honest, lucid, and intelligent people, who had survived in this country, which, sometimes, in the darkness of exile, I feared had perished, drowned in ignorance and conformism.

**L. V.** Do you have the feeling that culture is democratic in Romania today?

**I. V.** I found there a young generation, those in their '20s, who had all lived Ceaușescu's last years as the absolute evil, and now rejected all compromises flatly. I was so glad to see that. The relationship among people had a color and an intensity I had forgotten. I felt nostalgia more than ever. Consequently, after my return, I began to live a kind of double life, divided between my profession in Switzerland, and the constant thought of the country.

**L. V.** What traces did the time you lived in Romania leave on your life, and to what space do you consider you belong now?

**I. V.** Whenever I was in Romania, especially in the house in Andrei Mureșanu Street, where I was born and where my sister continued to live, I experienced a kind of ecstasy, euphoria. I relished the nearness of all those places, and meeting people I knew or recognized without having ever actually met them. Destroyed by communism as by a bombardment, Bucharest had cracked sidewalks, houses marked by smallpox, rusty and decayed buses. Still lucid, I felt it was a wonderful city, an El Dorado I had found again. My joy was insatiable. Of course, I was very much tempted, and I could return, but I found it hard to decide. I had made my life in Switzerland for quite a while. How or why should I destroy that, after all that had happened to me?

I felt compelled to ask myself very seriously the question: "What was the meaning of this long journey, which does not seem to have come to an end yet?" There is a word in Homer, *nostos*, the return, and it describes Ulysses' trajectory after the end of the Trojan war, his way home. I had, and still have the feeling that my *nostos* is not over yet, and that my return home, even posthumous, maybe, includes a lot to come yet, a lot of adventures are still possible.

One of them, which may interest my contemporaries, those who experience the same things I do, and all Romanians, ultimately, is the adventure of memory. In the few things I have written through all these years, I find a common trait—it is the concern with memory. First of all, we must not forget. We must not forget all the suffering we experienced, and, especially, we must not forget the others' suffering. We must not forget them, even if they were not our own. We have a sacred duty of solidarity.

Memory does not mean spite or desire for revenge. Memory was a muse for the ancients, even the most important one. *Mnemosine* has a kind of higher, superior indifference, a kind of self-contained emotion. To remember is to remember *only what actually happened,* without interference of passions. But it also means to remember *everything that happened.*

Without any claim to glory, I should like to help all Romanians remember never to forget. Forgetting, they might repeat the mistakes of the past. But the thought of revenge is alien to me. Romania is in the margin of Europe. This simple geographical remark is heavy with consequences. All through the stages of her history, Romania, the territories inhabited by Romanians, have been menaced to break with Europe and fall—I do not think this word too strong— into Asia. I am not preaching a continental racism, but I do think that for us, Romanians, it is better to stay in Europe.

But we can hardly stay there unconditionally. During these years, when all the games of history are made all over again, Romania risks an easy departure from Europe. The frontiers of our continent have not been settled forever. The powers emerging now that the Soviet empire collapsed, Turkey's revival, especially, and the revival of all Turkish peoples, can push these frontiers way up towards the West. Romania can easily fall into this trap.

What can deliver our country from this trap of history? First of all, the respect for the great values of Europe, above all for the democratic institutions. But we must not forget that this is connected to a certain urbanity of dialogue, no personal attacks, that is, and the respect for principles. I found so little of all this when I returned to Romania.

Joining Europe requires great tolerance for neighboring peoples, or the peoples whom we must deal with. I say tolerance, because I know that certain antagonisms are inevitable. We must tolerate one another, and pave the way for syntheses that history will provide us with, anyway. Today's Romanian ideology resurrects nationalistic and simplistic theories, pushed to the extreme sometimes. This mistake must strongly be indicted.

The reason is that such theories tend to widen the feeling of isolation and awkwardness, which the Romanians have experienced fervently for a long while. Things may have to be discussed *sub specie veritatis,* too. Why should the image of a peasant, pastoral Romania be the true one, necessarily? Our history, our civilization is one of half breeds and contacts. All civilizations are the same. I can't see any reason why, precisely now, we should favor an ideology that preaches isolation, the artificial creation of a state of siege.

The right extreme Romanian ideologists, who, by a strange coincidence, also happen to be those who used to extol the tyrant, talk about a severe danger which menaces Romania today. The danger comes from abroad, they say. It is the result of a consensus between Hungarians and Jews, who, supposedly, are both determined to ruin the Romanian people. This is hard to imagine, and it takes a conscience in delirium to do it. I am not going to do what a psychiatrist would be too easily tempted to do, that is, to analyze this invention from a psychopathological point of view. I have fought too much against the use of psychiatry to political purposes to fall prey to this.

On the contrary, I shall say that there is a grain of truth in this statement. The truth is that the Romanians are menaced by a very serious danger today. But the danger does not come from outside the country. It comes from within. It is caused by the fact that Romanians are faced with a choice. They are at a historical moment—one of many—when, according to the direction of their decision, the scales will tilt one way or the other. If they accept to or can—which is, in fact, one and the same—come out of, wake completely from the dogmatic sleep of communism, then they will arrive where they belong, if we consider their natural tendencies and their place in the world. I mean Europe, of course. If not, they will slip into another corner of the world, and will have a different fate. By far unhappier, of course.

This choice is the source of the danger. The extreme right ideologists feel it, but interpret it in the wrong way. As far as I am concerned, I cannot accept for my country anything else than the fate I wished to have myself. That of a European, in the middle of Europe. I hope the time will soon come when all Romanians can say they have appropriated this fate.

March 1992

# Dumitru Radu Popescu

**born 1935**

*Playwright, prose writer: editor in chief of* Moftul român, *formerly the president of the Writers' Union.*

## Burdened with the Censorship of Freedom

**Lidia Vianu:** How would you explain the idea and obstacles of censorship to an American writer?

**Dumitru Radu Popescu:** Hopefully we have one very important thing in common: that we have all read the Bible. From the very first chapter it becomes obvious that there was censorship even then. How does God begin his dialogue with man? Not with a statement, but a denial. "Don't do this," is what he said. Which amounts to having no conscience. This is censorship. Everything is allowed except one fundamental thing. More exactly, "Do not taste the fruit of the tree of knowledge." You may not be like me. You cannot be aware of the others, of where you are, even of yourself. Not knowing yourself, not even seeing that your body is naked, is total freedom. I believe this interdiction gave man energy and made him smarter. Censorship usually eliminates the lazy. Or those who are not gifted. Obstacles are made for those who know how to overcome them. All of Eastern Europe ran an obstacle course for a century against an opponent which was in fact not an enemy, but a phase which had to be overcome by means of some additional effort. It was simultaneously a physical and an intellectual effort. I think this effort cultivated unbelievable imagination in the people. When the East is more thoroughly examined, people will see that it staged the most interesting experiment, created the most interesting literature in the world. There were some compromises, of course, and lower periods, too, eras of exhaustion, but some of the books written in the East are essential to the culture of the twentieth century. I think that the East gave the deepest investigation effort to this century. Western literature deepened the themes of the last century, but, at the same time, it merely excelled formally. It did not necessarily look into man or society to find answers or to avoid what can't be said. The war created an extraordinary mood there; it almost compelled those writers to create masterpieces. One cannot live in an arid, unconscious heaven. Adam chose. And only after he had chosen freedom, was he chased out of Paradise. Compared to a poor censor who would eliminate a single chapter or a word, divine intransigence looks far harder to bear. But it is more stimulating to man.

**L. V.** Did you feel that the pressure of the communist ideology, which was imposed upon us, was an obstacle to your creative activity?

**D. R. P.** There were several stages. There were times when certain topics or characters were compulsory; you were forced to deal with them. That lasted until the '60s. The whole of society had to be present in a book. Around this time writers fought hard, and this pressure subsided until it finally disappeared. It was at first due to some writers' personal efforts, and later with the complicity of the censors. Sometimes, the censor was a fellow writer: he had graduated from a philological college, knew what was good and what was bad; he was affiliated not just with evil. He helped a book get published when things were at their best. He meant no harm; he was intent on emphasizing a cultural value. In this way, his prestige was enhanced and his salary was justified. And he appeared very moral. He actually helped a cultural phenomenon take place. Only plain statements could be accused of anything. If you hid behind a metaphor, no one could really catch you. You could say anything as long as you did not do it openly. It may sound paradoxical, but these obstacles enriched literature. They created a number of levels of meaning, which do not exist in more direct literature. Direct literature borders on journalism, and I, for one, do not even consider it literature. On the other hand, there are certain devices which may make literature less accessible, but more solid. I do not agree with those who talk about inner censorship. Inner censorship is a trick used by those who are not in the least gifted. Before, they claimed that society prevented them from writing well. Then they blamed inner censorship for the same thing. I read a writer who said that at the age of fifty, after writing I don't know how many books, he decided to become honest and write a book which could not be published at that time. But it could appear in the West. Well, if that is true, he was more than a coward. It means that until that moment he had never been honest and free. He was a mercenary; he wrote for material profit. But that was all that he could do. So he had made compromises and still had not been able to rank well. It is a pity that obvious literature can go free, without being censored. Though I do not mean to say that censorship made anybody happy.

**L. V.** Could you name some negative effects of censorship?

**D. R. P.** I will not slander the dead.

**L. V.** Can you imagine what you would have written if there had been no censorship? Would you have tried other topics?

**D. R. P.** I wouldn't know.

**L. V.** Was the literary code your defense mechanism against politics?

**D. R. P.** These literary codes were used by many others, and they were deeply involved in politics. Some went so far as to use documents as such. These codes did not hide politics; they merely avoided making it too obvious.

**L. V.** Now that censorship has died, what will happen to our literature? What are its chances?

**D. R. P.** I have no idea what its chances are. In the past, writers were protected socially, so to say. They were not forced to give up their art for the sake of journalism or to adhere to a party in order to win. They could win only by means of their art. But now they can win in other ways as well. The social protection they had was, at the same time, a cultural one. Culturally speaking, it also protected the young. We all tried to discover the values. It happened with the generation of the '80s. I can't see this cultural protection any more. I can't imagine who will take the trouble of publishing their poetry if they do not make the editor rich. Still, I think ways can be found, and we will manage, even though we are burdened with the censorship of freedom.

July 1991

# Marin Sorescu

1936–1997

*Poet, playwright, novelist, essayist, editor, painter: he has been the winner of*
*many Romanian and international prizes; his work has been translated into*
*many languages*

## This Age Belongs to Primitive Energies

**Lidia Vianu:** What does censorship mean to you?

**Marin Sorescu:** There are two kinds of censorship. It is very hard to stand
practical censorship, and it is exactly that which afflicted us for a very long
time. Censorship is one way to stifle anyone. It was used quite often in
Romanian administration. Consequently, censorship was used directly, which
meant that they banned books, words, ideas, and authors. And it was also used
indirectly, which implied the existence of a second kind of censorship, which
was, in fact, slowly becoming more dangerous than the former. If, for a long
time, you see that certain things are not allowed, you form a kind of conditioned
reflex and avoid those particular things.

**L. V.** I have the feeling that this self-censorship has never afflicted you. Did
you fight censorship? Did they ever mutilate your texts?

**M. S.** I would even go so far as to say that, on the contrary, censorship stimulated me. I am used to facing huge obstacles when I work. The greater the
obstacle, the more active my stubbornness becomes, and sometimes I get good
results. I saw censorship as a kind of incentive. Paradoxically, I looked for sub-
tler outlets, metaphors, parables. In my case, as in the case of many other writers, censorship proved to have an unwillingly creative effect. As a matter of
fact, our literature became more literary, so to say.

**L. V.** Do you mean a code?

**M. S.** Yes. We created codes in our struggle against censorship. I really think that our literature existed by hiding and exhaling codes. These codes came quite close to transfiguration, which also implies that they came closer to the essence of art, which is not supposed to be rigid mimesis. Paradoxically, that is how an unravelling literature was created in the countries of Eastern and Southeastern Europe. This literature has its own value. When it could not be published, it gave rise to the samizdat. On the other hand, a parabolic literature and a literature of the absurd appeared. There censorship was absolutely powerless because it did not know what to catch on to.

**L. V.** Your poetry is teeming with what we call "lizards" in Romanian—things half said which suggest what is impossible to say. How did you manage to make the censors accept them and let them appear in your books?

**M. S.** These lizards are living animals, dinosaurs adapted to our days' climate. They originate in the brontosaurus of Mesozoic freedom. They were, in fact, knots of meaning, ambiguous messages. Ambiguity is creative in art, and, as far as I am concerned, I tried my hand at finding such formulas, impossible to forbid.

**L. V.** How did you do it? Did censorship inspire you to find them, or did you protect yourself before being attacked?

**M. S.** I defended myself beforehand, and my writing is generally all polemical: essays, plays, prose. Even my painting, I would say. I threw arrows at the official literature written at that time. I favored a literature which would be literature, which would not humor politics in this primitive way. This forced me to look for more and more codes. I wanted my works to be original, personal . . .

**L. V.** Inflaming?

**M. S.** Yes, for the others. I discovered a kind of collective subjectivism, or intimism, so to say. Things which I considered extremely intimate, personal, only mine: my most intimate thoughts, my discontent, my fears, the feeling of oppression. All these became the mirror of a large group of people. Discovering this common self of mine was a great amazement to me. I react like thousands, millions of people, I thought, and this gave me great confidence in myself and in the world at the same time. I was considered popular, and I think I was among the first postwar writers who, in fact, suddenly reached this spontaneity, this spontaneous communication with lots and lots of people. I was criticized for being too popular. But, in fact, I felt that this was my most important quality, or at least one of the qualities I needed to cultivate.

**L. V.** Would you agree that your lyrical nature was forced into politics by censorship? Now that censorship has disappeared, are you returning to lyricism?

**M. S.** This is a very interesting remark indeed. . . . At that time, it was very important for the writer to be politically active. A specific political line was imposed. I did everything I could to avoid politics. In my theoretical works, I pleaded to preserve the autonomy of the aesthetic side of literature, to preserve the value of art, no matter what the political line was. Subconsciously I have always been an "anti." The lyricism you mentioned acquired a political bent because of censorship. At present, we must make an effort to return to pure lyricism.

**L. V.** Does the disappearance of censorship inconvenience you in any way?

**M. S.** It would certainly be out of place to speak out in favor of censorship, after having dreamt of being rid of this immense burden for a lifetime. I have carried the rock of Sisyphus in my pen for so long. Now that it is gone, I might feel a kind of nostalgia, as if I had been deprived of pain. I am like the cured patient who is unhappy because he has lost his pain.

**L. V.** You were an extremely prolific writer during the time of censorship. Have you experienced any postcensorship writing block?

**M. S.** If not a block, perhaps a state of noncreation. And I am not the only one. Lots of writers mention this. The cause is first and foremost the general confusion, both social and political. We have suddenly entered an era of numberless possibilities and, strangely enough, we are now the victims of too much choice. We feel unable to choose. As the Romanian saying goes, we are like a calf in front of a new gate. Many new gates, actually.

**L. V.** What do you think you will choose?

**M. S.** For the present, I have returned to normal and am writing poetry. I have started several things which I hope to finish. I consider my instinct to be better than my theory. I trust my instinct, and I feel that it has already found its bearings. I guess I am going to write a kind of lyrical diary, in a way. I have no intention of reinventing censorship or self-censorship; I will allow my inspiration to ramble. As far as I can tell, we are crossing a field full of electricity, lightning and thunder. Many are even thunderstruck. One can easily be hurt while coming into contact with our time. But there are so many opportunities available here that I would call it a fertile area. I want to choose the creative side of this time of ours. I hope I will be able to find it. There are so many quarrels and misunderstandings, discontent and the confusion of tendencies. . . .

**L. V.** Before the revolution you were associated most obviously with the opposition. You played no direct political part. Where and how are you these days?

**M. S.** I border on neutrality. I prefer a more discreet angle. I do not expect my work to yield any profits. Therefore I have not experienced the need to act as a discontented fighter in the street. I have always stood apart from these gestures, which seem to me to be more rhetorical than true.

**L. V.** A delirium of censorship has appeared, too . . .

**M. S.** Yes. A delirium of previous suffering. Those who were fervent leftists are now fervent rightists, so to say. And of course, they derive some benefit from this change of attitude. Since I want no profit, I keep my previous aloofness. I remain an independent person.

**L. V.** You are reticent to talk about censorship, although censorship has affected you a lot. For instance, in your novel *Three Front Teeth,* I felt a certain block. You did have to fight a writer's block when you wrote that novel.

**M. S.** Yes. That's right. That is a novel in which all possibilities are blocked. Now, I am trying to publish an edition of the integral text.

**L. V.** Did they cut out much of the novel?

**M. S.** About 150 pages. But I can't say for sure. I must take them and fit them all back together.

**L. V.** Did they force you to change the ending?

**M. S.** No, I never compromised. But I did accept the alterations. The ending, like all the rest, belongs just to me. I cooperated with censorship in that I had to accept these mutilations. I am an old client for censorship. I even have the feeling that I am the most censored writer in our country. Words, cues, whole texts were rejected. For poetry, a poem would sometimes appear in the next volume, or it was never approved. I have edited those poems now. If, in the meanwhile, the censor changed, a milder period came or the atmosphere was a little more open. . . . You know, censorship was not a unitary phenomenon, like a monolith. That is what they wanted. But it did not work like that, because the whole thing was based on humans. So it became the art of crossing.

**L. V.** You are a world-famous writer. Did they dare touch your texts?

**M. S.** At the very beginning I was not famous. Later, I admit, they rejected only some poems. But when I became fairly well known, they left me alone. But lately I was severely censored again. They even forbade me completely. Some plays could not be published; others were only performed, and then forbidden afterwards. I used much energy in talking interminably to the Ministry of Culture, so that the plays would pass the censors. For a play like *The Cold* to be performed, I had to attend endless performances for a whole year, with the show completed. I had to talk to people at the Ministry, to committees and subcommittees every week for an entire year.

**L. V.** How did you react to this harassment? Could you still write?

**M. S.** They irritated me in a creative way, but consumed much of my energy. I could have written at least twice as many plays if I had not tried so stubbornly to see those already written performed at that time.

**L. V.** Does that seem a waste to you now?

**M. S.** I don't think so. This energy was useful to others as well. At that moment, I succeeded in keeping close to Europe, to the European theater. Afterwards, the plays could be performed abroad. If the plays were not allowed to be performed here, the Ministry of Culture would not allow them to be performed in any other socialist country. Only now, for instance, have I learned that *Iona* or *The Third Pale* were interdicted by the Ministry of Culture in Poland and Czechoslovakia. There were cooperation contracts between these countries. Interdictions, which I could not possibly have known about, circulated inside the socialist countries. At least I know now. It was life-consuming.

**L. V.** Lots of the poems translated into other languages were "anti." Were they usually like that?

**M. S.** I was in no danger as long as they were published in Romania first.

**L. V.** Have you ever been in trouble because of your attitude?

**M. S.** I was not sent on official delegations. I was never sent on any cultural delegation by the Writers' Union, nor could I cooperate in cooperation contracts with other countries. I was not considered an official person.

**L. V.** Have you met your former censors, now in this new atmosphere of freedom?

**M. S.** Yes. And they are most deferential. Some even say that they always liked me.

**L. V.** Are they experiencing a guilt complex now?

**M. S.** They probably expect me to experience that.

**L. V.** Do you think enough time has actually elapsed for censorship to disappear?

**M. S.** No, I don't think so. We can't even realize how much we were changed. More time must pass first. Most of us try to rid ourselves of this burden by willingly joining the opposite side. Some parade a freedom which borders on pornography.

**L. V.** What do you think of such reactions to the disappearance of censorship?

**M. S.** They are useless. There are ways to show that we are free, of course. In time, everyone will adjust properly. Criticism can help a lot. Right now the papers barely do their job.

**L. V.** Would you say that the Americans write better poetry than we do because of, or in spite of their freedom?

**M. S.** I would say that they don't always write better poetry than we do. But that's not because of their freedom. It is because of a certain way of understanding the idea of freedom. If they created more obstacles for themselves—not censorship, but obstacles of common sense, maybe—it might be better. First of all, we must take common sense into account. One must have good artistic intuition. We must understand the distinction between art and journalism, immediate reflection of mass-media. Each has its own function. But the two must not be mistaken for each other. We are still very confused about that. The two can be confused, even in countries which have reached an advanced stage of democracy. Or in order to avoid mixing them up, people overlook common sense. That is how poetry is often divested of all meaning. Western countries are not very astonished at the strength of Eastern poetry. Wherever I go—Germany, France, England—my poetry is looked upon as an oddity.

**L. V.** What led you to painting? Does it have anything to do with censorship?

**M. S.** That story is older. In the final stages, it actually is connected with censorship. I had a kind of social shock and was under extreme pressure in 1981, when they raged against transcendental meditation, the famous scandal*; and I was named among those plotting against the state. That was a kind of dissidence that preceded the one known internationally as such. The accusation of being part of that plot was very serious and could have had extremely unpleasant effects. It made me experience a social shock which took me by surprise. I tried to overcome it by giving up writing, which had brought me into all this in the first place. I remembered that, as a child, I wanted to be a painter. I practised drawing and coloring. . . . Ostentatiously, I started painting in my courtyard, in oil, while the Securitate agent posted at my gate watched.

**L. V.** Would you be willing to say that these paintings came out as polemical poems too? Or are they only color and shapes?

**M. S.** There are many stages to discuss. The stage where I am now is closer to my poetry. My paintings gave me the joy of communicating through color. It was a very somber period in my life, and I needed light. I rediscovered the joy of colors and drawing. I became a child again, rediscovering the simple shapes and colors.

**L. V.** Do you think that the disappearance of censorship has positive or negative effects on literature?

**M. S.** Both. But we must see only the positive ones. We wanted so much to be rid of censorship. We must be happy that we are at last rid of it.

---

* A huge political trial was set up against many intellectuals who went to the meetings of a group of so-called transcendental meditation. It was harmless, but many dissenters frequented it, so it became the best reason to persecute them, which the communists did, fiercely.

**L. V.** Do you like what is being written these days?

**M. S.** No. People hardly write at all. Everybody wants to plunge into journalism, into scandal. Almost every writer has passed through his small scandal. It is like toughening people's sensibility. In the West or in America, generally speaking, people think that the censor is a hangman who comes and tells you that he will either cut off you head or spare your life, depending on whether you are willing to change your text or not. But the censor often happened to be a friend. He would come to you complaining that his career would be destroyed if you did not get rid of this passage or that one. When an official edited my text, I got terribly angry. But when the same person came begging that he would be ruined if I did not change something, asking me to understand him, saying that those things might be published later, in a better context, then I found it very hard not to give in and give up the passage in question. This was in a way complicity with censorship.

**L. V.** As editor in chief of a literary magazine, did you censor anything?

**M. S.** Well, that is an interesting question. First of all, all I dealt with was the poetry page. I let everything go that I knew would be rejected, and sometimes it actually passed through. I was the first to write an essay about Emil Cioran (Romanian philosopher who lived in France), and I had to speak harshly to the Ministry to have it accepted. I also wrote about Mircea Eliade and Eugène Ionesco. I was in deep trouble many times because of Constantin Noica's (reclusive Romanian philosopher) articles. So, I would say that I acted as if censorship did not exist.

**L. V.** Did you reject any articles?

**M. S.** No. On the contrary, I was content making life difficult for the censors. If the texts were published, that meant I had managed to enlarge the borders of what was allowed to be published. Several times I was successful in doing so. This normal behavior of mine, apparently normal, had a hypnotic effect, gave more self-confidence, both to those who had to censor and to those who wrote what was published.

**L. V.** What is your view of the future fate of the literary genres in Romania? Now that censorship no longer exists, anything can be said. Which will benefit more from this freedom, poetry or prose?

**M. S.** In my opinion, we are facing a much more demanding censorship: economic censorship. I have already felt it. *Poems Chosen by Censorship*, the title of my latest book, which includes poems I could not publish before the revolution, however hard I tried, and other poems which I did not dare submit because they were really dangerous, was very difficult to publish, even after the revolution, which is unbelievable. For two years, I talked to various publishing houses. They all said that they could not afford to publish it or had no money to print it because poetry was no longer in demand. So, I guess, less poetry will be written.

**L. V.** Does that mean that literature will lower its standards in order to meet the requirements of the public?

**M. S.** Prose will come to the forefront, I think. At first, what I would call "base prose," immediate and vulgar prose; the weeds will come out. The vigorous weeds may win for a while and become the standard, stifling the true grain. The great energies are peripheral. This is not the time for great aesthetic refinement; this age belongs to primitive energies. As the Romanians so often say, "Do not fight a stupid man because his mind is well rested." In my opinion this is now true. Later on, when people have had enough and feel that some attitude is necessary concerning so much wasted paper, we may reach a phase of aestheticism which will be as useless as the vulgar literature we have now. Now, we also face the danger of pluripartitism. Before, we were all on our guard because there was just the one party, but now we are terrified by the number of parties which have broken the artistic unity, and which, more often than not, come with dogmas which, I would say, look very much like those of the Romanian Communist Party.

July 1991

# Poetry

### I Caught Sight of Light . . .

I caught sight of light on earth,
And I was born
In order to see how you were.

Are you doing fine? Are you all right?
How about your happiness?

You do not answer, thank you.
I have no time for answers,
I hardly have time for answers.

But I like it here.
It is warm, it is fine,
And so much light that
The grass grows.

And that girl, there,
Watches me with her soul . . .
No, my dear, do not bother to love me.
I shall just have a coffee, though,
Out of your hand.
I like the way you make it
Very bitter.

### Early Morning

We wash in your foam, oh, sun,
Our basic soap,
Placed at hand
On the mantle of the sky.
We keep holding out our arms towards you
And rub ourselves with light thoroughly,
Until our bones ache with so much happiness.

Oh, what gaiety
There is on earth in the morning!
Like the washroom of a boarding school,
When children fill their mouths with water
And spit at each other.

For the time being, we still don't know where to find
The best towels, too—
And we wipe our faces with death.

## The Road

Thoughtful, hands behind  my back
I walk along the railroad,
The straightest road
Of all.

From behind me, at high speed,
A train is coming
A train which has never heard of me.

This train—old Zenon can tell you, too—
Will never reach me,
Because I shall always be ahead of things
Which cannot think.

But even if, brutally,
It runs over me,
There will always be a man
To walk ahead of it
Thoughtful
Hands behind his back.

Just like me now
Ahead of the black monster
Which is drawing near at terrifying speed,
And which will never reach me.

## I Blindfolded . . .

I blindfolded the trees
With a green kerchief
And I told them to find me.

And the trees found me at once
With  laughter of leaves.

I blindfolded the birds
With a kerchief of clouds
And I told them to find me.

And the birds found me
With a song.

I blindfolded sadness
With a smile
And sadness found me the next day
In a love.

I blindfolded the sun
With my nights
And I told him to find me.

You are there, the sun said,
Behind that time,
Stop hiding.

Stop hiding,
I was told by all things
And feelings
Which I tried to
Blindfold.

## Flight

One day
I shall stand up from my writing desk
And I shall begin walking away from words,
From you
And from all things.

I shall see a mountain at the horizon
And will walk towards it
Till the mountain is left behind me.

Then I shall follow a cloud,
And the cloud will be left behind.

The sun will be left behind me, too,
The stars and the whole universe . . .

## Creation

I am writing on earthquakes,
And if some words

Slide too far,
Only the surface of the earth is to blame
Because it is so unstable.

You can't foretell
When a volcano opens under your writing desk,
And after a day's work
You can sign your name on the very ashes.

All things change
Their places,
The lamp from the ceiling has come lower than my chin,
The mountain at the horizon has filled my mouth
Like a gag whose last bits
Will be spat out
By my descendants seven generations later.

The leaves at the top of trees
Have all moved into the ground
For fear of earthquakes,

Very many of my ancestors
Moved into earth
For fear of earthquakes.

I alone still try to bind together
Like rails after some derailment,
These two words,

Which run this
And that way,
Maddened with fear.

## The Flute

A flute screams all of a sudden
Behind a passer-by
Whose body is filling with saw dust
Like a tree, when it feels
The saw
At the edge of the forest.

However, I shall not turn my head—the man tells himself—
It may be meant for somebody else.

Or anyway, I shall allow myself
A few more paces.

The flute is heard loudly
Behind all passers-by
Who turn blue, pale, green, red
And go ahead stiffly,
Without turning their heads.
It may be meant for somebody else—
Each thinks—
What more have I done
Than one or two wars?
I have my wedding tomorrow,
My wife will give birth the day after tomorrow,
The day after that I shall bury my parents—
I have so many things to do,
It can't be for me.

A child
Bought a flute,
And came out to try it
On the boulevard,
Jokingly blowing it into people's ears.

## Illness

Doctor, I feel something deadly
Here, in the area of my being,
Everything hurts,
In the daytime the sun hurts,
At night the moon and the stars.

I have a shooting pain in the cloud in the sky
I had not even noticed it before
And I wake every morning
With the feeling of winter.

I have taken all kinds of pills in vain,
I have hated and loved, I have learned how to read
And I have even read some books,
I have talked to people and I have thought,
I have been kind and I have been handsome. . .

All these have had no effect, doc.
And I have spent so many years on them.

I think I fell ill with death
One day
When I was born.

## Fear

Wherever I go
I take my body along,
Because I have no place to leave it.
The earth steals it from me,
The sky and waters.

In happiness, in love,
In sadness and sorrow,
I must feel my hand and forehead close by,
I must feel my heart beat.
I should be worried otherwise.

Oh, how we tremble
For the dust of our body,
Rather primitive,
And out of which, after each rain
Earthworms still creep out. . .

## The Shadow

If our shadow
Had five senses too,
We would live much more beautifully,
With both hearts at once.

But between us and our shadow
A long process of abstraction
Took place
And all our insensibility
Has reached its peak in it.

Some people
Only live with their shadow
And even the shadow is not whole,
They take in turns, an eye,
A hand.

## Alone

I am cold in this shirt
Made of letters
Through which anything
Penetrates so easily.

The wind through a,
The wolves through b,
Winter through c,
And I am trying to protect my heart at least
Behind a darker title,
But the cold which comes in through all the letters
Gets me.

I don't like this shirt
Made of letters
Through which my breathing and heartbeats
Go out at once.

Through a,
Through b,
Through c,
The alphabet is full of me
For a moment.

## We Engrave Our Faces

On a huge wall of cells
We engrave our faces
And go by.

Sometimes on the wall there is also left
What we happen to hold while we are alive:
An amphora, a woman, a knife. . .

Our descendants crowd from behind,
As if in a museum,
And watch us full of curiosity,
They learn from our history
And keep making mistakes
In theirs
Nearby.

## Who

Let us examine well
Who is hiding below us,
Let us be very careful
Whom we call
I.

One can no longer
Trust blindly
Anyone.
Let us be very careful
Especially whom we call
I.

Squeezed by some knee
Under such conventional
Masks,
Laughter, tears, love,
We try hard and clumsily
To be familiar with ourselves.

We may even succeed
At a certain point,
But we are frightened to death
When we hear our own voice.

## Precipice

God is deaf
And when I have something to tell him
I write it on a sheet of paper.
This is what one does
With all deaf people.

But he does not understand my handwriting
And when I see him scratching his halo
When faced with some conjunction,
I think it would be so much easier
To scream it in his ear.

That's what I actually do,
But God shakes his head
He does not understand
And beckons me to put down on paper
Whatever it is I want to tell him.
I am besieged by despair,
I go out into the street and stop the passers by,
And show them the words I wrote.
They are written as best and legibly I could
For God's eyes.
But people are not deaf,
They are just in a hurry,
So they push my paper aside,
And ask me to tell them quickly
Out loud.

Then I find myself howling
As if from the bottom of a precipice,
As God howls
When he makes his prayer.

And for fear I may also have lost my hearing
I forget what I had meant to say.

## The Hour

The hour
When, tired with so much meaning, things
Fall asleep on top of him,
Like watchmen
Chin kept up
By the tip of the lance.

Walls, ceiling, sky and universe,
Do not lean too heavily
On me
However,
I am only catching at a single thought,

A single word even
Which has already stopped existing
At one end.

## Adam

Although he was in heaven,
Adam was walking down alleys, preoccupied and sad
Because he could not tell what he was longing for.

Then God put Eve together
Out of one of Adam's ribs.
And the first man liked this miracle so much,
That the very same moment
He felt his next rib,
And his fingers were thrilled
By strong breasts and sweet thighs
Like outlines of musical notes.
A new Eve had come to life in front of him.
She had just taken out her little mirror
And was spreading lipstick on her lips.
"That's life!" Adam sighed
And created one more.

In the same way, whenever the official Eve
Turned her back,
Or went shopping for gold, myrrh and incense,
Adam brought to life another odalisque
Using his ribs as a harem.

God noticed
Adam's dissolute creation.
He called Adam to him and swore at him in his godlike manner,
Then drove him out of paradise
Because of surrealism.

## We Never Wonder

We never wonder at anything,
Wonder has been exterminated,
It was an atavism which brought us too close to the ape.

The temperature of the human body dropped
From 36 to 15 degrees
Out of the energy saved
An artificial sun was created
To heat diesel engines.

The engines make such an uproar,
Human temperature drops,
Feelings point to zero,
We never wonder at anything,
This is uninterrupted progress.

## Actors

How easy going—the actors!
With rolled up sleeves
They are so good at living our lives for us!

I have never seen a more perfect kiss
Than the actors' in the third act,
When feelings start
Coming to light.

With oil spots all over,
With true-to-life caps,
Holding all kinds of offices.
They start and end cues,
Which fit them like gloves.

Their death on stage is so natural,
That, compared to its perfection,
Those in the graveyards,
The real dead,
Tragically made up once and forever,
Seem to budge!

While we, so stiff inside a single life!
We don't even know how to live ours.
We talk at random or keep silent for years on end,
Awkwardly and unaesthetically
And we simply don't know where the hell we should keep
                                        our hands.

# Ileana Mălăncioiu

born 1940

*Poet, editor: she has written ten books of poetry*

## The Only Obstacle Was Myself

**Lidia Vianu:** How did literature survive under censorship?

**Ileana Mălăncioiu:** It was, in fact, our way of survival. But it has become harder now. At that time, we could not complain to anyone. It was not a question of complaining.

**L. V.** Did you fight censorship?

**I. M.** It is too easy to come now and brag about it. The fight was led by our editors, on our behalf. As an author, I merely fought not to censor myself. I did have this fear, and I always thought that if censorship took hold in my mind, it would later be a disaster. My primary concern was my mind. I wanted to say what I had to say. I was lucky because editors of magazines and publishing houses fought and took risks on my behalf, because the author merely does his duty, when he writes. But when someone fights on behalf of somebody else, that person should be praised. In our country we talk too much about those of us who wrote, and much less about those who took risks for us. That is unfair. At one magazine, for instance, a man was fired because he published one of my texts. It also happened at a publishing house. To me, it seems fair to talk about those people who fought for other people's books. In Cluj, Victor Felea was fired because of some of my poems which were published in 1982. Mircea Sântimbreanu was fired from Albatros publishing house. Even the censor, Mrs. Doxănescu, who turned out to be a person who loved and really fought for good books, suffered because of me. These people deserve due attention. Lately, they seem, in fact, to be treated all the same. There was a clerk at the Ministry of Culture, Ecaterina Țarălungă, who simply burned an issue of our magazine when it had hardly been printed. She is now a very respected editor.

Nothing has changed for her. She was taken over by the National Salvation Front and protected by them. On the other hand, Mrs. Doxănescu was punished by Ceauşescu, and now, no one is trying to make amends for that. I do not think one must cut off people's heads. But we must examine what each of us did under the conditions in which we were working before. Now we run the risk of rehabilitating people who are not really worth it, and not doing anything about people who are being punished because they did something important for us then.

**L. V.** Did it ever happen that you were not able to publish a book because of censorship?

**I. M.** By the end, I was almost unable to write. After *Climbing the Mountain,* I was suddenly unable to have a single line published. The last time I managed to squeeze in a poem was the second issue of *Romanian Life* in 1989, which was burned as soon as it was printed. There were two risks: writing in vain, and not saying what was on your mind. In my opinion, the risk of not telling the truth is greater.

My troubles with censorship were a bit older, in fact. In 1971, I was working for state television; for three years I was a TV editor there. Everything that happened in Romania had the strongest possible effect there. At that particular time, anything new from above was imposed as law; you had absolutely no right to object. One day I dared say that I disagreed with the Party documents of July. I was not actually that brave; I said, in fact, that I did not agree to their publication. This meant implicitly that I disagreed with the entire thing. They actually stated that we were no longer allowed to have cultural television. We no longer had the right to culture. Consequently, I had to leave my job at state television. For twenty years since then, I was not allowed to appear on TV. Some people talk a lot about things like that. But I did not really suffer because of that. I suffered only because an illegal thing was done to me, but the institution worked so badly that it was desirable not to go there at all. In fact, I suffered because of the stance taken by several people about this decision, considering that if I was never again seen on TV, the tyrant would be satisfied. So, radio and TV censorship lasted for twenty years for me because I objected to the Party documents of July 1971. It seems to me that our situation got considerably worse at that time. I just could not write for a while, because I had the feeling that nothing I said would be published. It was very hard for me to say things only half-way. And then I started writing something totally different, in order to escape from contemporary literature. I defended my dissertation among other things. My dissertation dealt with the tragic, and in a way I was speaking about the same things, but my pain was transferred to another time. My dissertation dealt with tragic guilt in Greek literature, Shakespeare, Dostoyevsky, and Kafka. Theoretically, I spoke about the same things that hurt me, but I left out references to the contemporary world.

I did that until 1981, when it suddenly occurred to me that what I was doing was no longer enough, because the country was in bad shape. At first I did not write political poems. I even despised that. But at that time, politics had penetrated our homes, had become part of our life stories; it could no longer be avoided. So, in 1982, I wrote my first political poems and published them in *The Tribune.* In March 1982, they published a poem entitled "Buried While Standing" and one entitled "Nightmare," in which I equated Ceauşescu with Hitler. A month after the paper had been published, they tried to withdraw it from newspaper stands, but there were not many copies left to withdraw. Anyway, they wanted to change all the departmental heads at the magazine. They summoned everyone who worked there at that time. Those who could speak better got away with it. When asked how he interpreted the poem in which I mentioned Hitler, Buzura said that he saw it as an anti-Hitlerist poem. So he got away. Felea admitted that he had been wrong in publishing it, apologized and was punished. It was a matter of finding your way deftly among dangerous things.

These poems were included in a book which was being printed by Romanian Book. It was ready, in fact. The book bore the title, *The Line of Life.* It was rejected by the censors five times. Every editor who asked for one more censorship check asked me to take out more poems. In the end, I decided to withdraw the entire book. They did not like that because everybody knew that it had already been printed. Burning an entire book is a great waste of money, so they made a deal with me. I took out twelve poems, and the book was released. It was the next to last one I published. The last, *Climbing the Mountain,* came out in 1985. It caused a real scandal in the publishing house. The director was fired, and the editor was moved somewhere else. They also punished those who had let it get past the Council of Culture. I was never summoned there, but the president of the Writers' Union was, and he defended the book, no matter how badly he is attacked these days. Afterwards, none of my poems were published anywhere for four years, until the revolution, that is.

A collection of articles appeared, rather by chance. Because there were so many scandals, they did not want to have too many books rejected, and even a tyrant like Dulea had no time to check. He asked the people from Romanian Book Publishing House what the book dealt with. I had sent some letters saying that, because I was forbidden to publish, to submit anything to the radio or television and to travel, I felt forced to leave the country, although I wanted to remain a Romanian writer. I also said that I wanted to know what conditions I had to fulfil in order to remain a Romanian writer. That prompted their decision to publish my articles. So Dulea asked the people from the publishing house what the book dealt with, and Liviu Călin defended me. He said that it was a book of articles about classical writers, testimonies about writers I had met. In fact, each article, each testimony was used to repeat the same thing. Only they understood that very late, and I got away with the book.

**L. V.** What did the book discuss?

**I. M.** Some of the prose poems were a kind of nightmare which bordered on my poetry. They contained the things I had not been allowed to put in my poems. One dealt with the destruction of villages; another hinted at the Securitate via Caragiale, but quite directly. I used Caragiale's *At Căldărușani* as a starting point and discussed the permanent surveillance, which occurred even in the monastery. In another article, I mentioned Emil Botta and used him to talk about De Gaulle's visit, how people in the street commented on it. I finally reached the contemporary world by other means. The nightmares openly alluded to the destruction of villages and the state of affairs at that time. I dealt with what was on our minds most at the time.

**L. V.** Did you get into personal trouble after the effect of your books became obvious?

**I. M.** The censors did not have much to do with the author of the book printed. The author was interdicted, but nobody told him. I for one learned from the paper that my poems had been removed. I was not to know that I had been interdicted, not in so many words. They had their own ways. But I was never afraid. Once, when they refused to let me travel to Germany on a grant for the third time, I complained to the Council of the Writers' Union that I felt compelled to leave the country because I could not lead that kind of life. I was called to the Press Department only once, by Ghiță Florea. Every five minutes he told me that I was a "very good" poet, but I would be an excellent poet if I would write something else. Especially if I said nothing at all and did nothing. I explained to him that if I was a good poet, that should prompt him to let me go. In any civilized country—and not only in the civilized ones—even in Uganda, if a writer is good, it is not possible that the police would forbid him to go away. My police record was all right. The only thing wrong with my record was me myself. So the police did let me go. But the Ministry of Culture prevented me from going. I told them that in a civilized country it is the duty of the Ministry of Culture to release really good writers from the claws of the police, not to leave you in their hands, not to wait for the police to let you go abroad. I was finally allowed to go. But my departure was cancelled once more before I left. I later heard that it had been Mr. Dulea who had cancelled it. In the end, I was allowed to leave, when half of my scholarship was lost, as it happened toward the end of the year.

**L. V.** What was your mood when you wrote, considering that you fought so hard to stay free, even from the thought of censorship?

**I. M.** The time came when it seemed to me so important to say what I had to say that it seemed natural to take that risk, if not more. I tried to be as convincing as I could. During the last few years, I was terribly afraid of self-censorship because censorship itself was so strong. I thought that was more than enough.

Now, the situation has changed. So much is being said that a certain code of honor compels you to self-censorship. So many people who really were not victims have appeared that it affords no pleasure at all to appear to be one of them. A lot of false statements are being published and bring about public scandal. Lots of people who used to do ugly things now come to the forefront. Quite a few people try to find a way to become well known whenever a crossroads turns up, like now. These people are beginning to join all the parties, not just the National Salvation Front. So, from time to time, I feel the need to censor my own words. I don't want to be like many of the others. For instance, I felt that I had to declare that I would not sign any more collective protests because I found myself on a list which said, "Down with the Securitate!," and I saw that two Securitate agents had signed before me and two after me. That is unfair. When I took those risks, I did not do it in the company of these people. The name of a person who contributed to the destruction of the issue of the magazine in which I was trying to publish was on the same list, just above my name. So I said to myself, "Let me be a witness right now. I will sign only texts which I have written myself. Otherwise everything gets mixed up." I know it is very difficult, and it is good for people to be politically active now, but it is very hard to change something in a country in which so much harm was done without any interference on our part whatsoever. And there is another thing, too. I know myself: I am not good as a leader. My gift is writing correctly on paper. Maybe this is not so bad. Maybe there must also be witnesses, who support the Alliance from the outside, as far as we consider it good and useful.

**L. V.** Do you believe in the Civic Alliance?

**I. M.** I think that there are valuable people involved in it. And they stand a good chance of getting something accomplished. There are also certain risks, such as the risk that it would belong to a kind of elite group, which makes it less accessible. But my hope is that these extremely capable people, qualified in their fields, will find the right way from practice, will realize that democracy has much to do with the number of people involved. You cannot do without the people who voted for you. I do hope they will understand that if you intend to participate in politics directly, you must work for as many people as possible. In the end they will somehow reach the masses. They will reach the masses, just as their books have gradually done so. But for that, you must give in a little and even lower your standards, because for a politician whose goal is democracy the numbers count just as much as his democratic ideas.

This kind of education has to be undertaken by someone, and it is a good thing that some intellectuals have started doing so. Unfortunately, they still do not have the popularity they had hoped for. I have the feeling that the reason for this is that life in our country is even more difficult now than before. People need answers to very concrete questions. As long as only theory is resorted to, they might come to a meeting once or twice. But then the question of tomorrow's food becomes more important. Of course, all standards cannot be reduced to what they are going to eat tomorrow. There is a vicious circle here. It takes a long time to educate the people, and you cannot educate them when they are hungry. Ceaușescu decreed that every family must have four children. And now Iliescu is forcing them to starve their children. However deeply these people may want to listen to theory, the cannot, nor do they have time for it. It just is not enough for them, even if it is well done. Of course theory is important for the future; this is my opinion, anyway. It may even become more important than right now.

**L. V.** Before, you were in the opposition without being involved in politics. Have you become politically active now?

**I. M.** I did get involved in all the important moments. I wrote about my view of the revolution for the newspapers, or what I think actually happened, about our present government, about the miners coming to Bucharest to bring order (in 1990), even about dissidence. In regards to dissidence, I would say, using a well-known cue, "There were few of us, but look how many are left." The mere gesture of siding with the opposition does not lend one credibility; I can't believe everyone. I talked, or rather wrote, about all these things, as far as I felt it was my duty to do so. But my wish is to return to culture, because I feel that culture is the most endangered "species" in Romania these days.

**L. V.** Have you written any poetry at all since 1989?

**I. M.** Too little. I have, but not like I did before, because it takes me a long time to write anything, including journalistic articles, and I had to get involved. I also work as a journalist. It takes me a long time, and writing comes hard for me. I was not a born journalist. I do it to the detriment of literature. A time will come when we will look back, as we did in 1945, when we saw with great pleasure those who had managed to steer literature off that evil track imposed on it. What happened then, I am sorry to say, happened in the name of democracy also, because then, like now, many considered dealing with culture unimportant.

The most important field was always that of social change. But a nation's progress is caused by culture, and this cannot be ignored. What remains of a people is always its culture. There are moments, like the one we are now experiencing, when culture is so seriously endangered that someone must take care of it. The government has no time, and I understand that. They also say they have no money. I really do not believe that. So many party representatives from so many parties travel so much, while Romanian culture is left squeezed in its small place. A little more could have been invested in it. A little, at least. Consequently, if the government has no time to think about it, each party has its own policy to obey. Even the Writers' Union has become a trade union which deals with generalities. . . . Because it has been led by a dissident, the Writers'

Union is the quietest place in Romania. So, if no one has any more time to think of the future of culture, at least a few writers ought to do so, because it is so representative for a people.

**L. V.** The disappearance of censorship changes something in the way of writing. Do you think that it brings about a writer's block?

**I. M.** There are good and bad changes. What I mean is that we are witnessing a general outburst which surpasses the decency known in civilized countries. Not only in the National Front press, not only in *Great Romania* which is a disaster, but almost everywhere. It seems to me that people have understood that the absence of censorship means general upheaval. This is a danger. The disappearance of censorship ought to have been followed by a heightening of cultural standards, politeness, and respect for the Romanian language in the press. In poetry and fiction no essential books have appeared as of yet; it has been impossible to write in this atmosphere. This may be one good side to the lack of censorship. Before, literature replaced the press, which was unable to say anything; it was a subterfuge. In poetry, prose, essays, we could say what the press could not. Now, for better or for worse, the press does far more than its duty. Under these circumstances, literature finds itself forced to exist within its boundaries. This is a very dangerous limit. You have to determine how far you can go with social neutrality, if you stand any chances of being heeded right now. Or the extent to which you can get socially involved without repeating the dirty tricks of the press. This is a way which is awfully hard to find. In great literature, the social aspects were part of the background. Literature remained literature, without ignoring what belonged to the social side. Literature must not live on what we are used to calling "lizards."

The fact that literature survived on what the press couldn't say in a way reinvigorated literature. But it also endangered it somehow, because I am not sure how many of the books we read with excitement back then will mean anything to us ten years from now. Persons of remarkable quality find their way with difficulty now, and I can understand that. This crisis of culture about which so much is said, which we should treat with certain signs of respect, has a better quality than the previous ones. If the world has not gone forward as if nothing had happened, that is not bad, because culture cannot ignore the misfortune and chaos all around it. It may be a positive crisis, out of which something valuable will be born.

July 1991

# Poetry

### Night Almost White

It was a night almost white (Good God, what a night it was!)
I was in front of Hieronymus and his body was lit
Through to his bones. Mr. Hieronymus, I called out
(Since at that time I would call him Mr. Hieronymus).

Please, forgive me for telling you, but I am afraid
All that is left of your body is
A rather vague luminous halo
And inside it I can see all your broken bones.

You can take my word for it, that night I could see
All the broken bones inside Hieronymus' body
Even the forehead bone, which was hanging
And shone on the silver side.

The night was white, my God, what a night
And I was so scared to be left alone with Hieronymus
And his body was light
It showed all its broken bones right through.

### Water of the Dead

Hieronymus, I have scoured the fields today
And I saw the waters of the dead for the first time
And I ran towards them and in the midst
I saw you naked, ready to bathe.

You seemed to be trying to cover your nakedness and someone
Whom I don't know had stolen your clothes from the bank
And as I came closer to you
You ran away in shame and took the waters along.

And I was so unhappy you were running away, Hieronymus,
As I suspected you were ashamed
Because through that water around you
I could see huge scars on your body.

And I kept looking at the scars and chasing
The water of the dead in the fields...
(You were such a handsome man, Hieronymus
And I was so unhappy I could not come near you!)

## Wing of a Sparrow

Hieronymus, my bed is surrounded by dark pillars
That night I went to sleep in it only by mistake
Ten horses were pulling at it slowly
Nobody knew which way they were taking me
And you alone were crying by my side.

But I saw you, Hieronymus, lying by me and weeping
I seemed to hear the long roar of a beast
My fervent prayer was for a holy man to come
So that when he came close
The pack of animals might run away.

And then, at last, I don't know how it came to pass, Hieronymus,
But you approached me and you were so bruised that
Your body, hardly pieced together, took so long to come to life
That I could see how the living water of the soul soldered it
And I was afraid and ashamed of my death.

No, Hieronymus, I did not die that night
But I wept as much as a man and woman together could weep;
My right eyelid is a sparrow wing
Somebody tells me it is ill omen if it twitches
And I am afraid of everything that is in store for me.

## The Way

Hieronymus, the face of your son on the wall is so pale
That it looks like the halo of a saint in the night
When I am left alone with him to watch your sleep
On the white stones at the entrance.

Madam, he tells me, standing still
And trying hard to come near
To the stone I am sitting on, I could
Show you the way to my father.

Try to get on the wall by my side
Do not be afraid, just keep climbing;
Which way, Nathanael, I ask,
Madam, he whispers, I am that way.

And I keep standing at the gates of the city
On the same white stones
And I start catching sight of you beyond his pale face
Like a saint's halo.

## I Had Had No Idea I Could Put You to Sleep

I had had no idea I could put you to sleep
But, my sweet lord, I touched you by mistake
I am now sitting by your side and weeping
And I am afraid you might die in your sleep.

The earth shakes
I am sure it's true
Your bones knell
Like a silver bell at midnight.

A nymph is drawing near me
I pray quietly and witlessly
She teaches me how to make
The sign of waking on your forehead.

## Eden

I find myself facing the gentle queen
We talk like two dead beings
We died through our lost love
We had the same fate.

I whisper to her I had a lover on earth
I too had one, she says
Mine was the rising sun
Mine was the setting sun.

Then you come too, the one who died after us
Or the one who never dies
I had first loved a queen, you whisper
And a young girl afterwards.

So we all talk quietly
Since none of us knows any more
Whose the bone we see is
It looks like a body in another eternity.

## My Love, Maybe

My love, maybe we are clay dolls
Meant to be mere toys
And maybe the pale piercing our breasts
Looks for someone more important, dead forever.

Maybe the repeatedly redeemed body of your lover
As if in a boundless grave
Has the shape of a being not yet dead
But ceaselessly haunted.

Maybe our tears are not tears
Just a huge disarray
While real sorrow
Is silent and  unknown
And while real death
Is still looking for that living being
In whose likeness, our bodies
Were made just for the sake of black magic.

## Reveal Yourself to Me Now

Reveal yourself to me now for some day you'll be looking for me
A
nd I'll have ceased to be
My soul will shed its body like a premature baby
And will go naked down the road of all souls, will not know
At least a name to call you by.

Then you may want to be my transient flesh
And my once hot blood
And its caress gently following up the spine
Caress as pure as my thought of you

Or you may want to be my anguish or the breath
Called life, which you stoop to take away
Just like the bird left in my palm on purpose
Which silently picks its millet grain

Or you may want to be his image in my eye
Vanishing under your stare, which will blind me
At the very moment I feel I am heading for you:
Reveal yourself to me now for some day you'll be looking for me
and I'll have ceased to be.

# Virgil Nemoianu

born 1940

*Literary critic: he is a professor of comparative literature at the Catholic University of America, Washington, D. C.*

## Break of Contact with Reality

**Lidia Vianu:** What was your reaction when you first became aware of censorship, of the lies and slogans of totalitarian propaganda?

**Virgil Nemoianu:** Born in 1940, I grew up with censorship as a fact of life. I took it to be something unchangeable, in the nature of things.

Looking back to the 1940s, 1950s, or 1960s, I would say that the worst thing about censorship is the way in which it encourages nihilism, and a certain break of contact with reality. You tend to think everything is false, all writing mendacious.

**L. V.** Did censorship have any good effects, too?

**V. N.** Yes, I think censorship may encourage some individuals to be more skeptical, to develop their own theoretical frames, to seek for individual answers. But I guess the price for such individual acts of salvation is too high.

**L. V.** Can you remember the good underground Romanian literature, which we all read in complicity with the shrewd writer, who managed to reach us by cheating on the censors? Do you think there were any good books written during the totalitarian years in Romania?

**V. N.** Yes, a lot of good poetry was published in the 1960s and 1970s. Similarly, literary criticism played host to debates about broader sociocultural issues: a complicated system of coding and decoding took place, but for precisely *that* reason, the message was often garbled.

**L. V.** Did you have any direct fights with the censors? Could you describe the publication of your books there? How did a young writer join the tight system of book publishing? Is the situation there similar to that in the United States?

**V. N.** I did not have many fights with censors. When something of substance was touched, I just withdrew my article. At the same time, I exercised a lot of self-censorship. When I knew that some idea or argument could be subjected to censorship, I simply did not submit or did not even write it out (I kept it as a note, or filed it away, for "later" use).

**L. V.** Do you think Romanian literature is in a better position now than before 1989? How do you see the future of Romanian culture, literature, literary taste?

**V. N.** Too early to say. Government price controls on paper, print, equipment and the like are very stringent and they seem to be effective in restraining literary activity. I assume that in the future there will be more consumer-oriented literature.

**L. V.** Do you consider the idea that politics must no longer have anything to do with literature correct? Where should we draw the line?

**V. N.** Any literary work has a political context or a political dimension. In turn, any political utterance has a literary component. This is just to say that in human life everything is connected with everything else. It is equally important to recognize that literature and politics are different kinds of human activity and that they are both corrupted when their mutual otherness is not respected.

**L. V.** What made you leave the country? Was it the pressure of politics, of lies and slogans on culture?

**V. N.** I left the country because control was stifling and overwhelming creativity. Censorship was *one* among a number of other factors that I would group under social control.

**L. V.** How do you view Romania from abroad? Do you feel some of your cultural life still belongs there?

**V. N.** Romania seems to me somewhat exotic and alien. I believe that I continue to relate emotionally and culturally much better to nineteenth-century and early twentieth-century Romanian culture.

January 1992

# Mircea Martin

**born 1940**

*Literary critic: he is presently the head of the Univers publishing house*

## Pact with Censorship

**Lidia Vianu:** What was your experience of censorship?

**Mircea Martin:** Romanian literature during the Ceauşescu dictatorship had nothing of the samizdat in it. Romanian writers preferred to have their books published legally. Nevertheless, they tried to tell the truth by means of allusion and metaphor. Was that proof of their strength or of their weakness? Was it weakness or shrewdness on the part of the censors to tolerate such subversive forms, especially those coming from well-known authors, whose books could not be forbidden without causing scandal?

It is quite difficult to find a clear-cut, all-embracing answer to these questions. Anyway, even during the toughest years of the dictatorship, literature was written in Romania, and through its major representatives, this literature had good standing, it placed itself on the correct side of the barricade. In recent times, the mere appearance of books which did not support the official propaganda loudly was really kind of a miracle.

In the '60s, the thaw years, which brought about spectacular changes in Romania, especially as far as ideology was concerned, Romanian writers merely took the freedom (granted, rather than gained) of playing, dreaming, imagining. In short, they resorted to artistic gratuity. They rediscovered their own means of expression and traditions, which an artificially imposed ideology had forced them to abandon.

But after 1971, after Ceauşescu's domestic policy changed due to the Chinese Cultural Revolution, the same writers realized that aesthetic autonomy was not enough, that it was only a concession made to them by the ruling power. Their consciousness hardened; it became radical, if that is not saying too much. And thus, when the *politruks* least expected it, they found themselves confronted with a literature that only seemed to observe the party line of drawing inspiration from the realities of the socialist era. The image reflected was, in fact, far from the idealism of the revolutionary pathos. It was similar to the sadness and tragedy of the world, pinpointing the moral and physical decay, the injustice, the deportations, the crimes.

Such books could only be published if they dealt with the period before Ceauşescu's rule. Nevertheless, readers could easily understand that propagandistic deceit and economic inefficiency did not exclusively belong to the recent past, but to the present as well. The readers became silent, but extremely perceptive participants in the game which undermined the system, but which, as a rule, was forced to spare the Great Leader's image.

Was it a good thing for the writer to accept this pact with censorship, and, ultimately, with the ruling power? Of course, we are more intransigent today than yesterday when we read certain novels, poems and even critical essays filled with underlying political implications with subversive satisfaction.

Except for a very few writers, such as Paul Goma, Romanian writers tried to have their works published, even during the most difficult times of the dictatorship, sometimes running the risk of being compelled to accept changes, mutilations of the text, additional explanations, etc. The extent of that kind of dispute varied, because they depended on the social and literary status of the author, on his strength of character. Even censored, these texts told, though half-openly, the truth which no other cultural medium could voice at the time. Consequently, literature became a substitute for contemporary history, journalism, depth psychology, even for philosophy. Whatever could not officially appear in print was pushed into the literary world, which assumed a multitude of functions, which were, in fact, not in the least foreign to it, even if unspecific. The advantage of imagination, of ambiguity, as well as the significant detail that the ruling couple were not in the habit of reading, turned literature into one of the few refuges of truth in Romanian society. In spite of all the officials' efforts to displace the writer, he still occupied a central, privileged place in public conscience, enjoying a status any visitor from the West would envy.

During the last months of Ceauşescu's tyranny, and in the context of the rapid, radical changes in Eastern Europe, several prominent writers protested openly against the regime, thus becoming instigators of the December revolution in 1989.

After the revolution and the euphoria that followed it, which did not last long in Romania, the writers joined the political opposition, trying to make use of abilities which had been left unused until then because of the totalitarian restrictions. Now they have decided to be journalists, political commentators, witnesses and critics of the change, feeling that these are not the times for novel-writing, or even less so for poetry, on the contrary, for argument and straightforward debate.

However, besides economic difficulties (i.e., the shortage of paper and printing facilities), which represent another type of censorship, a new problem arises with extremely serious consequences. Once freedom of speech has been won, all forms of culture and mass media resume their functions, and literature loses its central, privileged place.

Moreover, the truth is harder to grasp because it is uttered by a multitude of subjective voices, which risk smashing it to pieces in the end. Before, one could tell the truth only partially and then only indirectly. But its impact on the audience was great: truth brought people together and made them feel that they shared a common bond. Now, everything can be shouted out loud, even the truth. But this does not mean much. In fact, it means very little. The writer has to redefine his means of expression and status in this new society. He will probably have to accept a minor, but no less efficient role, have to give up the privileges resulting from silencing his fellow intellectuals (or from compliance with the submissive eulogy), in favor of a number of rights he is to exercise and defend.

In fact, we have to make a new start because the revolution did nothing but create the premises, the opportunities for changing the structures. This process is only incipient in our country, and extremely painful. But what is infinitely more difficult than the change of economic structures is the change of mental structures, the modes of thinking, mentalities. It is only now that we discover the long-lasting and enduring effects of the communist propaganda and especially of totalitarian terror. The totalitarian system, generally extremely rigid, had the shrewdness to be permissive on occasion, in strictly individual cases. But the moment the faintest attempt at building a common cause became apparent, it was immediately and severely repressed. The feeling of civic solidarity that any democracy should rely on was altered profoundly, even annihilated, unfortunately, I would say. When I speak of obsolete mentalities, I mean the passivity, or more precisely, the insensitivity to civic morality of a majority of the population.

The writers, all artists, will have to fight as best they can against the social and moral indifference of a number of people who have become insensitive in this respect. They will also have to fight the recrudescence of nationalism, which turns out to be an only apparently paradoxical outcome of communist dictatorship. Literature, once again, will have to exert its far-reaching effect on people's consciences. In the long run, the synthetic instruments of imagination and fiction might prove to be more convincing and efficient than the analytical ones of the political essay.

We are all going through distressful times. This is, as always, more obvious in the East than in the West. As far as I am concerned, I think that these distressful times will prove fruitful for literature. Literature and culture in Romania will be forms of humanism. Humanism may seem outdated in the West, but we are still in great need of it in the East.

May 1991

# Mihai Ursachi

**born 1941**

*Poet, fiction writer: he has written five volumes of poetry, one of short stories, and several essays; he defected to the United States in 1981 but returned to Romania in 1990*

## What Future Do We Expect for Mankind?

**Lidia Vianu:** Do you remember your literary debut?

**Mihai Ursachi:** As far as I remember, my first poems were published in January 1968, almost simultaneously in three literary magazines: *Cronica*, in Jassy, *Gazeta Literară* and *Viaţa Românească*, in Bucharest.

**L. V.** Was it hard for you to get them published?

**M. U.** Not really.

**L. V.** Does that mean that you knew anyone?

**M. U.** My first three poems had been taken from my house without my knowledge by a friend, who was a well-known writer at that time. He published them. I did not intend to publish them. I never believed that my poems would be published by the communist press in Romania, because all the press in this country was controlled by the Communist Party, by the institution of censorship, and by the Securitate itself, and I was a former political prisoner, so very harshly discriminated against.

**L. V.** Can I know the reason of your political imprisonment?

**M. U.** Yes, you can, but this is a long story, and I am not sure that this is the right place to recall it. But you can notice that, at the age of twenty, as a philosophy student, I was sentenced to four years of hard prison, and I was lucky to get out after only three years, because of the political amnesty given by the former communist dictator, Gheorghe Gheorghiu Dej, in 1964. I came out of Jilava, the famous political jail, in April 1964.

**L. V.** What was the accusation?

**M. U.** I was caught in the middle of the river Danube, trying to cross the border to Yugoslavia. In fact, I was trying to escape an imminent arrest because of my so called counterrevolutionary activities as a philosophy student in Jassy.

**L. V.** In what way did the prison change you?

**M. U.** This is another long story. Actually, I became a poet at Jilava, the political jail.

**L. V.** What did poetry mean to you before you left Romania?

**M. U.** First of all, it was my real and deep vocation. And my only reason to exist. Secondly, I can think now, after many years, that poetry also meant for me, and probably for many of my colleagues at that time, a kind of spiritual resistance.

**L. V.** How come, then, that you only discovered it in prison?

**M. U.** I intended to pursue an academic career in philosophy. I was sure that would be possible for me. In prison, I understood how wrong I had been, and started to write poems. "To write" may not be quite the right word for it, since we never had paper or pencil, we were not allowed to write or read in prisons. So, I composed for myself some poems, and then, when I was free, I continued to do so, and even for others.

**L. V.** How old were you when you were imprisoned and started writing poetry?

**M. U.** I was arrested at twenty, as I said before, and I was in the last year of my philosophy studies in Jassy. I wrote my very first poem, "wrote" in memory, that is, when I was put in solitary confinement, a place where you were expected to die.

**L. V.** How did you survive and how did you write in the larger prison you found when you were set free?

**M. U.** I think your question is interesting. In principle, I didn't count on publishing my writings. I still think it was a pure accident, maybe happy, that I got to publish some books, or even short stories. I think it is appropriate to quote a very well-known Latin poet: "Habent sua fata libelli" (books have their own fate).

**L. V.** Once you were caught in the game of publishing, though, how did you cope with it?

**M. U.** Very hard, it was a continuous fight, every day, every hour, every second.

**L. V.** Whom and in what way did you fight?

**M. U.** First of all, censorship, which was official, and which was a branch of the Securitate, led by the communist party. Now, this is abstract. In fact, I fought people, who happened to be censors. I had an established policy on that, which I used quite successfully. First of all, I never accepted a word to be changed or erased, or replaced in any of my poems. If the censor did not give up in our face-to-face conversations, and he said "we cannot publish this poem because of this word," my answer was, "I shall not publish this poem." So we kept negotiating. If they did not give up in any way, my policy was not to publish the entire poem. I did this all my career long. But I accepted, when publishing books, to take out the poems which could not be published from their point of view. Even the book that appeared in 1974, in Cluj, at Dacia, under the title *The Purple Poem and Other Poems,* was a good example. Four parts of the title poem were taken out. The Purple Poem has ten parts, and they were all rearranged, as order, although the poem in its entirety had been published in România Literară in 1972.

**L. V.** Could you write freely, feeling this very concrete burden of censorship?

**M. U.** I never established any connection between my writing poems and my business with censorship. I knew that this censorship was arbitrary and stupid, so I never took it in my deep calculations.

**L. V.** Were you happy to see your books in print, even at a socialist printing press?

**M. U.** Yes, I sure was.

**L. V.** Would it have made any difference for your poetry if you had been able to write it abroad, as an American citizen, which I understand you are now, although you have returned to live in Romania?

**M. U.** As a native of the Romanian language, no really good poem could be written by me in another language, whether German or English.

**L. V.** Did you try it ?

**M. U.** Yes, I did.

**L. V.** What were the results ?

**M. U.** I wrote a few poems in English, in American English, when I was living in Southern California, among poets and artists over there. I read those poems to my friends and colleagues, and even to my students, in the literary workshop, in La Jolla. I even published two of them, in some magazines of no importance, whose name I have forgotten.

**L. V.** Do you feel you have made the right decision in returning to Romanian literature, or are you paying too high a price from the point of view of everyday life?

**M. U.** I still think that I did the right thing when I left Romania, twelve years ago, and when I came back, two and a half years ago.

**L. V.** What future do you expect for Romanian literature?

**M. U.** What future do we expect for mankind?

December 1992

# Poetry

### Ad Lectorem

At first you'll see
leave and forget;
then come again, and if you do,
you'll hear, and live, too.
The third time
hey
you'll stay.

### Mount Cain

Waste and remembrance,
the rotten maple trees now know no more.
The moss sofa of love,
the same.
Mount Friday hangs
over the forest, huge rock
dangling from a spider's thread . . .

Trees, woods know nothing.

. . . Childish remembrances,
a golden flake clutching at a ray. . .
Cain, Cain, Cain,
a mount of fear
from a mere
spider's thread
                hanging . . .

Waste and remembrance,
trees, woods know nothing.

### The Dog Miriapodis

Deep sleep,
untroubled by voices and shadows
or bird flight.
Only the dog Miriapodis
prowls about me, narrow and long,
but inexistent.
The dog Miriapodis

is just a remote memory
of the vague suspicion
that somewhere, among the trees, there is a kind of forest.
But this so very doubtful dog,
although prowling—long earwig
at my feet,
the dog Miriapodis does not even exist.
Except in the forever stagnant waters of sleep.

## The Wedding

Look, I am coming now
for the wedding that can't be postponed.
I'm wearing the white sign, silver trivets
and the seven marks under the trivets.

      I know, I know, it is so very late,
      as if this were never.

I have ordered joy for all those present
ice cold joy, since such duty
can be fulfilled only once in a lifetime
and for ever and ever.

The Priest's blind, well, so what,
all those present, the bride and the groom
laugh like fools and pinch their butt . . .

      Everything's O.K. at last,
      just the bride has no cast.

Bride, bride, what scythe
is that?
the last

## Victory

"I myself have defeated myself," the self-defeated bounced,
"and my vanquished self is my slave."
At that very moment his defeated self
shouted his victory: "I have defeated myself."

### The Daybreak Cocks Trigger the Bow

Co-co-hoo-hoo, the cocks scream, a million cocks at daybreak,
I bang my skull fearfully against the ceiling
while the cocks squeak all together,
a million dreamy cocks.

I am a bluish steel bow
tense, cuddled in my bed all night,
hoo-rico, the cocks crow, I have blown,
I dashed up to the beams, my head is all sore.

Their dreamy bellow scares me,
fool, damn it, these are ghosts,
they shriek in tombs
which are hazy and rainy.

### The Zero Hour

It's sheer madness to be at this hour.
Small watches, like insects, have been eaten by average clocks—
round, fat brood hens which cackle
and protest when they are swallowed unchewed
by abulic, monstrous clocks.
The bigger clocks in their turn
are slowly digested by the pontifical clock
in the belfry,
dating back from the twelfth century of
all ages.
The twelfth being the last hour, then,
it gnaws at itself from the inside
until it eats itself up
and nothing is left of itself.

It is foolish to be at this hour.

### No Chance

We are the gift moments
having existed on other planets
and even constellations whereinto
our eyes fail to peer.
But now, see, the crystal spheres of our eyes
will rot in the dust which is eternally the same
all over the Universe.

Oh, the specks of cosmic dust which once
just once, had been Me
will they forfeit for ever and ever the chance
that happened to be left out?

## The Last Letter

Listen to the voice of grass
and you'll hear mine.
Don't miss me:
long ago, I hid at the bottom of waters
and drowned in azure.
Just listen to the voice of leaves
and you'll hear mine.

Look carefully at the acacias
on a certain day of May:
I am among the flowers, listen to the story
of my immortal life...

## Watery Discovery

In a lake in the Suceava district
a small, tubular animal was found
and inside it we suspect
the map of an unknown planet was drawn
to the least details

## Epistle

I'm telling you again, then,
it's useless to strive,
useless to reach
to ridiculous
foundation.

What word
could be heavier on the scales
than the enormous silence
meant to be
the only chance?

Beware, the enormous
silence, do you think

can be removed?
It is
as big as the Cologne dome.

## The Song of the Dumb Snail Adeodatus

From one leaf
to another
it's endlessly
far away.
I'm carrying a letter
from the magic circle.
Everything changes
the secret language
it was written in
was a dream.

There is no leaf
that can decipher
what has been written
on the shell.

From one leaf
to another
it's endlessly
far away.
I'm carrying a letter
from the magic circle.

## The Child's Belief

That little girl, whom I so much loved, still believed
that the snail had left its shell
for some far away place
only to come back,
so she lovingly kept the shell
and waited for him.

## Century of Iron

Godless
through abysmal outskirts
ruins
of furnaces

iron
in the rain
red
the spring

Thus I go
deeper and
deeper
into the century
of iron
into the century
of iron

O, stella maris!

## Self-Portrait

Oh, if after death
one could write poems
I dream
of having died
long before
the Universe was born

# Ana Blandiana

born 1942

*Poet, essayist, prosewriter: she is head of the Civic Alliance (a large civic group) and president of the Romanian Pen Club*

## Nobody Exists in Vain

**Lidia Vianu:** What was your experience of censorship?

**Ana Blandiana:** I keep saying that I am the author of twenty-three books, but I am not sure that the twenty-three books were as important for my literary fate as my three interdictions. Anyway, it is obvious that the three interdictions were extremely important for the Romanian reader. The first interdiction, the longest, lasted for four years. It did not have as much to do with me, as with my father. I was still in school, about to graduate, when I sent two poems to a literary magazine, and they were published. Although I signed them with what was to become my pen-name (but which is really a pseudonym), the officials discovered the truth. I lived in Oradea at the time, and they let all the reviews in the country know that I was the daughter of an enemy of the people; my father had indeed been imprisoned for years. I was not to be published again. And so, before becoming a real writer, I was a forbidden writer. In a way, and in time, this even had a positive effect. When I started publishing again, I was more than just a young girl who was publishing: I was "that" girl who had been interdicted.

This interdiction lasted four years. Afterward, the times were a little better: it was a period of more openness, around 1965, and I began publishing again. In fact, this was my real beginning, because, until then, only two of my poems had been published. This was possible because the man who headed *The Contemporary* then was George Ivaşcu, a big name and a brave man, who had himself been in prison not long before. He had fought on the side of the left before the war and was prestigious. He published my poems and took responsibility for me. So, that was my first interdiction.

Afterward, my destiny continued in the usual way, as did my contemporaries', which, when compared to the generations before and after me, was better off because the situation was more relaxed for a few years. Nichita Stănescu, the oldest of my generation, made his literary debut in 1964. We followed in his footsteps during the very good years between 1968 and 1971. After these few years of openness, we started closing again. But by the time the situation was at its worst, we were already too well known to be stifled easily, because we had won international recognition.

The second scandal took place in 1985, because of some of my poems which were published in *Amfiteatru.* They appeared by accident, in fact. My final conclusion was that no one got around to reading them.

**L. V.** Did you have the feeling that you might get into trouble when you wrote them?

**A. B.** I never thought about publication when I wrote. I have always believed that it is, after all, the duty of writers to speak their minds, to write what they think, and then, if possible, try to publish what they have written.

**L. V.** But they were polemic poems, quite different from what you used to write.

**A. B.** They were not so different from what I have been writing lately. It so happened that Constanța Buzea insisted that I give her a few poems. I told her that I did not have any that could be published. She replied, "Just give them to me. You're probably just exaggerating." I gave her several poems, of which some were much more dangerous that those which were finally published. These poems represented a degree of exasperation which so far had not reached the press. They appeared by sheer chance. Constanța gave them to the editor in chief without putting her signature on them. (Her signature was needed because she was responsible for the poetry page there.) It seems that the editor in chief did not even read them, but they were left on his desk. It was Christmas Eve, a holiday, so he left, went camping. The layout was done in a hurry, and my poems were included. They had been taken from his desk, in the assumption that they had been accepted for publication. When the scandal broke out, on January 15, the editor in chief was fired and transferred to another magazine. I felt both guilty and grateful to him at the same time. To my great astonishment, I learned that he verbally attacked me. He even refused to talk to me. As a matter of fact, he is currently the head of the paper *Today,* which explains a lot of things. But there is no use talking about people here. The poems appeared, immediately went into samizdat, were copied and circulated. Some people were imprisoned, though only for a short time, just for possessing these poems. It was a huge scandal.

**L. V.** Was there no censorship at that time?

**A. B.** Well, you know, the magazine belonged to the students. But, in fact, it was dependent on the Central Committee of the Communist Youth Union, whose head was Ceauşescu's son. Everything was a mess there. The heads of the paper were his drinking buddies. It was an abnormal situation.

**L. V.** So, censorship did not function at that time?

**A. B.** Well, no. They were considered to be above the others.

**L. V.** But, afterwards, censorship did work against you?

**A. B.** I still had no idea that the poems had been published. On January 15, there was a meeting of the Central Committee. I heard about it for the first time when this meeting took place. And I also learned that I had been interdicted. The meeting was presided over by the Secretary of Propaganda, who called all the editors in chief in the country to him and scolded them harshly, saying that what had happened was a scandal. It was against all morals . . .

**L. V.** Did they do anything against you personally?

**A. B.** They took away my right to publish. That happened right away—that very moment—but lasted less than three months. During that time, Ceauşescu's image in Europe was still fairly good, but his last years completely destroyed it. He was very keen on keeping this positive image. As soon as I was interdicted, people began to side with me. In Italy, for example, a list of about 300 signatures was drawn up. Mostly people from the Italian universities. It started at the University of Padua. It was signed by well-known journalists, famous writers. It was then published, and broadcast in various places. The International Pen also protested. They finally gave in when confronted with all this.

**L. V.** Have your poems already been translated?

**A. B.** Quite a few have. I think there are already about four English versions.
     But what I meant to say was that Ceauşescu's international image was important. In 1988, that was no longer possible. That was my third interdiction, brought about by a poem written for children. It was about a tomcat named Arpagic. But Ceauşescu did not have anything more to lose.

**L. V.** Was it a total interdiction?

**A. B.** It was certainly different from the first one. I do not know what the first would have meant for me if it had lasted any longer. At that time, the only thing I could see was that my books, all of them, were banned. But in 1988, starting on the day I was interdicted, a car with a man in it appeared in front of my house. He was there all the time and listened to what was being said inside. That was, by far, the hardest part. I realize I am subjective and sound superficial, but being forced to whisper in my own home for a year and a half seemed the hardest part to me. Even when I asked, "Would you like some more tea?", I whispered. I felt like I was being watched, naked. Imagine being in your own home and knowing that someone outside could and did hear absolutely everything!

**L. V.** Did you have microphones in the house?

**A. B.** I cannot say with certainty. It seems that there was no need for that. I asked the electricians about it, and they told me that a special little object attached to the exterior of the house was enough to hear as far away as 200 meters. It was not even 200 meters from my house to the car. The purpose of that car was very complex. On the one hand, no one dared enter our yard any more. They did not stop anyone, but no one would come. Then, they made a point of being seen while they were listening. Everyone was scared, the whole block; their whole lives were changed by terror. Their small affairs and all the rest. They were all afraid and did not hide anything. Everything was meant to scare. Once a neighbor saw me in town, and told me that when I had left the house, he had heard the woman in the car saying, "She has just left. She went to this or that street. May I leave for an hour? I do not think she will be back before then." It was summer and he often had his windows open. The neighbors heard all of it, and I think that was exactly what they wanted, in fact. The terror was meant for the others as well. Well, the protests in Europe were stronger now, but they were of no use. Ceauşescu had lost all credibility abroad.

**L. V.** Between 1988 and 1989, they did not reconsider your interdiction?

**A. B.** Certainly not.

**L. V.** You could no longer publish anything?

**A. B.** No, and in addition to that, my books were taken out of the libraries and books which were in the process of being printed were stopped if they mentioned my name. That was the case of a book by a very good literary historian, Mircea Scarlat, who died in the meantime. It was a history of Romanian poetry from the beginning to the present day. He wrote a volume dealing with the post-war period. My name appeared in two places, just footnotes, because I did not belong to that period. I suppose you can imagine what that means, how much it costs to do something like that. Well, the volume was cancelled because my name was mentioned in two places.

**L. V.** Who was behind all this? Cabinet 1, 2 or censorship in between?

**A. B.** I have the feeling that it all came from denunciations sent from below. Maybe the paper *The Week.* Of course, I do not have any proof. But then they are the parents of *Great Romania* these days. There were many such dirty places. Let me tell you something that might sound like a joke. It was very hard for me to get a passport when I received the Herder Prize in 1982. I did not get it until the eve of my departure. It would have been a scandal if I had not gone because the prize was being presented by Austria's president, and it was a whole ceremony. A friend of our family, who happened to know Petru Enache, the Propaganda Secretary at the time (the only one who could grant me the visa), met someone we knew since he had been Secretary in Jassy while on holiday. This teacher from Jassy said that he had met Enache at Lacul Roşu and Enache had asked him, "You once told me you knew Blandiana. Do you think she will come back?" "Sure," he said. "Oh! I am relieved to hear that! I have decided to let her go, out of fear of scandal, but I have 32 letters from writers asking that she not be allowed to go." Few things have impressed me so deeply as this. It impressed me in two ways: first of all, because a Secretary of Propaganda, which meant the second or third most important person in the state, could be so insecure in his position as to be afraid that he had made a mistake in granting a mere visa. That implied that everyone was afraid, no matter how high up they were. Secondly, because 32 of my fellow writers had written against me in this base way. I have no idea who they were, of course; I do not know how close they are to me. You know, after the revolution they talked about showing each of us our Securitate files. I have always said, "Even if my life depended on it, I would not want to read it." I could not stand the idea that I could have read and found out that people whom I had considered my friends were just the opposite. I prefer, by far, not knowing.

**L. V.** Did you write as if censorship did not exist? Did censorship affect what you wrote in any way?

**A. B.** I hope not. I was obsessed with being free from it. That seemed like the most serious thing that could happen to me. If censorship did exist in my life, it took this negative form: my fear that it might affect me. And there was one area where it did not exist at all. About six years before the revolution, I began writing a book which will come out in the fall. It is a kind of novel, although I prefer calling it a poem, just as Gogol said that *Dead Souls* was a poem. What I mean is that its meanings surpass those of a novel. I began writing it and I believe that I would not have been able to survive these last years without it, the last year and a half. I would even go so far as to say that reality almost ceased to exist when I entered its world. I wrote this novel fully aware that it could not be published during my lifetime. I never would have imagined that Ceauşescu would die before me. I always thought that this book would be published after my death. I actually wrote it without any hope of anyone ever reading it. Censorship did not exist there, that is for sure. For the rest, there was my obsession with not allowing myself to be influenced by it. It also existed to a certain extent in my selections of texts: I did not submit everything I had written for publication. But I did submit quite a lot, about 85 to 90 percent, because there was a kind of complicity, too. The reviews were headed by our fellow writers. Censorship had many levels. The higher stages were unrelenting. But in the lower levels, they were writers like us, who could close their eyes and pretend they had not understood. That is all we asked of them. And they actually did it.

**L. V.** Your highly sensitive lyricism generally does not have much to do with politics. What pushed you to defy censorship?

**A. B.** I did it because it was infinitely harder not to. I got involved in politics naturally. Not doing so would have meant permanent self-censorship which would have been catastrophic. I lie so badly that I find it much easier to tell the truth. Lying does not come easily to me. It seemed to me that if I had not done it, the results would have been far worse. I am no hypocrite. I did what I did because it came easiest at the time. Or rather, it would have been infinitely harder on me the other way around.

**L. V.** Your revolt against censorship at first took the form of small, so-called lizards.

**A. B.** Yes, it did. In time they became a true complicity between reader and author. They were not disparate lizards; there was a system of lizards, and all the readers could have the key. My permanent columns in *Literary Romania* and *The Contemporary*, which were widely read, almost always had a key. Sometimes people made keys which had not even existed in my own head. They were metaphorical comments on what all of us experienced. These people felt a little revenged for what they had gone through when they found these lizards in the text.

**L. V.** Now that censorship has disappeared, do you still feel the need to find a code, a key to hide the meaning?

**A. B.** This is a loss for literature. Aesthetically speaking, it may sound cynical, but I could write an essay on the aesthetic virtues of censorship. Right now we are all far too hysterical to be able to be real readers or writers of poetry. I believe it is even more difficult to be a reader than a writer, because the writer's subconscious usually bursts out somehow, but as a reader we need concentration and inner peace which we have lost. I still hope we can find it again sometime.

**L. V.** Did you ever directly fight your censors? Fight for a particular passage? A certain line?

**A. B.** Absolutely everything published was the result of a fight. My column in *Literary Romania* had brought me to sheer exasperation. I wrote three, four, or five texts every week so that just one might be published.

**L. V.** What did you think of that? Did you consider it a waste? A necessity?

**A. B.** I did not do that in my poetry. I would rather forfeit the entire poem. I never accepted changes. Hardly ever. For instance, in my book *Projects of the Past*, only two pages are missing. I fought quite a lot. In the end, I realized that it would be a pity if the book were not published, since it included a lot. Even without those two pages, which were a description of the Securitate building in

Oradea and of my childhood fears when I walked by it. Of course, the word was not mentioned. But there were all sorts of hints, including the fact that the building bore a name which means "certainty" in the dictionary.

**L. V.** Did censorship block in any way your creative power at any time?

**A. B.** No, because it was not connected with the act of writing in my mind. Not with writing literature at least. As far as the columns were concerned, they were influenced by censorship because I would always write bearing in mind that the text had to be accepted. It was almost like a game. Like a crossword puzzle, to some extent. I made a code and knew that the readers had the key to it. I had to write in such a way as to suggest the key to the reader. And I had to hope that the censor would not discover it, or that he would pretend to ignore it.

**L. V.** You relied heavily on the reader's complicity?

**A. B.** Immensely. I would even say that we met half-way.

**L. V.** Do you think that literature will survive the disappearance of censorship, with its high standards?

**A. B.** It could have survived if prices did not grow so outrageously.

**L. V.** Are you referring to economic censorship?

**A. B.** Well, yes. Censorship is now economic, and it is even stronger, because the price of a book is now a huge obstacle for us, poor as we are. The relationship between poet, writer, and reader was so strong in Romania that I would venture to say that it was the only social dialogue which functioned during this whole time. Books were printed in incredible numbers. When I went to the West, I am sure that they did not believe me when I spoke about that. My book of poetry which was published in *Everyone's Library* cost 8 lei; it was sold on the black market for 100 lei after it had been withdrawn. The number of copies published could have been at least twice as large. People in the West cannot imagine that this is possible. Now, in Romania, this is no longer possible. Not because we lack readers, but because they no longer have any money.

**L. V.** So, censorship no longer exists. How do you view the fate of poetry?

**A. B.** Besides economic censorship, it could be that people do not want as much poetry any more.

**L. V.** Do you detect a writer's block, maybe, because the writer must expel self-censorship from his mind?

**A. B.** Maybe. But I am not sure because even if the writer feels the lack of a code, which in a way impairs the quality of his metaphors, there is something else too. There is the rough material of our suffering, the best rough material for literature, and that has to mean a great deal to all of us. Nothing was experienced in vain. This is my only philosophical conclusion. Nobody exists in vain.

Everything we experience stays somewhere, in the artists' souls. And they are obliged to express their experiences. I am certain that for many decades in all the countries of the East, maybe even more so in Romania than in others, extraordinary poetry will be written because our suffering was greater.

July 1991

# Poetry

### Rain Spell

I love rains, I love rains passionately,
Mad rains and calm rains,
Maiden rains and raging woman rains,
Fresh rains and boring endless rains,
I love rains, I love rains passionately,
I love rolling in their tall, white grass,
I love to break their blades and squeeze them between my teeth,
And see men grow dizzy seeing me doing it.
I know it is not nice to say "I am the most beautiful woman,"
It is not nice, it may not even be true,
But, when it rains, let me,
Just when it rains,
Utter the magic formula "I am the most beautiful woman."
I am the most beautiful woman because it rains
And the curls of rain suit me as they hang from my hair,
I am the most beautiful woman because it is windy
And my dress tosses desperately to hide my knees
I am the most beautiful woman because you
Are far away and I am waiting for you,
And you know I am waiting for you,
I am the most beautiful woman and I know how to wait
And I wait, all the same.
The smell of living love floats in the air,
And all passers-by sniff at the rain to feel its smell,
In such rain you can fall in love on the spot,
All passers-by are in love,
And I am waiting for you.
You are the only one who knows—
I love rains,
I love rains passionately,
The mad rains and the calm rains,
The maiden rains and the raging woman-rains . . .

### Coming Back

I come back home victoriously
After the adventure of having been honest.
How many generations ago did I leave?
I don't remember where it was or when.
I am carrying all the stars with me to show them

The garden which they must keep warm,
And the mountains ask me to take them to the land
Where they can place their height.
The birds hover above and ask
Where to make their nests, and endless flocks
Come after me and wait for the place
Where they can settle and breed.

I say: "Wait just one moment longer,
The place I came from is very near,
Just one more minute, there must be
Some fixed place, only one . . ."

But everything is flowing all around. I keep looking about
And I am tired because of death and walking,
Since I am forced to carry within me the point
Against which the whole universe leans.

## Parents

Our parents do everything for us at any time—
They give birth to us and bring us up until we
are taller than they,
Then they discreetly lag behind,
They usually do not disturb us.

They are ashamed they are too old and ill,
Too modest and too simple for us,
Guilty for the lost time
They watch us silently, quietly.

Then they look up at a star at last,
Till the ray rooted in the sky grows thinner.
And, tired, they do not hesitate
To lie down in earth, to be our very foundation.

## Morning Elegy

At first I had promised to keep silent, but then, in the morning,
I saw you turn up with ashes at the gates,
Sowing them as one would sow wheat,
And I could not wait any more, and I cried out: "What are you
doing? What are you doing?"

I have snowed for you above the town all night,
I have made night whiter for you: oh, if
You could understand how hard it is to snow!
Last night, as soon as you went to bed, I flew out in the air.
It was dark and cold there. I had
To fly to the only point where
The void makes the suns spin around it and puts them out
And I was supposed to flicker a moment longer at that point
In order to return towards you snowing.
I have thought over, weighed and tried each snowflake,
I fashioned and polished it with my eyes,
Now I am sleepy to death, I am exhausted and have a fever.
I watch you sowing the dust of dead fire
Over my white work and I smile while I let you know—
It will snow much, much more after me
And you will be drowned in all the white of the world,
Try to start understanding its law now,
Huge snowfalls will come after us,
And you will run out of ashes,
And the children will learn how to snow very early,
And the white will cover your weak denial,
And the earth will join the spinning stars
Like another star burning with snow.


## A Time Will Come

A time will come
When I shall need leaves
And shall be cured by grass,
When, growing old, I shall acquire a set of false teeth
The song of birds,
When I shall miss the moon pill
On sleepless nights.
Don't worry, a time will come
When I shall not be able to live without all these.
When I shall be forced to admit
The whole universe
Is important.
A time will come,
But, for God's sake, leave me now,
Leave me alone with myself.

## Humility

I cannot prevent the day from having twenty-four hours.
I can only say:
Forgive me for the length of the day;
I cannot prevent the butterfly from flowing out of the worm,
I can only ask you to forgive me for the worms, the butterflies;
Forgive me that flowers turn into fruit, and fruit into kernels,
And kernels into trees;
Forgive me that springs grow into streams,
Streams into seas, seas into oceans;
Forgive me that loves turn into newborn babies,
And new-born babies into solitude, and solitude into love . . .
No, I cannot prevent anything,
All things go their way and never ask me,
From the least grain of sand to my own blood.
I can only say—
Forgive me.

## Connections

Everything is a part of me.
Give me one leaf which is unlike me,
Help me find one animal
Which does not moan with my voice.
Wherever I walk the land splits
I can see the dead wearing my face
In one another's arms, breeding more dead.
Why so many connections with the world,
So many parents and forced descendants
And all this mad resemblance?
The universe harasses me with thousands of my own faces
And I can only defend myself by striking at myself.

## The Boundary

I am looking for the beginning of evil
As in my childhood I looked for the edges of rain.
I ran as fast as I could in order to find
The place where
I could sit on the ground and gaze
At the rain here, the non-rain there.
But rain always stopped before
I could find its boundaries
And started again before

I could realize how far the blue sky went.
I have grown up in vain.
With all my might
I am still running to find the place where
I can sit down on the ground and gaze
At the line which parts evil from good.
But evil always stops before
I have found its boundary
And starts again before
I can find out the place where good ends.
I am looking for the beginning of evil
On this earth
Both cloudy and sunny
In turns.

## Travel

I travel inside myself
As about a strange city
Where I know no one.
In the evening I am afraid to be in the street
And on rainy afternoons
I am cold and bored.
I feel no wish to travel,
When just crossing the road
Is an adventure,
No memory from previous lives
Can answer the question
"Why have I been brought here?" . . .

## Condition

I am
like
the sand in the sand-glass
which
can be time
only
while it
falls.

## Psalm (I)

See, the cranes betray, the trees give in,
Wisdom spreads,
My careful father.
Will you like that?
See, word by word,
I have been taught not to talk.
But, God, can you promise me
That in this silence
You will keep my words alive,
That the birds will remember the way back
And the leaves will find
The branches they fell off from,
That everything will come back to life
When you are strong enough
For me to ask you—
Instead of sadness give me hatred?

## Everything Is Simple

Oh, if only I were a candle,
Gradually burning
From one end to the other,
Uncomplicated, as in children's
Arithmetics . . .
First my head would melt
Oh, how good!—
People would say:
"This girl has no mind at all!",
I shall have forgotten everything
And would not try to understand anything any more
Then my heart would melt,
And I should stop loving,
I should stop hating,
No suffering could affect me
And the people would say
"This girl is heartless!",
And so on.
Then I should forget all about desires,
And passions,
And my blood where ships sail
Would vanish,
Only my dry knees would be left,

Shaking dignified or bent,
No one would take the trouble of saying anything any more.
In the last silence,
The wax pool
Would get cold, punished on purpose
For all the terrible shadows which
Its light brought into the world . . .

## In Winter the Stars

In winter the stars
Are so far away
That you can't see them
Through solitude.

In winter the seas
Are so alien,
That they do not even acquire
The murmur of springs.

In winter the dead
Are so cold,
That they freeze the land
Of the everlasting hemisphere.

## Homeland

In you I miss no one,
Land sunk in sleep
Through green orbs,
I am a stranger if I pass the border
Of your tired hair.
I can only talk
Your tongue in my dream
And tell tales only for you
My transitory paradise,
My transitory master.
It's cold outside
There's dense fog in the house,
Evening comes down,
Time slowly descends,
But it's so good and warm at home,
When you're my homeland and I yours.

# Nicolae Prelipceanu

**born 1942**

*Poet, prose writer, journalist: he has written thirteen volumes of poetry and five of prose*

## Censorship—The Wooden Shoe

**Lidia Vianu:** How did you make your debut? Did you or didn't you know what censorship was? Were you or weren't you hampered by it?

**Nicolae Prelipceanu:** I did not know much about censorship when I made my debut. I did not feel at all like believing my poor father, who kept telling me, beginning with '58, '59, '60—he was not a man of letters, he was quite the reverse, I should say—that, before publishing anyone for the first time, a review was compelled to gather information about the person who wrote, the author, from the party committee of the district, region, or the institution the writer worked for. Later I began to find out that I could not publish this and that. Censorship had been in me, of course, for quite a while, since my second childhood, when they proclaimed the "Popular Republic of Romania." In spite of this, I have often been blamed by editors that I was writing too "darkly," that I was not optimistic. Optimism was in fashion, as a variant *avant la lettre* of the "constructive opposition" of our days. But I was a naive young man who wrote about his grief.

As soon as I had published my first poems in a review, and I tried to publish some more, I bumped against the arm of censorship, which was as long as that of the "proletarian revolution." I very vividly remember the editors and those who published in that Cluj review—*Tribuna* was its name—waiting on Monday afternoons (the review was issued on Thursday) for the answer from the Press Directorate, which was the name of censorship. It was a euphuism. Later on, when censorship was "abolished," the answer was still expected on Mondays, but it came from the "department," meaning the press department of the district party committee. Among those who published in that review, were rejected or maimed by the "department," were such writers as Ana Blandiana, Ion Alexandru, and so many whom you may not know. Or not yet.

**L. V.** What do you think of the good and bad effects of censorship?

**N. P.** I believe that the effects of inner censorship are deplorable for anyone's life. For a writer's too, therefore. The writer is a human being, too. It may be commonplace to compare it to that wooden shoe used to change the shape of little girls' feet in Japan, I think, in order to obtain the desired shape for a geisha, or a courtesan, to use our European-American term. After all, the party meant to change into courtesans those who were not wise enough to avoid the field of literature. I am certain that, had I not lived in a world dominated by general, total censorship of communist totalitarianism, censorship which penetrated my inner being sooner or later, I should have been a different man, and anyway, a different writer.

But, after all, anyone can say that, had he lived in another country and/or another century, he would have been different. I take it, consequently, that this was our fate, here, in the wild East. Censorship was our destiny. For us, who have lived to see what it is like *without* it, after we had only lived *with* it, it seems a blessing at first sight, and a misfortune if we peer closer. The misfortune is not that censorship died (I am not so self-censored), but that we were not born the very second day after its death. But maybe we must not envy anyone. We may have to try and peer farther ahead. Who knows . . .

**L. V.** What was your relationship to censorship and censors?

**N. P.** It was fairly abstract. I have only been able to set eyes on one or two district censors. I never met the important censors, who maimed my books. What they did to my books can best be seen in the volume *Ask the Smoke*, published in 1975, which, having been censored, contained no more than a third of the initial list of poems. Lines and words had been cut off, too, especially the decisive ones, as far as the meaning of the text was concerned.

Unfortunately, the censors were not stupid. I know I should not have accepted that they should publish that book as it had come from censorship, but I did not have the strength. Let the one who was brave enough throw the first stone.

Later on, things went far better, probably because I had become "smart" and learnt how to "fool" censorship. In a volume of 1978, I even managed to publish a poem entitled *What Did You Do during St. Bartholomew's Night,* where I was wondering plainly "how long St. Bartholomew's night had lasted and how much longer it would be." In the meantime, the poem was published in translation by Andrei Codrescu's journal, *Exquisite Corpse.* It really was a corpse! The poem, I mean. A corpse that censorship had not managed to kill. I also published prose and interviews. At the least false step, censorship would cross whole chapters or answers. This was our life. We waited for the answer of censorship, especially at the time when censorship, according to the statement of the party and state leader, did not exist. It was abolished for a few months, in the '80s, but it was resurrected out of its own ashes, like the phoenix. The statement "we have no censorship" was kept for the sake of "Romania's image in the world."

**L. V.** Did censorship, self-censorship, affect your relationship with your readers?

**N. P.** I guess so. I have no idea what my relationship with the readers would have been if so and so had happened. The same as I would not know whether I would have been a writer, and what kind of writer I would have been, if I had been born in another century and another country, without censorship.

**L. V.** What can follow totalitarianism in literature? What new censorships can emerge?

**N. P.** In literature, aesthetically speaking, in 1989 there already was pluralism. In politics we fail to achieve that pluralism even now. Censorships have already started to appear. The economic one comes first: the price of a book is too high, it does not sell, so printing becomes very hard. As you know, the human being is very hard to explain; it must be the only being dissatisfied whatever the circumstances, eternally dissatisfied. In order to preserve this eternal dissatisfaction, the human being invents its own barriers, obstacles, censorships. As society is a sum of beings, it is also a sum of dissatisfactions. . . . A Romanian hymn says: "Heroes we had, and heroes we have/ And they will exist for as long as there are Romanians." I used to replace *heroes* with *errors*, as a *joke*. I shall change it for you, and replace it by censorships.

May 1993

# Poetry

## What Did You Do during St. Bartholomew's Night

I know you'll say you were alone at home
you pondered
all alone
against St. Bartholomew's Night
you put down your thoughts on paper
all alone
you had not even been born
you pondered against St. Bartholomew's Night
unborn as you were

who were you on St. Bartholomew's Night
and why didn't they enter your house
it was so easy, wasn't it
your brain was on the white paper tray
you operated on it with your quill
one false move would have made a dead man out of you
one false move of the quill
on the white paper tray where your brain sprawled
why didn't you make that false move

why didn't they enter your house
and why weren't you killed
on St. Bartholomew's Night
who can certify you are not lying to us
that you were not one of them
what's your alibi
no one who thinks at night alone
has any alibi
if in the meantime St. Bartholomew's Night
has already happened

you should have chosen another night
to sprawl your brain on paper
(as if you could postpone sprawling it there
as if postponing did not equal
the false move of your pen)

you can't be
alone on St. Bartholomew's Night
the traces of the night on paper are not enough
in order to understand St. Bartholomew's Night
it is not enough
to be alone it is not enough
you should have called someone to join you
even before you were born

concerning St. Bartholomew's Night we do not trust you


## You Can Do Without

You can do without a man
as you can do without a bird
you can do without a leaf in May
as without everything in October

when rain goes up around you
you can still scream in tears
that you are happy optimistic
future
you are to be
you will be

when a tree falls over your shadow
it is as if you passed
by the shadow of a barely started wall
and the shadow were taken from you

in a foreign town
you were compelled to stand still
for five minutes joining the others
until the statue arrived
with the arm up in the air
you called the stone crowd
to follow you
to cry and applaud

## Afterwards

They will wash the stains
on their hands with cloth dipped in blood
and the stains will be replaced
at last
by others
the same shade

and we shall say
justice has been done
to the old stains in the soul
                    which reached light
                    with such difficulty
that there is only one perfection
                    that of stains
and one imperfection—of thought
pulsating in sleep moreover
moreover silently
revealing in hiding
                    the tough flesh
                    the young flesh
                    the immortal

## The Houses Once

The houses that once were
still linger in a halo
over our heads

in rooms closed forever now
only the cigarette smoke
of the past

The moon sometimes brings to light
white walls closed windows
doors we used to go out
once and for all

whole streets
floated up in the air
bearing our footsteps as well

before long
we shall go back there
holding hands like of old
our soles will touch
silently
the stones of the sky

## Self-Portrait

I am sitting in a restaurant
chewing the same gum
I had last year
and I look out
with one closed eye
in front of which
grey
all mine
relatives and friends go by
and strangers
and moreover myself
in dozens and hundreds of copies
urging them all to hurry up

## The Black Cat

I can no longer rest even when asleep
you, a stranger, come and grab my arm
asking me to join you
but I won't go wherever you do
I know what happens there
only you are so strong
you take me, dream and all

sleep and all
bed and all
house and all
town and all
earth and all

the black cat follows
slowly
licking our steps
so that they may say
we have never been true

## Gone Down the Drain

The feeling there is no more time
days come yet never begin
and never end
just fog farther and farther away—
life

you bite from an apple
its middle grows red
with your blood

you avoid eating
lest you should be swallowed
unchewed

when you drink water your soul
flows with the spring
along with the white rocks
darkening them slowly

you avoid drinking
lest your soul should be sipped
black blood moreover unseen

you can hardly write words
47 years old
this age is already lost
torn from you
swallowed unchewed
down the drain which is supposed to be a spring
it slipped and rolled
long silence
final
your only refuge
from now on

## Continuation

I guess I was in the bathroom
where
naked in the hot water
washed
hypothetically

of all sins
as one could receive the call
towards the other world
as if one received
the key to an apartment
in this world

## Before and Now

I know love ought to be reinvented
I know people keep telling one another lies
about one another
which ends in a world of one-eyed people
maimed imbecile knaves
a world issued from their own mouths
multiplied by millions
but I refuse to believe them
I doom myself to loving them all
with their speech defects as well
with their crutches and sticks
breathe mouth to mouth
listen ear to ear
stare eyes in eyes
from a three millimetres' distance
so that I may love them all
without their being aware of that

## Before December 22

We shall not give you all the paper
we happen to have at home
so that you may fill it
with lines of untrue words and lies
because we no longer want
to write anything
no word that you will afterwards translate
into your language
and make it mean
what you please
after you have bound it tight
and filled its mouth
with wool

## Tomorrow

What I'm afraid most of is
poplar branches

what I'm afraid most of is
sea waves

what I'm afraid most of is
tomorrow
when the poplar branches
sink into the sea
carrying my eyes along
my eyes which watched
first the branches
then the sea
then
today's night

## Dreamless Sleep

Now when it is late for so much
I turn my face to the wall
where my vanished friends
bring their shadows at night

I ask them and they answer me
take care
what is happening to you
happened to us too

do not make our mistakes all over again
or make them, why not
keep dreaming of worlds
you will never see

lay your ear on these dreams
imagine they are soft pillows
listen to remote seas
wash your body in the dust of roads

bend down so we may bless you
put on the sheets of unwritten paper
and be patient till the thunderbolt

strikes you

## There Is Time

More and more fellow beings
say eagerly about themselves
excellent very good

the sheet of paper is ever narrower
someone pulls it away with my hand on it
my soul slips away
from off my feet

## Never Scared

Why do you always phone me too late
and ask me if we are both dead
my friend, let me tell you, we are still alive
"a day," as you well know by now, is much "longer
than a century"
and the century, my friend, "the century goes by"
the day too
with the speed of its own light
and some may believe night does not budge
the speed of darkness has not been calculated
we are told it is everlasting and we must
fear its everlastingness
but we are never scared
not even of our own shadow
we are
n-e-v-e-r  s-c-a-r-e-d

## One Joy Alone

While you party and phone me
telling me every now and then we feel
I settle the bandages on my eyes
lest

while you shout and are happy with yourselves
I rejoice I am blindfolded
so well that no one can untie
the large white bandage

stop for one moment your enthusiastic call
and your joys
not everything that happens to you must necessarily
happen to me too

blindfolded there is only one
joy
late very late

# Lucia Negoiţă

**born 1945**

*Poet, journalist: she is editor in chief of Romanian National Television*

## To Save Our Souls

**Lidia Vianu:** You have been writing poetry since 1966, and you have worked as a literary editor (for the Romanian Broadcast Corporation, then television) since 1967. What is your experience of censorship, especially during the last decade before the fall of communism?

**Lucia Negoiţă:** In the Orwellian world of communist dictatorship, the mechanisms of censorship had reached a devilish threshold of perfection, especially during the last decade. Aggressive, obvious, or hidden, these devices were a sure way towards the alienation of the individual. As in Eugène Ionesco's famous play, we were all in danger of becoming rhinoceros.

The whole system, well planned in its structure, condemned a whole people to a slow but sure death of the soul. The kulturniks of the age, those who, higher or lower in ranks, carried out the instructions received from the Party, from Ceauşescu himself, had an inexhaustible imagination in heightening suspicion, fear, and terror. The "comic" and the absurd mingled with the tragic. The individual himself was doomed to being a mere number in a monotonous, mortifying series.

How did Television play its part as a tool that was totally the slave of power? It was no secret that the presidential couple were paranoic as far as their image on the screen was concerned. Television was their private asset. Every step, minute, and image had to be carefully supervised, dominated, stifled.

We all know that in the early 1980s the television shows did not last more than two hours a night, daily. During these two hours, from the news to the so-called entertainment, mostly political, too, everything was focussed on the "two comrades," the presidential couple. The two Ceauşescus, who had only attended elementary school for a few years at best, were certainly conversant with everything, from the basics of a farm to high-brow medicine, architecture, music.

The ideologists of the time had created a true communist mythology. They had exhausted all praising figures of speech. Nicolae Ceauşescu was called "titan," "colossus," "the genius of the Carpathians," "the absolute Leader." Elena Ceauşescu was praised as everybody's mother, her face and smile were goddess like, and, on top of it all, illiterate as she was, she had become a "world-renowned scholar."

The zealous and fearful censors of the television had reached the stage at which they actually counted how many times the two sacred names were mentioned. They were the pattern of history, science, culture. Nobody else had any part in it, they were all anonymous. If their count was not satisfying, the shows would be filmed and worked all over again. The price was unbelievable. There existed a board of over-censors who approved of the final show, and you could easily be sacked if your opinion was not "convincing" enough.

Romanians remember in despair the years before 1990, when they were reduced to watching Bulgarian TV. A Polish or Czech film, cartoons for children offered a minimal escape, although the language was totally unknown and a small one, after all, belonging to the family of the Slav languages, which had given rise to a real allergy here. The danger of becoming alienated from their own language and nation was immediate. The television was a confiscated medium. In December 1989, preceding Ceauşescu's execution, the question a military man asked him in the Court room at Târgovişte, ran as follows: "Why have you stolen our television from us?"

Another instance to illustrate the perfect absurdity of communist censorship was the blacklist of forbidden words and images. Here are some of them: death, angel, church, cross. Churches were shown without steeples, the crosses were ignored by the camera, left out, cut off on the assembly table. Nothing inside a church could be filmed, actually. The above-mentioned words were replaced by new ones, the classical writers were rewritten, new rhymes were created, meanings that those writers had never even contemplated.

Old books, objects of religious cult did not have a better fate, either. The titles of books which belonged to early Romanian literature were forbidden, too. Romanian culture had huge blank areas, meant to be left unknown for the only fault of having belonged to a Christian tradition.

Another kind of censorship, successfully used for years on end on the screen, could be called the "censorship of faces." Cultural anonymity was complete. The remarkable cultural personalities were always absent. Some of them cannot even testify to having lived in the age of television; they were utterly ignored by it. The exception were cultural aparatchiks. Romanian intellectuals were ruthlessly doomed to forgetfulness.

The editors who were allowed by the power to be seen on the screen were very few: two or three read the news, two or three unkempt women, most often with Elena's hairdo and a modest appearance of a mere party activist. One of the editors, a woman, was famous for the wildly pathetic fight against imperialist ideology, another one had specialized in announcing the folk music that the two liked best.

Reading these notes now, one may find them unimaginably absurd. Yet, we lived days, weeks, years, decades of lie, exposure, alienation and death of the soul. The spirit itself was censored and imprisoned. Those who came to its defence, resisted, opposed, paid their revolt with their own life. The sacrifice of the young people who died in December 1989 was the death of the innocent. For truth. For the freedom of the mind. For tolerance. Against lies. To save our souls.

June 1997

# Adriana Bittel

**born 1946**

*Fiction writer: she is the editor of* Literary Romania *and has written four volumes of short stories and one novel*

## Evil Sieve

**Lidia Vianu:** How much of censorship have you experienced?

**Adriana Bittel:** Censorship was a kind of evil sieve, which became less and less permissive during the last years of dictatorship. It rejected ideas, sentences, words—anything that seemed to hint at our two "Leaders" and at the details of our miserable daily lives. Fortunately, the censors were not cultivated; their minds, which were perverted in order to find all the things on lists of interdictions, stopped in front of the trees without seeing the forest, as we say in Romania. Consequently, they could be fooled if you had in mind a strategy for misleading their search when you wrote. This, of course, limited freedom of creation and brought about a division of the self into two parts, an alienation from yourself, because you had to scrutinize the text with their eyes too, you had to keep inventing traps, passages written especially to be censored. In addition to them, you squeezed in things which were, in fact, much more "subversive," but which stood a chance of making it past the censors without being noticed.

The most diabolical invention was, by far, the fact that the editor of the book himself was under pressure; he would be fired if he allowed uncensored manuscripts to get past him and reach higher persons. This was a very complex situation because the editor was a professional, and, more often than not, a friend of yours. He had his own family and life; you could not ask him to risk his job for you.

So there were several stages: self-censorship, the benign censorship of the editor's sentimental blackmail, which often proved to be worse than the child who dreads fire after being burned once, and trying to foresee all possible objections the censor might have; and finally the real censors with their lists.

You could make a deal with the editor, since you were generally on the same side. You weakened the emphasis, changed or used Aesopic language, placed a contemporary story in the past, switched the action to another place. The fight was fair; you faced each other. But with the censor there was no question of discussing or making a deal. The author was never supposed to know who suggested the changes or mutilations of the text. As a matter of fact, the censors did not forbid anything. They "discussed," that is, imposed changes on the editor. The editor did that himself, so no concrete documentation of censorship remained, because censorship had officially been abolished.

After the book had been printed, a thorough "postcheck," as it was called, was made on the first copy of the book. The censors from the Council of Culture (called "instructors" or "readers") checked whether or not their instructions had been followed. If they had not, the books were destroyed. Party or administrative punishment followed, anything from fines to firing.

Under these conditions, a language of hints was created. It could not be understood by someone outside totalitarian Romania. Readers got used to understatements, and, anyway, you hoped for a reader who would be more intelligent than the censor. The latter was usually a shallow, uncultivated activist. Writers used parables, polysemic metaphors, Aesopic style, while the truth of everyday life was subversively squeezed in, in disguise.

As for myself, I worked as a proof-reader in a literary magazine, so I knew about the list of interdictions and the censors' absurd way of reading. They managed to see an allusion to the two Ceauşescus even in the traditional formula beginning every Romanian fairy tale: "Once upon a time there was an old man and an old woman. . . ." There was also an absurd prudishness which censored the very names of undergarments from various contexts, even if there was nothing sexy about them. Knowing all that, I gave the censors the satisfaction of doing their jobs by eliminating unimportant trifles. They were insignificant, as far as the epic construction was concerned, and the censors could then be satisfied with their vigilance. At the same time, I impregnated the book with the atmosphere of everyday life in the conditions of "multilaterally developed socialism."

I was not a victim of censorship. The four books I wrote during the last four years were finally published, with changes which were, in fact, insignificant, and I am not ashamed of them as they are now.

There is a risk in claiming to have been a victim of censorship: what seemed very brave at one time but did not have true literary value and gift to support it, has become obsolete. The truths which were formerly forbidden are now commonplace, and the books which include them are not even valuable as documents, like so many documents devoid of literary pretensions. And they replace the literary substitute which had no aesthetic value.

The positive effect of the disappearance of censorship is that writers can now prove their gifts without the excuse that they are prevented from doing so. Today, they are no more or less than their writings bear witness. On the other hand, censorship was an obstacle which forced us to use all kinds of stylistic tricks. It stimulated our capacity for symbolic invention, pushed the epic toward a psychological level which had many undertones, and created a complicity between author and reader, above the head of official stupidity.

Now that we have complete freedom of expression, it has become useless to write things which are too sophisticated. The force of the realistic narrative, with subjects which were once forbidden, is what counts. People are mostly interested in confessions, true experiences which touched the limit of the understandable, and suffering during the communist regime. This is paraliterature (memoirs, documents, etc.). It is a period of transition, of release, which will be followed by the writer's return to the significant narrative.

As far as literary currents and tendencies are concerned, they were happening at the same time as great world literature, even before. We did read a lot, translated and theorized. Recent news from the West was known to writers. In the universities, the best philologists encouraged their students to value aesthetic elements and the courage to express one's opinion, despite ideological pressure. The literary circles which existed at the University until 1989 created two generations of writers: those of the '80s and those of the '90s, all of whom are very interesting. They are all poets, prose writers, critics, and essayists who had to fight censorship hard, and all of them are extremely interesting. Some of their books could be published only after the "revolution," or whatever it was. They could not be published before, precisely because these two generations had been educated in the free, iconoclastic and cosmopolitan atmosphere of these literary circles which were interdicted during Ceauşescu's last years.

June 1991

# Prose

## Walls among the Living

It was the name of a street at the eastern outskirts of Bucharest—Madam Puşa lived there. Out of cheap, rationed cloth with dots, she made me the same kind of dress every year. It had a big hem, which grandma kept letting down, so the old dress ended in line after line, stains and patches. For a while, I was not allowed to go play in the new dress, I could only wear it on special occasions, covered by a small apron.

The fitting for the new dress was something I disliked: I had to "stay still," which I could do for no more than two minutes in a row, and this only if I swore in my mind, using the swear words I had learned in the big yard at number 24. On the other hand, I liked Puşa's chatter while she stuck pins in the stiff cloth and made signs with a little bit of tickling chalk under my arms and at the waist. She most often talked about her daughter Jeni ("clean, refined and having graduated from high school"), whom she was determined to marry to a serious officer. To this purpose, she went to the Military Circle every Saturday, to balls. Jeni was invited to dance, then the dancer sat down at their table, they ate, they drank, they talked, and at the hour of the last tram, they allowed him to accompany them to the gate of their house. If the lieutenant or whatever he was tried to enter the yard, Puşa became dignified, raised her forefinger to the level of her temple, and uttered solemnly: "No more!" adding that beyond that gate only those with *serious* intentions, officially declared, could pass. She also said that there, on the Walls (her street), everyone knew them, and thought well of them. They were not like those women, you know, they were serious.

Listening to her talk and doing my best to stay still, although I felt like scratching my head, picking up some pin left on the carpet, or nibbling at the scratch on my elbow, I concentrated on the words which kept coming back—*Walls among the living*—and I suddenly saw in front of my eyes a maze of rotten walls which divided groups of people who had open eyes, blinked, breathed moving their chests—they were the very opposite of dead people, with closed eyes, who held their breath and refrained from bursting into laughter (in our games at 24 I sometimes had to play the dead one, and it was just as difficult as the fitting).

The phrase "No more!" suggested to me a barrier beyond which an area full of obscure gussets and pleats began, an area where you were allowed to go only if you were *serious*, meaning frowning, angry, silent—more precisely, dead. To my mind, in order to be allowed to enter as a stranger the walls among the living, you had to be dead, and especially not to laugh, as I did at the fitting, when she tickled me with the chalk, and mother kept telling me, "what the hell, can't you be serious."

At that time I had no idea how often the walls among the living would come back to my mind, how many times I would pull them down or forget them, or see them turn up out of the blue, when I least expected it, in the middle of a crowd with which I felt one, or in the solitary interval of my reading, at a party with friends or in a talk with unknown persons on a train.

The last time I saw Puşa I had turned six, and she had been summoned to make my school uniform, which was a totally different as pattern from my old dresses with dots. It was towards the end of summer, when children play at their best, and I was in the yard at 24 with my friends, who had just returned from the countryside after the holidays, and had a lot of new phrases and crazy stories to tell. I was called three times over the fence: once by the name they used as an endearment, second time by my full first name, and the third time with both first and last name, as an order. These were the three stages of grandma's patience.

I jumped over the fence and ran into the house. The annual meetings with Puşa took place in the bedroom, in front of the wardrobe mirror. This time it was a special meeting, the uniform was the second step towards the new identity which was being prepared for me, that of a schoolgirl—the first step had been a visit to the doctor. With her meter tape round her neck, the box of pins and her scissors at hand, Puşa reminded me of the anxiety I had felt when facing the doctor with a stethoscope and cold metallic instruments. The black silky cloth sparkled gloomily on the bed. I was afraid as if she was going to cut me too, my living flesh, to make another me, and grandma and mother had consented to this torture.

"Please," I said, "just wait a little," and I sat down cross-legged on the carpet, in front of the mirror, because my knees were trembling. "Till the child gets a short rest, I'll bring you some preserve, Madam Puşa." "God bless you, I was really awfully thirsty," the dressmaker said and sat down at the table, sighing deeply. The mirror reflected the three of them, like a broken screen: in the background there was the open window, with the curtain and a plate with fly poison, in which corpses of dead insects floated all glued together. On the table, the dish with blueberries, like the corpses of glued insects, all swallowed by Puşa's greedy mouth, like an anthill that she slurped from the spoon, while mother and grandma looked eagerly—all viewed from below, sort of upside down. In front of it all, there was me, with scratched knees touching the mirror. I had just fallen and it was good to feel the mirror's cool touch.

I abandoned myself to that sensation with eyes closed— behind me I heard Puşa swallow with satisfaction, then she said:

"I actually wanted to tell you how unhappy I am. May you never feel what I do now!" Mother was curious:

"Well then, what happened, I hope Jeni has not done anything wrong."

"Oh, yes, she did, and to think I laboured for her with my needle, and withstood all the whims of ladies all my life, this comes from having children, as they say, I feel like strangling her with my own hands, and then I shall drown myself in Fundeni Lake, may God forgive me!"

"Come on, I think you are exaggerating, what could happen to make you feel so bad, is she *in the family way?*"

"That would not be so bad, after all, she can have an abortion, but you could not even imagine, forgive me for saying so, what she did to me!"

"Is she having an affair with a married man?"

"Far worse: it's a ZHID!"

She banged her fist against the table, the table rattled, silence fell. A new victim had fallen in the plate with fly poison and was dying with a lot of noise. My knees had left two pink signs on the mirror. The word accompanied by the banging of the fist was unknown to me, but I inferred that Jeni had done something terribly wrong, such as, for instance, to sleeping with the small pillow between her legs, or peeing in front of everyone. Though it was not good manners, I needed to understand, so I heard myself ask:

"What is it Jeni did worse?"

On the screen, mother and grandma stayed stone still on both sides of Puşa. One was all flushed, the other pale. On my spine I felt the tension in the air, irritating vibrations, like the buzz of a fly. No one hastened to answer my question, so I cleared my throat to ask louder, and then I heard grandma with her tone of the third stage, the one of the full name:

"Madam Puşa Dobre, you have come to our house for so many years that it would be amazing if you did not know that *we are Jews.*"

"Oh, oh, oh, that's altogether *different,* you are nice people, do not misunderstand me, you can't even tell you are, not really, and besides, a customer is not the same as a son-in-law. Why couldn't she find one of us, a Christian, what will the neighbours and the relatives in the country say, and what wedding will they have, a Zhid wedding, no, no, nobody in our whole family did a thing like that. . . ."

"No more . . ." mother suddenly said, very tired, old, even older than grandma, "I have heard enough."

"So what, I couldn't care less," Puşa stiffened, "I have enough work on my hands, I go to colonels' wives, priests' wives, actresses, you'll be sorry, that I can say. I shouldn't have opened my heart, this is no time to be honest about anything, to believe in human good will. . . ."

She began gathering her boxes with pins, the meter tape, the scissors.

"What about the uniform?" I asked frightened, but also glad, hoping my age could stop at the dress with dots, the games in the big yard at the 24, and that the autumn when school was to begin for me would not come any more. Then grandma seemed to realize at last I was there too. She stroked me with a kind of pensive pity, while the dressmaker was leaving and slamming the door behind her.

"No more!" my mother mimicked her, raising her forefinger to the level of her temple, and I was the only one to laugh at that, and it did not last long.

# Dan Verona

born 1947

*Poet, author: he is the author of many volumes and an editor at the Romanian Broadcast Corporation*

## The Nightmare

1971. Start of the cultural revolution modelled on the Chinese Cultural Revolution, following Ceauşescu's visit to China. The "famous" July Theses. My generation started publishing in this unfortunate climate.

1. *Silence Required.* Poems. Manuscript submitted to Romanian Book publishing house in 1970. Edited by Alexandru Paleologu. In 1971, after the above mentioned theses, the manuscript was rejected due to censorship. The accusation: "orphism." The title was considered to be a "lizard," alluding to Ceauşescu's speeches. The book was never published.

2. *Migrating Nights.* Manuscript submitted in 1971. Edited by Alexandru Paleologu. Although this book was just as orphic as the previous one, it was returned with changes which made it acceptable, as well as congratulations from the censors. I am still young and perfectly confused. I receive the prize of the Writers' Union.

3. *The Olive Tree Sign.* Manuscript submitted in 1972. Edited by Alexandru Paleologu. The censor rejects several poems which are considered "mystical." Words such as "God," "church" and "death" are crossed out. It is released in 1974.

4. *The Book of Runes.* Submitted to Eminescu publishing house in 1974. One-fourth of the book is left out. Reason: "No paper." It is released in 1975.

5. *Order the Magnolias to Bloom.* Manuscript submitted to Romanian Book publishing house in 1975. I abandoned "orphism" in favor of a more direct kind of poetry with ironical undertones. With this book, the nightmare continues. Edited by Alexandru Paleologu. Paleologu

is forced to retire, and I fail to understand the reason why. Gradually, the undesirable persons, those who do not humbly approve of the regime, are displaced. The exodus of intellectuals begins. Not just intellectuals. They defect. The exodus is even worse after 1980. Paleologu's report on my book is rejected by the editor in chief. My book is left without an editor. Nobody wants to "get into trouble." At last, the manuscript is taken over by Florin Mugur, whom many considered a real "rescuer of books." During this period, the so-called syntheses come out. They are meant to check the artistic value of books. Actually, they are a kind of hidden censorship, exerted by clerks from the Council of Culture. The manuscript arrives at syntheses. It comes back missing eight poems. The endings to many other texts have been cut, and others are added in pencil. What they add is more "optimistic." Thus mutilated, the manuscript is subjected to official censorship. When it returns, seven poems have not been officially approved. I cross out the endings added in pencil. The manuscript is printed in the summer of 1976. The Council of Culture asks to review it. Six more poems are removed. Stanzas or lines are crossed out of other poems. I am accused of using "lizards." The main criticism: "Why didn't you keep writing in the orphic manner?" At last, in the spring of 1977, the book comes out. Only half of my initial manuscript is in it. A disaster. To me, of course. And on top of all that, half the copies are destroyed at the printing house by the earthquake of 1977. Or at least that is their story.

6. *Life at Thirty-Three.* Manuscript submitted in 1977, in fall, under the title, *Life at Thirty.* (Although I feel tempted to give up, I continue writing.) Edited by Florin Mugur. The manuscript is rejected by the censors, and a laconic explanation is given to the publishing house: "It won't work." The publishing house keeps it in the plan for the next several years. The Council of Culture crosses it out. In the meantime, Ceaușescu abolishes censorship. It was a mere trick to bait the intellectuals. In fact, censorship continues to function, but in secret, within the Council of Socialist Culture and Education. A few years go by. I change three-quarters of the book. It is released in 1981, entitled *Life at Thirty-Three.*

7. *Bald Angels.* Novel. Subject: life in an orphanage. Manuscript submitted to Albatros publishing house in 1977. It suffers the same fate as the previous book. A kind of "to and fro" from the publishing house to the Council of Culture and back. They dislike the title. They dislike the subject-matter. The reason the book is rejected: "It won't work. This isn't the right time for it to come out." They suggest that I add some positive characters. (The same happened to other

writers: the Party secretary's obsession with positive characters, more often than not.) I refuse. The book is left in an ambiguous situation. Years pass. The head of the publishing house continues to support the book, although he is warned to let it go. The Council of Culture constantly crosses it out of the plan. I write to the Council of Culture and the Party's Department of the Press. The book is released in 1982, five years later. It is awarded the prize of the Writers' Union.

8. 1983. I give Florin Mugur part of the manuscript for *The Vaviloniad,* so that he might include my work in the plan. I withdraw it in 1984. The way it looked, the book did not stand any chance at all. Discouraged and hopeless, I can no longer work. It is a hard time for me. Like many others, I feel that I am affected by the most insidious kind of censorship: inner-censorship, the one that numbs you.

9. *The Ballad of the Announcer and Other Poems.* Another manuscript, which I mustered up enough courage to take to the publishing house in 1985. Edited by Florin Mugur. I employ all the experience I have and, resorting to traffic of experience, get my book past the Council of Culture unexpectedly well, completely accepted. But I have bad luck: it gets stuck at the publishing house.

A different editor in chief. The new editor in chief is required to review the book before it goes into print. He sends the editor a bulky stack of paper containing his comments. I recognize the censor's handwriting from "syntheses"; it is the one who pencilled in endings to my poems. We haggle for a while. The book comes out—minus a few poems and many lines crossed out of other poems.

\*

Almost two decades of tearing agitation, resignation, weariness. I kept waiting for that happy moment of literature, which never appeared. An unfair fight with tricks I used, small local victories, and a slow defeat of the body and of the mind. The result: a few books in which the author sees his face as it is reflected in a mirror which was broken by a stone. Are they worth the wasted energy the way they are? The life maimed to fit into Procustes's bed, that devilish contraption which will neither allow you to live or to die.

# The Path from Manuscript to the Printed Book

Self-confident and enthusiastic, the poet enters a publishing house carrying a manuscript under his arm. He is excited, of course. If he has even the least bit of experience, he is a little reserved. But he cannot help but hope that things will work out better this time. If it is his first book, he is to be pitied. He believes that everything works without the least bit of intervention on his behalf. If he thinks so, he really is to be pitied. As soon as the manuscript is submitted, the first barrier appears.

## The first barrier of the nightmare

First of all, the poet was supposed to obtain a space in the publication plan. The book had to be read by an editor. If the editor accepted it, the book was placed on the editor's list of suggestions. If it was not, the poet was powerless; he could spend years looking for another editor who was more favorable to him. He kept being postponed all the time. But let's assume that the editor was willing ho help him. At the first meeting, when the editors decided on the plan of the publishing house, they all came with their suggestions. After several meetings, the plan was worked out. If the number of books was larger than the number allowed for that year, they began crossing out titles. If you overcame this first obstacle, you felt relieved. If not, you had one more year to wait. And then another, and another. And so on. One could find manuscripts ten or twelve years old in the drawers of the publishing houses. And they still had not been given a definitive answer.

The plan made by the publishing house was then forwarded to the Council of Culture. Here, it was added to the plans of other publishing houses. If you submitted two books during the same year, one was eliminated. Especially after 1980. They said that the decision was made by Elena Ceauşescu. Maybe it was! It could be true. But I know for sure that some decisions were made at the Council. Persistent authors were then told, "It is the decision of Cabinet 2." That meant Elena Ceauşescu. You could not reach her, of course. Comrade Elena could not be held responsible; no one would have dared do that.

The Council of Culture made other decisions as well. It reduced the number of books to be published. The usual reason: "No paper." They also revenged themselves on people. If some clerk happened to dislike an author's eyes, his name was instantly crossed out. "Damn him! He can wait." The adjusted plan then returned to the publishing house. After a while it was again requested by the Council of Culture. Again they crossed out more titles. And, finally, it could be printed.

# Personal Diary of a Nightmare

I take the manuscript *Order the Magnolias to Bloom* to Romanian Book. Book editor: Alexandru Paleologu. Paleologu is the kind of editor who takes and puts his signature only on the books he likes. I tell him I am afraid I might be blocked by censorship this time. He tells me it's a good book, nothing wrong will happen. I remind him what happened to my first book, *Silence Is Required.*

He encourages me. I wonder whether he believes what he is saying. Considering everything that happens, I can hardly understand him. And I can't think him naive, either. He draws the report. Usually, the head of the publishing house will not object to any book accompanied by his report. The book goes to syntheses. It comes back. I have to work on it again. Paleologu does not ask me to change anything. He draws another report. Although he has not reached the age of retirement, he is forced to retire. The editor in chief rejects his report. I am left without a book editor. The editor in chief promises he will take care of my manuscript himself. A few months pass by. I come to the publishing house from time to time to find out what is new. No news. He tells me every time he has not had time. Come next week, he says. I come next week. No news. At some point he tells me: I have drawn the report, it has gone to censorship. I leave. I feel "happy." A month later I go to the publishing house again. The editor in chief tells me: it has not returned yet. The same answer a few weeks later. An idea occurs to me: I ask the secretary what she knows about my book, has it not yet come back from censorship? It has not even left, she tells me. It's here. It has no report on it. But, I say, Mr. G. made it. He made no report whatever, she says. I go to the editor in chief. He is in a hurry. We are waiting for it to come back from censorship. He has a meeting. But the book is not in censorship, it has no report, I dare tell him. Can't be, I made it myself. I change my tactics: maybe the report was lost, the book is in the secretary's drawer, I tell him. He looks at me in astonishment. Come tomorrow and we'll see to it, he tells me. I come the next day, as he told me. I have been too busy, he tells me. I am working on the plans. Come next week. I come next week, too. Look here, he says, I have read the book, it is not what I expected. You are not your old self. Here are my remarks. Work them out. He hands me some sheets of paper. Come when you have finished working on it. It was true, I was not my old self, I had given up the "orphism" I had been accused of. I reach home. I change the order of poems and a few titles and I go to the publishing house again. Have you revised it? I have. Leave it here, I shall draw the report. I come back in several days. I have had no time, he tells me. I am going abroad tomorrow. But I shall leave the report with the secretary. I return the next day. The editor in chief has left, indeed. He has left no report behind. I find myself on the corridor, in disarray. I stay there for a while. Florin Mugur, who is an editor of the publishing house, comes in. What's wrong? he asks me. I tell him the whole story. Give it to me, he says. I give him the manuscript. I have new hopes. A few days later, Mugur phones me: I have read almost half the book, it's fine. A few days later he phones again and says: I'm afraid I was optimistic. Come to see me, we'll see what we can do. I go to his house. We talk for hours, studying the manuscript. We try a few tricks:

  1. We change the order of the poems.

2.  Have you been abroad? Like hell, I tell him. Never mind. Choose any town and place it at the end of the text. He shows me the poems to which I have to do that. I write under all of them: Paris 1970. The reason is that we mean to show I am talking about western reality, not ours.
3.  I don't capitalize God any more.
4.  We change a few titles.
5.  In few poems, we insert the word subway. (It obviously reminds of Western reality, again. The Bucharest subway had not been started yet. Later on, these texts will not work any more.)
6.  I replace the following lines in the poem *Woman with Peaches:*
    Never had the Militia had till then
    So many Doctors in Peachology . . . .
    I write instead:
    Never has the University had
    So many Doctors in Peachology . . . .
    Nobody was allowed to mock at the Militia, but you could do that to intellectuals . . . .
7.  In the poem which gives the title to the volume, I replace the following line:
    Comrade Minister, I apologize for the disorder
    I write instead:
    Comrade Mayor, I apologize for the disorder.
    (Ministers were taboo, too.)

We are done, at last, and have the feeling that we have not compromised so much. Mugur shrugs his shoulders: what are you going to do about it?

A few days later, Mugur gives me his report to read. An "optimistic" report, which interpreted "optimistically" all dangerous poems. In many cases, his interpretations had nothing to do with my poems at all. I am not convinced it will work. But he hopes we may still trick them into it. Anyway, the report is better than that made by Paleologu. Paleologu did not know how to make reports. The head of the publishing house, Marin Preda, signs and approves the sending of my manuscript to syntheses, on the basis of Mugur's report. Included within the Council of Culture, these syntheses employed "trustworthy" people, writers some of them. The smarter, the more dangerous, Mugur, my "rescuer," warns me.

The manuscript returns from syntheses with eight poems missing. No explanation given. I talk to Mugur. They picked them at random, he says. It could have been others. Everything I had discussed with him had been left, though. Many other endings had been crossed out and others added in pencil, to replace them. This must be C., he tells me. He usually does so. He wants "optimistic" endings. I am grieved, but can't help it. No one will listen to me. The manuscript goes to censorship. It comes back with seven poems missing. I'm giving up, I tell Mugur. Does it help? he asks. That's what they want. Censorship did not touch the texts with endings added in pencil.

These endings obsess me more than the missing poems. I get an idea: I talk to Mrs. V., who is in charge of technical editing: Can I give up some lines I don't like any more? Sure, you can give up all the lines, just don't put anything in. I cross the added endings and the lines which crossed my own endings. I feel a little more satisfied. One more step towards "happiness."

The manuscript goes to the printing house. The first copy comes out. I am at peace. Nothing bad can happen now. I did not yet have the experience of maimed first copies. A little later, the first copy returns, deprived of six of the poems which I considered extremely important for me. I go to see Mugur at once. I am in despair. This is no book, I tell him. I had thought I had compromised enough resorting to his tricks. You must go to N. if you can, Mugur tells me. N. was the head of the direction of publishing houses in the Council of Culture. He asks me if I know anyone who can help me reach him. I'll try to find someone, I say. A few days later, I find the man at last. He makes the providential phone call. One night, N. himself calls me up. I am close to stammering. I hear you are in trouble, he tells me. I don't know much, I have just returned from Portugal. There must be some mistake. Come to see me at the Council tomorrow. Who wrote your report? Mugur, I say. Oh, that one. No wonder. He's a . . . .

I did not understand the connection between Mugur's report and my missing poems. But I realized how perfect the mechanism was. You floated in haze like a blind man. They all slipped through your fingers. It was never anybody's fault.

I go to the publishing house the next morning. I tell the editor in chief (just returned from abroad) what it is all about. I don't want him to think I do things behind his back. I realize my naiveté. I'm coming with you, he says. We leave together. N. is waiting for us. He seems surprised to see G. In spite of the fact that the latter (I heard from the corridor, the door was ajar) had phoned him he was coming. We all sit down at a table. The head of the publishing houses leafs through the first copy. Why did you give up orphism? he suddenly asks me. That's where great poetry lies. You have switched to the opposite, as far as I can see. Let the others be ironical. I tell him, however, that my first book was rejected precisely because of its orphism. That's different. God knows what stupid censor got it.

N. lectures me. I realize he has read my book. He takes a text at random. Look here, he says, is this a good ending? He reads:

> When tears refuse to touch my lips
> And raspberry closes the gate on me
> I shall only be left with a dead body
> Or have my throat cut in the bathroom.

How can you use such a word as cut the throat? It's ugly, it's primitive. You are an orphic, let the others speak like that. I dare reply I have no other word for that precise reality. Well, then, he says, why do you have to cut it? And he smiles to the editor in chief. I try to defend myself saying it is a metaphor, I do not really mean to kill myself. The manager keeps silent. He takes another text. *Woman with Peaches.* This is not bad, the editor in chief says. It's all right. O.K., the manager says. But not this one (another text). Or this. (He meant *Stranger with a Map,* which was published later, in *Life at Thirty-Three.* Many poets used the poems rejected in one book in the following books, and, unbelievably, they did come out—thus proving that we were in the hands of judges who did not have any rule to go by. It was the age of the absurd. Everything depended on the moment, the incidents, or rather the misfortunes of that very day. Poems previously published in books were rejected when the poet dared suggest an anthology. Poems published by reviews sometimes were taken out of books. In connection with whatever came up that day, new "lizards" were detected, and the one who knew least about them was the author himself.)

The manager takes another text. That's good, the editor in chief says. Another text. This is out of the question, the manager says. I was witnessing a show where I was only formally present. But they tried to make me believe they were on my side, they were trying to save me. I was given to understand this was a favour done to me, because I was who I was, that some poems could stay because they tried to close their eyes, as in fact they were not suitable at all. Others would not even dream of such a privilege. . . . Here they were right. Others had the right person to help them, the person who made a phone call where it was necessary. Others had very strong friends and had it much easier than I had it. Phone calls, interventions, former school fellows who were now high-placed, stubbornly knocking at doors which seemed to be made of stone, irritation, especially anger, a subterranean battle led by each one of us, an exhausting battle, which for some ended in a solitary victory that you had no strength left to enjoy.

Go back to orphism, the manager tells me when we leave. Then he addresses the editor in chief: see what you are doing, give up churches, they are too many already, and death too. . . . It's hard to work with them, the editor in chief tells me outside. I don't mean the manager or some particular censor. It's just *they,* a face that has no name attached to it. But you saw me, didn't you? I forced his hand! It came out all right in the end. You have nothing more to change.

That was it. He, the editor in chief, had fought for me. I had to be grateful to him. I had come out all right. A fake book. Half of it left out.

*

## The second barrier of the nightmare

You started working with the editor of the book. Editors usually tried to guess what the censors would object to in the book. They looked for "lizards," hints, especially those directed at Ceauşescu and his family. When carefully read, everything sounded subversive and alarming. The texts which were very pessimistic were eliminated. Even at the level of the editor, there was a mania of interpretation which did much harm. The editor was, in fact, the first censor of the book. In many cases, the first censor was the author himself, by avoiding dangerous topics. Afterwards, all religious hints were eliminated. Then any word that could be interpreted as or hinted at our "socialist realities." This was the first stage of manuscript maiming. The more famous poets had it a bit easier: the really important ones could keep their books intact. As for the rest. . . . It was the first stab in the heart. You were extremely disappointed. But, after a while, you got over it. "There is still some hope left," you thought. Especially after you had seen the report on the book, and the book went to "syntheses"; you were almost glad. But after a while, you became tense. What followed was:

## The third barrier of the nightmare

If you knew the fate of the book until now, once it reached the "syntheses," most authors placed all their trust in God.

From there, the book usually returned with a few more poems eliminated. You experienced despair but were finally cleared by censorship. Some of the poems you liked were still there. And then what followed was:

## The fourth barrier of the nightmare

Official censorship. Here, too, many texts were rejected. You stopped feeling despair or joy; you just leafed through the manuscript, which had become razor thin. Books did not have a better fate, though, even after the "syntheses" and censorship were abolished. Council of Culture clerks were even better censors than those before them. That meant that responsibility had increased.

## The fifth barrier of the nightmare

The manuscript was returned from being censored and was prepared for the publishing house. Here, the obstacles were of a different nature. If you had any experience at all, you would want the book to look nice. And if you knew some tricks, you found out where the book would be sent. You could go so far as the manager in order to obtain better quality paper or to hasten the printing process. You contacted the printers, bribed them, offered them bottles of various spirits, which you brought yourself. If you were not smart enough for that, you had to place your faith in God once again. At last, the first copy was printed. Now followed:

### The sixth barrier of the nightmare
The first copy was sent to the Council of Culture again. More sleepless nights. The text looked different when printed. Now the censor could see other traps, find other "lizards." It threw a different light on your work. If this happened during some ideological campaign, that was it; the book was postponed until some unspecified date. If it happened during a fairly relaxed period (since the time of Homer, there has not been anyone who has not at least dozed off at times), only a few texts were rejected.

### The seventh barrier of the nightmare
The first copy was sent back to the publishing house. Despair again; sometimes even tears, then resignation. Or, rather, a numbness of all your senses. You had to go to the printing house again, contact the printers, bribe them. . . . Sometimes it worked; sometimes it was all in vain. You felt cheated. You would wait fearfully for the first restricted number of copies.

### The eighth barrier of the nightmare
The copy went to the Council of Culture again. At this point, nothing much happened. Even if the book was maimed, you told yourself that it still contained some poems you liked. But you were still afraid. You said to yourself, "Please, God. Don't let a crackdown begin right now." You would not be at peace until you saw the book in the bookstores. Such as it was, you wanted it to be out. If they thought that you had put your signature on a book "with problems," you had something to be afraid of. Some books were removed from the bookstores and burned; some were merely withdrawn.

### The ninth barrier of the nightmare
This should have been one of joy. What joy? More often than not, you would find yourself confronted with a book which seemed alien to you. The editor tried to console you, "Don't worry. It's a good thing it is out. Next time . . . who knows?"

Really, the only thing you could do was be happy. After this mourning, joy. Was followed was:

### The tenth barrier of the nightmare
The book had to be sent to the literary critics, right? It had to be commented upon. You became your own agent. And then you stubbornly, and with a kind of belated, velvety revenge, started to reconstruct the book as it had originally been written. You did it for the critics. You added the stanzas and lines which had disappeared. Sometimes, you added complete poems. But the critics, of course, could only talk about what had been printed. What bitter sadness and disappointment! They would comment on a completely different book from the one you had in your soul.

However, after so much trouble and anguish, you would feel ready to start the next book, to overcome the barriers of the same nightmare. Let bygones be bygones. A new battle lay ahead; you felt much more experienced now. You knew more tricks, knew which editors were more generous and tried to make them side with you. You tried to find out who the censors were. You looked for a kind of protection, the miraculous phone call that would open doors for you. This was the moment when you had become a real Romanian writer. You actually experienced the literary life of the Romanian "Golden Age." With God's help, if you had ex-faculty colleagues in important positions, could make friends with the head of some publishing house, or had a car to drive around an important person, if, if, if . . . then you could hope to put out another book which should be closer to the original.

The barriers of the nightmare I have described come from my own experience. They can be more or less numerous, depending on the author. But the nightmare was the same. No matter how it was for different writers, it was a nightmare.

*

## The Ballad of the Announcer and Other Poems

Manuscript taken to Romanian Book in 1985. Book editor: Florin Mugur. The poems are inspired by the cell-like atmosphere we are compelled to live in. A cell, a closed space inside which we keep looking in vain for the smallest way out. The announcer keeps running, but has nothing to announce, because he doesn't know who won. The good citizen—a guinea pig which is constantly experimented upon. I use hints more than before. People keep looking for escape. They keep saying: we want to go home. As I had to help the reader, however, to make him understand I was talking about him, about all of us, I used a motto from the Swedish poet Lars Gustafsson: "It is time we went home. But we are home." This motto was extremely important to me. I used it to get in touch with the reader, who in the meantime had become expert in understatement. I relied on his complicity. Something amazing was happening: the hypocrisy which united reader and writer had become a virtue. So, the Romanian writer could say like Baudelaire: *Hypocrite lecteur, mon semblable, mon frère!* When censorship was cheated, the victory made both author and reader rejoice. Behind the scenes, till the book came out, a stubborn battle took place, an immense waste of energy and intelligence. It almost looked like a game (tragic, but still a game): the poet set traps for the censor, and the censor, searching the manuscript, exclaimed triumphantly for every trap he found out: I have caught you, you are not smarter than me. And he was smart. Very smart. Especially the censor who was an intellectual as well. Sometimes he was a writer himself. The last kind was the most dangerous: he always found more traps than the poet had thought of, he could always convince you that each of your lines was a bomb meant to overthrow the government.

Mugur reads the manuscript. He changes some words, we use some more Western cities to take our socialist reality abroad. Not too much, anyway. We'll let it go as it is, he tells me. Let's trust your luck. Official censorship having been abolished, the manuscript went to the Council of Culture. The manuscripts from Romanian Book were in charge of three censors. Mugur tells me they are one woman and two men. The woman is a witch. Avoid T., too. Try to make your manuscript reach Z. He is not too smart and you will reach an agreement with him. He doesn't usually change much in a book.

So Mugur must write the report and I must find the right person to help. After a long search, I find him. She works with me for the broadcasting corporation, she was in the same faculty year as the new head of the directorate for publishing houses. It's all settled. The book will go to Z., the director promises. But why, he asks, are there any problems? No, she says, he wants it out sooner, and Z. doesn't keep books for a long time.

The book reaches Z. indeed, and it returns intact to the publishing house. That's a great victory. Only in the meantime the editor in chief of the publishing house is changed. The new one is the man who changed my endings by adding others in pencil. A good censor, therefore. As soon as he comes to the publishing house, he asks to see all the books ready to go to print. He gets to read mine, too. Mugur is gloomy. This one is a tough guy. He was sent here on purpose. (Romanian Book was the publishing house of the Writers' Union, and, since it wasn't a state publishing house, it was considered a rebel).

I meet the editor in chief down the corridor. He congratulates me. He has read my book. He only has a few remarks. Nothing important, really. I almost believe him. But Mugur comes with a pile of sheets. The remarks of the editor in chief. I almost quarrel with Mugur, after reading them. I tell him I am withdrawing my book. It's a hard time, he says. Why quarrel with me? I cool down. Let's see what can be done.

We take it poem by poem:

- *Prayer of the Pharisee.* Interpretation: the pharisee is comrade Nicolae. He has underlined the lines: *As soon as I turn up, among people, full of joy/ Church walls fall in tears.* I can't save the poem. It falls.
- The subtitle of the *Prayers—from the cycle Radioactive Prayers* become—*from Mr. Shakespeare's Denmark.* (The radioactive catastrophe at Chernobil had just taken place—they took out everything that reminded people of radioactivity, lest the great friend from the East should get angry.)
- A stanza is cut off from *The Prayer of the Nail:*
  Just that. I feel sick. And I dare

> Say: if I have crucified the Father
> I shall not stop at that. When I feel no longer sick
> I dream of the son's flesh.

In the book, the stanza is replaced by dots. (Interpretation: hint at Ceauşescu and his son, the prince inheritor. Absurd interpretation, belonging to a sick mind. I never even though of that.)

- *Cheering up Song.* Cut off. (Remark: We shall all go to jail if this comes out.)
- Out of the cycle *Sonnets without a Visor* the added sonnet is rejected. (An attack against our socialist system. The first line is underlined: *Sharing the room with a candle.* A hint at the lack of electricity. The last line is also marked down: *Sleep! Sleep! A five-thousand-year rest!* He wrote under that: Who? The Romanian people?)
- Out of various poems, he crossed the words: God, church, disaster (forbidden, as a hint to the disaster in our own country), Doctor Honoris Causa (hint at Ceauşescu, our only D.H.C.), balcony (a hint at the balcony from where Ceauşescu makes his speeches), pyromaniac ministers (a question mark), comrade general (replaced by Monsieur le General, lest people should think I mean general Ceauşescu, the great comrade's brother), comrade captain (replaced by Mon capitaine, lest people should think I hint at our army), two speaking pigeons (hint at Nicolae and Elena Ceauşescu).

Here is what I could save, with Mugur's agreement:

- I saved in a few poems the word god, noncapitalized. (During the first proofreading I changed the letter here and there, so in the book it also appears capitalized in a few places)
- The poem *Wandering Gods* (censor's remark: a hint to our old people. The regime kept discussing the possibility of sending old people from towns to villages)
- The end of *Letter to the Civilizing Heroes:*
  > If you are still alive, if it's not all a joke
  > Answer us, we have our eyes riveted to the sky
  > Now, when here we are, deceived
  > Among ovations, in the last Summer.

  (a hint to the ovations that welcome Ceauşescu. Summer is Romania. I dated the poem: Vienna, 1984. So Summer was no longer Romania.)

Although I tried, I could not save the motto from Lars Gustafsson: "It is time we went home. But we are home."

I am in Mugur's office. The editor in chief comes in. Have you finished? Mugur assures him everything is all right. The censor looked satisfied. Then I won't read it again, he says. Let it go to print. Congratulations, old man.

One thing was left unsolved. What could happen to the first copy if it reached the Council of Culture? Shall I be lucky again? I talk to Mrs. V. from technical editing: what can we do to prevent the book from reaching the Council of Culture again? She says I must be out of my mind. Yet the first copy does not go there again. I used a simple trick: on the inner cover they printed the year 1986, and on the last page 1987. If a scandal had ensued, we had an explanation ready: the book was not put on the 1986 list because it was thought it would be included on the 1987 one, as shown on the last page. And it was not included on the 1987 list because it was thought it had been on the 1986 one, as the first page showed. A misunderstanding. But there was no scandal. The book came out in 1987.

*

Before I published the first book I published a lot in reviews. Ana Blandiana published lots of my poems in *Amfiteatru*. Then Dan Laurentiu, in *The Morning Star*. That happened in 1970. It was a good time. As I did not have the courage to go to a publishing house, Blandiana took the manuscript of my volume *Silence Is Required* and gave it to Paleologu at Romanian Book. It was not their fault that censorship rejected it. When Paleologu received my second volume, *Migrating Nights*, he published an article accompanied by a poem from my book, on a whole page in the review *Arges*. It had a smashing title: *We have a Hölderlin!* I am not going to discuss Paleologu's enthusiasm; even then I took it as his wish to attract attention towards a new writer. People often did that at the time. It was still the time of great gestures of generosity. But I must say that later many critics judged my books only according to this first welcoming exclamation. Some even brought arguments that I wrote in Hölderlin's line. Others did not. But many forgot that I had my own will and ideas in my books. When I refused to be the orphic poet any more, when I considered that no one could afford such a thing in Romania at that time, when my poems changed a lot, some were disappointed, others merely discussed my style. Very few, especially among the provincial critics (Cluj, Iasi) went to the essence of my poems. As the social order could not be discussed in articles, no political pamphlets were possible in socialist Romania; poetry tried (sometimes it even succeeded) to stir the reader—sometimes by a meaningful depressive mood, at other times through irony.

Generally, literary critics avoided pointing with precision at what we were doing. They reacted as if we all lived in normal times, I mean the more permissive years. To me at least, who was born the year the king abdicated and the dictatorship of the proletariat began, the '70s seemed the image of normality. I had no other image to go by. I can't really tell whether for our literary criticism the stubbornness to discuss literature as in normal times was a way of opposition or merely subtle self-censorship.

My debut in press was lucky. I became a poet although I had not yet published a book. The reviews asked me to give them poems to publish. G. Ivaşcu publishes my poems on a whole page of *Literary Romania*, the main review of the Writers' Union. I receive a prize from *The Morning Star*.

But after the July Theses of 1971, I also receive the first blows. In *Scânteia*, the paper of the party, a raging article appears against some of the poets. Poems published by me in *Amfiteatru* are quoted as negative instances. Anonymous voices from the working people accused me in various papers.

After July 1971, special pages began to appear whenever an important event took place.

At a first stage, this is what a special page looked like: first there was a poem dedicated to the party (it was still too early for the poems dedicated to Ceauşescu) and signed by somebody unknown, or some cultural clerk. Later, when writers refused the game, the poets among the editors had to write these poems and they signed them with various pseudonyms. Very many shockingly native names were thus launched, and disappeared forever, after just one or two poems.

On the special page, after the poem dedicated to the party, one or two poems about the homeland were published, signed by writers already known. Then one or two historical poems. Then more poems on bright topics, signed by very good poets.

Soon the phone system began to work. They asked poems for the special pages. This was the so-called social command. It first appeared as a friendly help. The writers who were editors as well helped each other. You help me with my page, and I'll help you with yours. Then various phone calls to young and old writers, more or less known, who had sometimes, once, or never published in their review.

If you were a young writer, the tone was intimate, warm, but sounding so that no refusal was possible. Old man, my friend, we need you. Here are the topics, choose one. If you did not sound enthusiastic about it, the call gave you something unpleasant to ruin your day. It was not yet a direct menace (soon that came too: you won't publish again if you refuse now), it was just a warning.

After 1972, when I became an editor at the broadcasting company, I also started receiving these calls. Gradually, I was learning that it was not good for you to settle down anywhere, to have your own phone, to have friends who were editors, that it was not too good to be well known—maybe that it was not so good to have been born at all. Being a writer and doing all these things flung you in the middle of the nightmare.

At first I did not realize what traps the special pages were. I was still young, healthy, I could afford losing nights writing what I had to say. I did not give a damn about "events." But when a well-known writer phones you, one who has helped you publish, how can you refuse him? Especially when he allows you to choose your topics. So I did write two or three historical poems, about Michael the Brave, about Alba-Iulia, two or three more about an ideal country of our parents, about the apple orchards, as I knew them in my grandparents' village, before collectivization. I became an "orphic poet of apples."

Later they began wanting more and more. Not at once, though. But I was lucky I realized what was happening in time. I could not really push my poetry farther than that. Old man, please, don't say no; you don't have to write about *him*, you could write about the project of the subway. There's nothing wrong with the fact that we are going to have a subway, is there? All great European capitals have it, why shouldn't we too? I keep silent for a while, then I agree, on condition it is an article and not a poem. The voice agrees. Who else is writing for this page? I hear a number of well-known names. I feel better. I write an article about the subway. It is a necessity for Bucharest. I deliver it. The review comes out. I can't believe my eyes. Whole sentences have been dropped, others added. I am answered without conviction: It's not our fault, old man. It's the Council.

Another attempt. Another phone call. The 23rd of August. National festival. Mr. Verona, please write an article. I hesitate. Please, Mr. So-and-So himself asks you to, he himself made me phone you. O.K., I say, I'll see. I write about the young soldiers dead at the front. I deliver the article. The paper comes out. I can't believe my eyes. Sentences dropped, sentences added.

I shall never write again, I decide. It is not our fault, Mr. Verona. It's the Council. I become suspicious. Please write several poems, Mr. Verona. The blackmail begins. I give them some poems. Only a few come out. Not space enough, Mr. Verona.

Another time, another phone call. An old friend. He wants a poem or an article. What about? It's a special page, the poet and the city. Greek topic. Agora. . . . Although I have sworn to myself I shall never write ordered things again, the topic looks innocent. I write *Poets in the City*. I give them the article. The paper comes out. Awful. My editor in chief at the broadcasting company praises me during a meeting. I was slowly entering the nightmare. Good God, there's no one to complain to. I get home and feel lousy. I go to the bathroom and start crying. I am still young and I have enough tears. Later, even those will be scarce. My wife knocks at the door: is anything wrong? No, I'm shaving.

Phone call from *Literary Romania*. The voice of a poet I respect, who is editor there. Comrade Verona, give us several poems for next week. I give them a long poem. I wait for next week. The poem does not come out. The respected poet phones me. Something came up. Next week. Next week, another phone call. Comrade Verona, come to do the proof-reading. I do just that. I correct the mistakes. Comrade Verona, we are preparing a special issue. I feel mad at once. Can you give us anything? Silence. When do you need it? Till Monday. Oh, my God, I say, I must leave town tomorrow. (At about that time I began to lie, it was my only defense). Maybe you have something ready. I don't think so, I shall see. Maybe you can write something before you go. I'll try. . . . The evening before the review comes out the phone rings. Well, comrade Verona, have you written anything? No, I'm sorry. All right, comrade Verona. Never mind. Next time, maybe. The poem will be out tomorrow. Buy the review.

I buy it next morning. My poem isn't anywhere.

A few months later: Comrade Verona, bring me your poem again. I don't know what they did to it, it was lost somehow. By the way, we are preparing a special page . . . .

I did not take the poem, of course. I have not published anything in *Literary Romania* since 1974.

In *The Morning Star* I have published nothing since 1980, except an article about Eminescu.

At about the same time I stop writing for *The Contemporary* as well, after they changed a few lines in one of my poems which hinted at nothing at all. I asked why. They didn't look good, old man. What do you mean, they didn't look good? Oh, forget it, they have changed even Eminescu's texts!

So I broke all contacts with the press. The phone kept ringing, but I never answered it. I taught my wife how to lie.

I avoided all public places, shows, walks. You could meet them anywhere. There was pressure, too. My editor in chief asked me weekly: Comrade Verona, when are you going to bring out a volume of patriotic poems? Write it, hurry up, we need it, even the president is waiting.

There were temptations, too. I was offered a permanent column by various reviews. But that would have been worse than suicide. The "events" were more numerous than ever.

Later it became worse. Bright themes were no longer enough. The *proletcultist* poets of the '50s were brought back. They invented worker-poets, peasant-poets, soldier-poets, sailor-poets. Retired people, housewives and pioneers helped, too. Ceauşescu himself came to the rescue, founding the festival Praising Romania, which meant praising him, of course, and also praising the extraordinary couple. Our whole people had to do it. Applause, huge popular assemblies, shows on stadiums, applause. Ceauşescu himself set the tone, writing poems such as: Let the nation fly towards communism. Magic formulas began to appear, such as PCR—Party, Ceauşescu, Romania. They became the slogans used by the whole people, so to say.

I hear that when Ceauşescu once met the writers (till 1985 he enjoyed these meetings and would often have them) he mentioned socialist realism. "If you bring that back into literature, I shall commit suicide," Marin Preda said. Listening to the great writer, Ceauşescu smiled. If I were to paraphrase the title of Ernesto Sabato's book, *The Exterminating Angel*, I should say that to Romanian culture that was the exterminating smile.

*

## Our Poor Three-Day Miracles

In 1972 I become editor at the broadcasting corporation, the cultural department. I am told to record interviews and poems read by the authors. Nothing
nightmarish, so far. The interviews were more like advertisements, I admit, but
it was bearable. People were nice and hardworking. No directions, so far, no
need to mention the big comrade's name. If the poems did not contain forbidden
words like God, church, etc., and if they were not too gloomy, it was all right.
Landscape and love poems reigned. Till quite late we had love poems broadcast. We even had a special broadcast, with the obvious title "Love poetry,"
recited by a masculine and feminine voice, alternately.

Censorship was exerted by two comrades: one of them was one of the editors, and he gave the political visa. The other was a clerk of the Press
Directorate. They were normal people. The editor would bring his broadcast for
a visa, and the two guardians would listen to it carefully, without anger, for the
time being. Their remarks were usually technical. In the end, it was not too bad.

I felt as if I were on holidays, somewhere in a provincial town. I went from
office to office, I listened, I noticed things. I would usually stop at office 642,
where a fellow who had been to prison around 1964 worked. He still works
there. Later this became the 642 club, as the editor in chief called it.
Ceauşescu had not yet become an obsessive topic to talk about, but soon this
happened. The editor in chief did not yet come in gloomily, warning us and
complaining at the same time: stop these talks, comrade Pavlovici, don't get
together again, stop joking. We were listened to, of course, and the editor in
chief knew all about it. Or at least I think so.

Things started changing gradually beginning with 1973, when they started
firing people. I was given more poetic broadcasts to make and I accepted gladly. Soon I realized I had been right. The time had come when Ceauşescu's name
had to be mentioned everywhere, no matter what you were talking about.

The well-known professional meetings on Monday began. The editor in chief
would come and start whining: the management has decided, it's our duty, comrade x, why don't you want to talk about comrade Ceauşescu? It's no joke, we
shall all be fired, etc. If you listened to him, you could believe a war was drawing close. He was really angry. We listened and kept silent. We pretended to
listen. My fellows tried desperately to go on making good broadcasts. Till 1989,
in our department that was possible. But it took energy, and despair. Each
broadcast allowed by the visa to pass unchanged was a great victory. Fights
every week. Everyone was looking for new tricks. The visa fighting the editors.
Or the other way round.

But the political visa was a fellow-editor. He told my friend from 642, who
had a broadcast entitled *Dictionary of World Literature,* that he must not come
again if he did not mention Ceauşescu. I failed to see the connection between
Ceauşescu and world literature.

The first man who gave me a visa told me: I don't care what you include in your broadcasts, just don't get me fired. Another told me: I have children to bring up.

In time, just like in the press or publishing houses, our visa-men tried to demonstrate how subtle they were in detecting hints, lizards. They seldom accused us directly, they just found out traps we had not detected, not because we were stupid and knew nothing about literature, but our political level was not good enough, they had to protect us from our own mistakes.

Here is an instance of how subtle they could be. The man with the visa listens to my broadcast. He suddenly jumps up. Stop! I start up. What's the matter? This poem won't do! But we broadcast it so many times. You did, but you can't now. Look at the title, it's very dangerous: Country gently lit by flowers. He stares at me. Can't you see? I do not reply. Just listen to it! I listen to the tape again. I don't see what's wrong. Haven't you heard there are no bulbs in the shops? So what? Suppose a worker at Reşiţa turns on the radio, and listens to this. What will he say? Aha, he says, no more bulbs, so they want to light the country with flowers. But this is nonsense, I dare. The worker in Reşiţa hardly has time for such conclusions. The visa: don't you teach me. Just drop the poem.

Another time. It is the national day of Greece. The tape starts. One minute, two minutes. Stop! It was a poem by Kavafis. Achilles' horses. The divine horses presented to Achilles by Zeus mourn Patrocles's death. Zeus scolds them: Why did you go to those horrible people? Can't you see? my visa asks me. I couldn't. Don't you know the president and his wife are in Greece? What does the listener hear here? That they have gone to Greece, to those horrible people. But my text speaks of horses, not presidents. Don't you dare teach me, I don't want political scandal with the Greeks.

In 1974 I learned how to counterfeit the signature of the visa and I started using it on the most complicated tapes, which would never have been accepted. I had so many tapes to make a week that I expected the visa-man to forget what had been signed and what not.

I had fourteen broadcasts. They gave me three more. I accepted, in order to reduce as far as possible the number of failures. All the events in the country had an effect on literature as well. If the steel industry went wrong, for instance, you were not allowed to mention steel. If there were floods, you could not broadcast poems about rain.

After I had started using the signature of the visa (the Press Directorate had been abolished), at least two or three tapes a week were broadcast without being listened to by anyone else. I tried to introduce some good poetry. I was extremely tense. I waited for something to happen any minute.

If anything happened, I had my explanation. While being listened to, the tape had been ruined, so I had replaced it and had not announced the visa. Years passed by, and, to my amazement, no scandal broke out.

When I managed to introduce unpublished texts by a poet and they were not listened to by the visa, things became even more complicated. The poets had to be paid for their texts. But in order to be paid, they had to reach the editor in chief. On the basis of those texts, he signed the list for the money. I could very well be discovered at that point. So, what did I do? Well, I remembered I was a poet, all the same.

I took the texts home with me and I started changing them. I dropped all lines that could irritate the editor in chief and replaced them. I made the poems brighter. In this way everyone was satisfied. The poet heard his poems broadcast as he had read them, and wondered that nothing had been rejected by the visa. The editor in chief was happy, too, and praised comrade Verona at meetings, reproaching the other editors that they could not get people to come, while I could.

This is how I filled the archives of the Radio with counterfeited texts. But the tapes had the real texts on them. That was what mattered to me.

When Ceauşescu went abroad to countries in Asia, Africa, the editor in chief compelled me to find poems from those countries. We had very few translations from those countries, if at all.

One day I find out I must make a broadcast of Philippinese poetry. I look everywhere, try all translators, nothing. One person found in a dictionary at the American library a small fragment from a folk poem. One minute out of the ten I needed. I had no other way out than to add lines to it. I imagine I am a folk Philippinese poet and get to work. I invent a name, after I have looked through various papers, to see what kind of names they have. I combine the first name of a minister with the last name of a rugby player. After the broadcast, I am congratulated. You see, comrades, comrade Verona could do it!

In 1988 I was forbidden to broadcast world poetry. I was hunted by those from the Council of Culture to write texts for various occasions, too. My only way out of the nightmare was the passage to "nonexistence." Helped by a number of people, I obtained a medical retirement, invalidity of the second degree. Once arrived at home, I cut the bell wires, I took the plate with my name from the door, and had my wife answer the telephone: he is out of town. I was preparing for a long winter.

June 1991

# Poetry

### The Ballad of the Announcer

More and more often
I tumble down in the city square
in mass editions
de luxe editions
at the feet of happy citizens
at the feet of citizens satisfied with
their position
in encyclopaedias and touristic guides.
And when I think it's all over
and I mean to settle down for good
among generals and artists and merchants,
the turmoil of a new battle
throws me out of the window
throws me into the street
throws me on the pyre
demonstrating to me how relative
eternity is.
I walk out of the flames
and see unknown faces
and see unknown uniforms
and ask: what is wrong with me,
why can't I tell the Greeks  from the Persians ?
And they all order me in an unknown language
to give the others the great news
to shout: we have won!
And I look each of them in the eye
hoping to find light
and I don't understand anything any more
and I pray again: good God, I am an announcer
which way shall I turn?
And god explains that to me
in an unknown language.

Allow me please
to unbutton my coat and ask:
who has won?
The trains still do not reach their destination
or anyway they do not arrive where
they are expected.

Tomorrow
walks the roofs
scaring children
with its two heads.
Who has won?
In a photo
the victors
cover their eyes
with their hands.
In another photo
they merely turn
their back on us.
Who has won?
My friend is attacked by a dog in his dream
and nobody can cure him
of the bite.
Who has won?
And what shall I say when I am asked
about the man absent from his own wedding?
What shall I tell the old dog
which can't die
till its master comes back
from the dead?
Oh, God, how many trifles, how much I ignored
while I was running,
how many defeats in one victory
which I never thought of
while I was running
burnt by the light which seemed to signify victory
while the trumpet sounded retreat
for the citizens
to drink their beer under their comforters . . .

# Mircea Dinescu

**born 1950**

*Poet: his work has been translated into English, German, and French; he is currently the artistic director of the opposition review* Cațavencu Academy; *he was also a dissident around whom other writers united and was under house arrest during 1989 as a consequence of his protests; he has written seven volumes of poetry and been the recipient of four Romanian and two international prizes*

## The Revolution Must Take Place in Their Minds

**Lidia Vianu:** How does Mircea Dinescu, the poet, feel after 1989, as president of the Writers' Union?

**Mircea Dinescu:** I don't have anything interesting to say as president of the Writers' Union. I feel very commonplace, because being president of the writers equals to being a clerk of the Writers' Union, taking care of the writers' pensions. I'm telling you all this for your own information, not necessarily for the interview as such. . . . No, I don't like it, I have nothing interesting to say.

**L. V.** How do people write at present?

**M. D.** If it comes to literature, most Romanian writers, including myself, have left poetry or fiction for journalism. I have written pamphlets for the *Cațavencu Academy* for two years. I used the weapon of irony in them, because irony really is a weapon, as long as the official power is solemn and has an allergy to irony. I have written very little literature. A few notes for a book of prose, which I am going to Berlin, on this scholarship at the Academy of Arts, to finish. Consequently, I must admit that, while I was under house arrest, I wrote a book of poems in one year, while for three years now, since I became president of the Writers' Union, I have only written two poems and a half. It was a time of accumulation, rather than creation.

**L. V.** Is the time following the so-called, or rather the false, revolution a period of disillusion for the poet Mircea Dinescu?

**M. D.** It was neither a revolution, nor a false revolution. We had in Romania a popular revolt, and we see its consequences today. A revolution must take place in the people's minds, and that revolution hasn't occurred yet. It was not a true revolution, because its consequences are not as shattering as they should have been. You can very well see that a restoration has taken place in Romania. Not the restoration of a communist system, because the old communists, the activists, and the security agents are the first capitalists in Romania now. They are prosperous businessmen. Those of us who, even when Ceauşescu was alive, wrote pamphlets against communism, start flirting with Marx, become leftist unwillingly, when we realize how prosperous the new capitalists, the former party activists, are. Consequently, for a true revolution to take place in Romania, we should first witness a trial of the communism that ruled in Romania after the Second World War, and which destroyed whole social strata, from Romanian intellectuals—imprisoned—, to the depersonalization of the workers. It was not true that, as they used to say, there was a dictatorship of the working class in Romania. I am amazed whenever I see photos of workers between the two world wars, the capitalist age in Romania. I see the workers' strikes or demonstrations, and I see that workers were gentlemen, with hats and ties, while, under communists, the worker was a poor tramp, with dirty overalls, who never dressed up. They were like cattle in a herd.

When the working class finds its real status again, the pride to work—because, in Romania, most of those who were workers used to say, "I'm going to be a clerk, soon," which means they were somewhat ashamed they were working, as work was a shame in itself, here, well, when work in Romania is no longer considered to be a shame, we shall be able to say a revolution has really taken place. When national institutions, beginning with the Romanian Academy, justice, and the church, admit and repent for having compromised for forty years, when they regain their independence versus the power, we shall be able to talk about a revolution in Romania. Until then, we see the consequences of a street revolt, which lasted three days, like any miracle that can't last longer than that.

**L. V.** The first man we saw in December 1989, the first moments after the change, on the TV screen, was Mircea Dinescu. What would you tell us now, if you were seen on the screen again?

**M. D.** I was on a show even a few days ago.

**L. V.** Yes, I saw that.

**M. D.** Of course, those were pathetic moments. I was after ten months of home arrest. During those days, I became pathetic. I do not regret it, not in the least. I do not say it was a coup d'état, or anything staged in December. Ceauşescu did it all, in fact, because he had the only extraordinary idea in his life: during a very tense period, when we knew from Radio Free Europe and the BBC that they were shooting at people in the street in Timişoara, he organized a huge assembly in the Palace Square. He was hooted at, and everyone could see, on the screen, with their own eyes, that he was scared. That was the sign. So, he is the chief of the conspiracy. Later on, of course, after three days, the professionals of power took the lead. There was no so-called second shift in Romania, by which I mean the organized opposition, like that in Czechoslovakia, to take over the power. We had a few weak dissidents, arrested at home, three or four, and for the rest, the greatest majority of the population and intellectuals compromised.

**L. V.** I shall repeat my question: what would you say if you were on the screen in that situation again?

**M. D.** If I did that now, of course I should not dare give the population the feeling that an earthquake is taking place in Romania, as beautiful as we expected it then. I refuse to spread such news. A kind of new moral A-B-C is needed. Something similar to the Nuremberg trial must take place in Romania. I do not think we need another revolution in the streets here. As I said before, the revolution must not take place in the streets any more, it must take place in their minds.

1993

*

Interview published in *Liberation, France,* March 17, 1989

*How does an intellectual feel in a state ruled by a dictatorship of the proletariat?*

About twenty years ago, there was a joke about an experiment performed in a socialist system with an intellectual mouse, a worker mouse, and a peasant mouse. Kept under identical laboratory conditions and examined after a while, the peasant mouse and the worker mouse turned out to have gained weight and became quite optimistic, while the intellectual mouse looked skinny and irritated. When asked if he had been given less food than the others, he answered, "The quantity was the same, but from time to time I am shown the cat."

Well, now the situation has become more democratic. Everyone is shown the cat.

The allergy caused by intellectuals is no longer in fashion. Around 1950, whoever wore a hat was labelled bourgeois and risked being sent to prison and being reeducated. According to Marxist dialectalism, things have developed and now, even in Romania, we do not have coffee, but ersatz coffee. Substitutes of intellectuals have appeared too. The former inferiority complexes have become superiority complexes. Now, the "comrades" have collections of English hats, collections of doctorates, collections of university degrees, and are more informed about the history of football than the Marxist philosophy they teach. Many of these collectors imagine that Marx's *Communist Manifesto* was a kind of illegal flyer which the bearded old man stuck on walls at night. Specialists in every field simultaneously, the new *illuminists* advise the peasants how to handle the hoe, explain to the workers where they have to hit the nail, and teach the writer how to write from left to right.

In the meantime, the true intellectuals are outside, waiting, paralyzed by the shock of this amazing replacement.

If I am not positive that, while fighting for socialism, the proletariat had nothing to lose but its chains, on the other hand, I have absolutely no doubt that the intellectuals have received those chains. They got even more than they could carry.

*People talk about a certain sleepiness of intellectuals in your country. How do you explain it?*

Because there are splendid conditions for hibernation, people hibernate professionally in all fields. I would not be surprised if the following advertisement were published in the classified ads one day: "Lost, Romanian Academy. Along the Calea Victoriei. Substantial reward for finder." Since 1969, no new members have been admitted to the Academy of the Socialist Republic of Romania. With two minor exceptions, that is—no names; they are VIPs. During these twenty years, half of the immortals began to die a little. The others have withdrawn into their houses and wear their galoshes only twice a year, for festive meetings. The Writers' Union is practically illegal. The last national writers' conference took place in 1981, although the rule is that a majority of the writers must gather every four years to elect new leaders by secret ballot. If professional writers are forbidden to assemble, the amateur peasant-poets come together every year to dance and sing the praises of Romania, clean, starched and photogenic, thus demonstrating that the best thing these days is being an amateur. In 1981, our Union had 1,300 members. Now there are about 1,000: around 150 have emigrated, and 150 have died. The situation is all the more dramatic if we think that no new members are received any more, so the young can safely grow old at the gates of the Union. The censorship which was abolished by the General Secretary of the Party in a fit of euphoria has been changed—now that its head has been cut off—into a three-headed dragon, which is today more careful and greedier than ever. . . .

*Why does no one react against all this?*

Cowardice has, in a way, become an institution. Individual voices have been stifled by official leaders who are specialists in forging reality. Private opinion has been abolished. Any attempt at uttering unpleasant truths—the pleasant truths have all migrated to warmer climes—is considered heresy and is promptly punished. . . . Our silence so far has various motivations, all ruled by a feeling of general paralysis and fear. The constitution of the country, if read today, seems like a fairy tale, one of the thousand and one nights of Scheherazade. Man's fundamental rights do not have a tourist visa for Romania. Even worse, the very institutions meant to defend them, justice and the press, to say nothing of the police and security, have become means of intimidating and frightening the population. If a Romanian tries to abandon his neutrality, he runs a greater risk than a Swiss, who runs none. Free expression of opinions is considered treason against the homeland, and the mere casual conversation with a foreign citizen is labelled espionage. . . .

*Is there any solution to the crisis which reigns in Romania?*

It may sound strange, but Stalinism was the best thing that could have happened to socialism because man was done away with as an independent individual and he could be made to function in a flock, which was far more efficient and productive. Do you want to know the secret of the pyramids, which has evaded historians, architects, mathematicians for so long? Someone ordered them to be built, and that order was carried out. That was all there was to it. Even then, there must have been a kind of socialism; but its name must have been different. Stalinism was just as good as slavery: people starved to death in misery, whole generations had alienated childhoods, dignity and conscience were trampled into the ground, innocents and geniuses were shot, artists committed suicide—the price for all that was the atomic bomb, building dams for hydropower, digging canals in the deserts, moving hills onto plains. All this because Father Stalin ordered it, and his order was carried out.

Socialism's recovery after the Stalinist virus, the attempts of returning to normal which have been made in several neighboring countries can hardly be accepted by professional Stalinists, who see danger and bourgeois inefficiency in the fact that people no longer want to work like cattle; they demand independent trade unions; they want brighter clothes, free Saturdays, and the right to say, "No!" when "No!" really has to be said. In an argument with the Genesis, the leaders of the party recently planned the creation of a "new" kind of human on Romanian territory. Unfortunately, the overwhelming majority of the population is comprised of people of an older kind, still affected by hunger and cold, unable to face the austere, freezing laboratory conditions necessary for the creation of this "homo ceausisticus," which is fattened with ideology and heralded by the gross rhetoric of party propaganda.

If the leaders could rediscover their lost senses: the sense of measure and the sense of reality, if they could give up party mysticism—that would be a solution that would bring light back to the faces of the other kind of people, those who still want to be citizens of old Europe.

*People talk more and more about a common Europeanness. What do you think of that?*

When political architects draw up the plans for a common European house in Paris and in remote Moscow, we can already bet that this house will certainly be deprived of one of its windows: Romania. Instead of the assumed window, you will bump into a wall behind which twenty-three million people are waiting in astonishment for the moment of official unification with a new continent. If the revolutionaries of 1848 had spoken French, if those who forced King Michael to abdicate a hundred years later could speak Russian fairly well, it seems we are witnessing a new influence on our language: this is Romanian with a North Korean accent. If we consider the fact that a letter from Paris reaches Bucharest—if it ever arrives at its destination—and its addressee, already read, in forty-five days, we are justified in asking the question: are we still in Europe?

Romania, which was said to be a Latin island in a Slavic sea, has really become an island. But this time it is placed in an existential geography, not a linguistic one. It is an island surrounded by the restless waves of political reformism, with natives who are eager to taste just a bit of the wonderful balms called *peristroika* and *glasnost*, which appear to be able to bring the dead body of socialism back to life, but which is strictly kept out of their reach, just as we were protected from evil Coca-Cola, which was supposed to be an American drug, when we were children.

Romania is in fact an island on land. It embodies the painful antagonism between politics and geography, because removing Romania from Europe and hitching it to the abandoned cart of the Maoist cultural revolution, to the new pharaonic North Korean formulas, fully demonstrates the idea that the maps of the world no longer reflect reality or that it is no longer true to say, "Tell me who your neighbors are, and I will tell you who you are."

The terrifying idea that power can erect a wall worse than the one in Berlin overnight, a wall separating Romanians and the "civilized" world. It can demolish a town with European traditions in order to pride itself, afterwards, on the concrete masses of Stalinist pagodas; it can poison air, water and soil with the flames of huge chemical plants. At last, we have to admit that, after almost half a century of socialist impetus, we have acquired the paleness of Asians: our children are pale because of malnutrition; their parents' eyes are made smaller by hatred and despair.

## Is Gorbachev a hope for Romania?

The Romanians have always looked towards the East in fear. The feeling is not hard to understand, historically, considering that we are a people located on the border of an empire. Besides that, Stalinism was not imported from Honolulu, but from the stocks of the Kremlin's ideology. Forced collectivization and the famous Black Sea Canal, where the intellectuals almost dug their own graves, well, these are only two exotic fruits which filled Romanians with distaste for a very long time.

For many years, we were told, out loud or indirectly, that the Romanian system could become more liberal if it were not for the "Eastern Bear." And the people even believed it. Soviet troops trained on the Romanian border. This was the statement which the officials drummed into our heads whenever we tried to rebel. The fact that Gorbachev appeared with his amazing reforms, brought to light the truth that the pretext of the Muscovite dragon was very useful to the dogmatic leaders of the other socialist countries, because thus they could control all kinds of opposition, and preserve their own style of Stalinism. I have no idea whether Gorbachev is considered a good czar by the people beyond the Prut, but for the millions of people who kept silent and endured humiliation for dozens of years in Poland, Hungary, Bulgaria, Czechoslovakia, East Germany and Romania, he is very welcome. He is the Messiah of a human-faced socialism. If he takes into account the theory of a physicist who used to say that an egg will not boil in ten tons of luke-warm water, but in a small pot of boiling water, that is, if he has the courage to realize to the bitter end his fervent vision of history, we may see worlds and people coming back to life again.

*The revolt (a strike that failed) in Braşov, on November 15, 1987, had no effect whatsoever. Why was that?*

"A car might run over you!" "Think of your children!" "You might be forced to leave the country!" These are the statements one hears from one's best friends when one considers sending the officials the least statement concerning the terrible situation of culture. A venerable prose-writer, the author of extremely popular novels, when invited to sign such a statement, among others, answered, almost transfigured, "I would gladly sign it, but at my age I am afraid that I will not be able to survive the beating at the police station." Why can an 80-year-old artist imagine such a horrible consequence in a country which is not fascist but socialist? Can you answer that? Why a few million people are whispering, instead of talking aloud in their own homes?

Few people are called to be martyrs. After what happened in Braşov, they spread the rumor that those who had organized the revolt had been irradiated afterwards. Who knows? The press did not even mention it. Justice is blindfolded, and also dumb. The fear of death is more prevalent in humans than in animals, after all. Even in the West, there was a recent song entitled "Better Red Than Dead." No one has the right to judge us from the outside. In a country where even the dead in the cemetery are uncertain of their place, because they are rearranged every year and brought closer together, you can easily imagine that the living are even more severely checked and kept in hand . . . .

*What would you do if Ceauşescu disappeared some day?*

That is impossible. His Highness is immortal.

*Do you consider exile an option for artists in Romania?*

An artist's raw material is liberty. I do not know how to explain it, but the oil and energy crises and the lack of other goods enhanced the liberty crisis.

The writer began being considered a potential delinquent, who must register his typewriter with the police annually, report what he had discussed with a fellow-writer in a neighboring country, submit his manuscripts to committees specializing in detecting understatements, and meet with his readers only with special permission. They just forgot to take his fingerprints. Otherwise the file would have been complete.

The collective neurosis which spread throughout the population has also infected the artists, who are pushed to the outskirts of society, humiliated, forced to submit to duplicity, condemned to slow suicide.

As they say in Romania, truth walks around with a cracked skull. But writers can no longer be called the surgeons of reality. They have been transferred to the cosmetics sections of the Power, adorning the Ugly, applying make-up to the face of Lies, praising Mediocrity. The compromise specialists have become aggressive when someone steps aside from the chorus of paid praisers. There are only two solutions for surviving: either you accept a life of deprivation, accompanied by drawers full of manuscripts, or you emigrate. External exile is most often a consequence of internal exile. There can be nothing more tragic than Romania's losing its own artists, who have been and are still the salt of this earth.

*Western journalists take more and more interest in Romania. Why do you think this is so?*

They are attracted by the fabulous social exoticism here, by those who fail to commit suicide because they cannot set themselves on fire in a public square due to the lack of matches and cannot hang themselves because of the lack of rope and soap. By Bucharest, too, which tends to become the first lay-city in Europe where policemen are more numerous than pigeons, and where the black market has managed to print the name of Kent cigarettes on the national currency. By the malady of giganticism, which considers man's happiness in terms of quantity of concrete. By the absurd region where border guards keep their guns aimed at those inside the country. The place where wheat is harvested on TV, but rots in the fields. Where workers are nicknamed owners in order to be compelled to buy what is rightfully theirs. The street car drivers are pressured to buy their street cars, the peasants their houses. . . . Wherever you go, tell everyone that God has turned his face from the Romanians.

—written seven months before the 1989 revolution

# Poetry

## God Forbid

History seems to be carrying us in its belly
and has forgotten to give birth to us,
the holy ones are nearsighted
they sip the borsch of dogma which drips in their cap,
and daily bow to all things
since who knows what archbishop sleeps
in the ladle, in the rag basket,
in the barrels of these sad guns
where the Madman hatches his crime
and kills us just because he loves us,
when we are hungry he draws fish,
when the cold comes he jails the weather
stop History—I must get off at the next stop
stop at the God forbid stop
                              stop

## The General Face

I counted 71 feet in the whirl of the metro
(the maimed was among them)
but good God
the left one fell apart from the right
the mud had defeated the strength of the tan yard
the shoe seemed tortured
the boot careless
the galosh pouting.
71 honest feet, my God,
and a general face
on which I could read nothing
at all

## The Door

As you lie on the bank of the dark water
you feel the summer fly circle,
and find its message easy to decode:
it has reminded you that you are carrying a corpse on your back.
Then out of the blue it just seems to you
that a terrible steamer floats up the Danube
cracking in all the joints like an empire,

dragging behind it forests and bridges
herds and houses, church steeples
glued like snails to the bottom hull,
a steamer driven by a law as it were
natural and absurd at the same time,
its belly full of country children
to be spat out like spawn at the source.

Awakened by the splash of some bottle
flung by some drunk who hates the stream
or by the siren of the sugar plant
you go back silently to your close room
and try to put together something out of nothing
to glue a frame around the painting
whose painter will never be born
or even clearer than that:
to fix a doorknob to a wall
which has no door
on it at all

## Wheat Watched by Poppies

If the poet  is peacefully sleeping among flowers
wake him up friends, harvest men are coming
with reddened palms hidden among poppies
if I keep silent you have no right to keep silent tomorrow.
For thousands of years, like a watch, the earth is wound
the same horses keep eating the same barley
where the grave embraces another grave
morning star bones fall like snow on a realm
and love goes up above us, up and up
we love the very sunrise which promised us sunset
as we sprawled at the horizon, our body like a bridge
we have tamed the snow coming from the North Pole
and the beasts freed from strange cages
(it was late and instead of bullets there were words in the guns)
we shall show them a country with wheat watched by poppies,
when I do not keep silent, you have no right to keep silent
tomorrow

## Rented Sun

an oil stain on tall windows, that's what I am
on your daily starched life
no power, no rain can make me fade away
the same as the change in the beggar's pocket
draws the lightning
among silverware
I shall drop
the rat killed by watchmen in the garden
on the melon you will find out
a poem I scratched there with my nail
and here is a crack in the wall
through which one of your daughters will elope with a poor student
but you withdraw under the cheap rented sun
celebrating your indigestions
let him bark, you will say,
let him bark,
don't even throw him a bone as you used to
just lie down peacefully under the rays of my sparkling fangs

## Dance on Embers

Today jealous of butterflies, milked by clouds yesterday
I didn't know what shade was when they struck me with the stick
like the tear on a foundling's cheek
I slipped down and I feel now the whip and the harness.

Pulling the stars apart I could have shouted
but I felt so sick at their savage laughter,
a pyre of cold was coming to life on my frozen lips
and now I dance in chains on thorns and embers.

I once flew over lakes and hardly mirrored my face in them
when the water closed its eyes at my spare rays,
now they are beating drums and send me daily
a bowl of black blood after some stabbing.

How can I tell them that the locust tree flower was to me
shrine of grace and chance of peace
when I stumble on rocks they call me idiot fool
because I cannot carry the dirty skins,

how shall I tell them that I cannot, the same as thoughtless bears
hop and scrape the sand with my claws
since my birth had been heralded by three magi
and of all the people only my mother still knows my face,

how shall I tell them that I cannot growl, but sing
how shall I tell them that my hand touched the harp
when all they left for me to see are earthen windows
and a muzzle which does not allow at least grass in

## Absurd Chess Game

Sweet innocence
to imagine that poetry can make a better world.
It is as if you were throwing a piece of sugar
in the cage of the tiger,
and the latter started reading Shakespeare.
Fattened by your own disaster
(as if you had your lunch in the mirror)
you whistle like a train in stations
until the mob tramps all over you
hastening to get the warm spot on your nape.
And since the dream is only the love child
of reality,
remember the absurd game of chess
in which the madman moved the villages
first sacrificing the horses,
and a thousand guys could not wait to praise his move

## At Your Disposal

misfortune wears my orange shirt walking about
friends greet it absent-mindedly
I milk the zeppelins withdrawn into the air
between the two world wars,
I answer them dangling the pails above the angry mob
they shout and point at me and swear:
"that guy wants to escape reality"
"why did you go up there
what were you insinuating
what do you mean to do with that zeppelin milk?"
"a doctor is what he needs
to put his imagination in plaster"

"damn you"
"boo"
"do you have a license?!"
At last I had to climb down.
I had got bored of being young...
In hospital five doctors stared at my death
as through a window pane.
One knocked my chest.
I said, Come in, although for some time now
I haven't been living in myself.
"So much the better," he answered, "we shall rent you."
So here I am now at your disposal:
cheap,
comfortable,
anxious to see you gamble my orange shirt at dice

## Love Story

A former pal
who proved to be a very gifted informer
after he had made three children with a woman
whom he married off to a dentist who was emigrating to America
(well done, good bye, good bye!)
grew even deeper roots into the native soil
and made honey with the help of some bees
whom he turned in at the police
because they touched pollen from plants turning to the West
then he made a few friends
who were even easier to turn around than hives
they were permanently efficient, winter, summer,
a yellow adder in each of his cuffs
when he shook hands, very convincingly
when he detected—a small cancer in the paleness of your cheek
     —a certainty in the rumour that your girlfriend cheated on you
when he sold you—a lamp which belonged to Ilitch in fact
     —a wardrobe without doors through which any woman could leave you
At last I had to tell him: be so kind
as to become a true enemy to me . . .
Good God, you should see how well he succeeded

## Walls

Stupid illusion:
to surround yourself with walls
and suddenly feel
so free


Manuscript Found in a Lamp Chimney
In the letter box a cold pair of scissors
to cut off fingers with
                              has made its nest.

On the hill of our metropolitan church there are windows
                              but there are no shops
In the tram stop a dwarf is walking about with his Phillips hump
waiting for customers.

Death is sold to anyone and is pretty cheap
but
one must save a lot of fuel, paper
                              and God

If fools were edible
there would not be such huge lines at the butcher's
                    where they sell
                              intellectuals

# Daniela Crăsnaru

born 1950

*Poet, editor*

## Recuperating Our Freedom

**Lidia Vianu:** How was your literature influenced by politics before 1989? Immediately after the revolution? Today?

**Daniela Crăsnaru:** Not at all. The starting point of my writing has always been a kind of inner duality: spirit and body, between lucidity and sensuality. There was a period when I tried to be revolutionary, so to speak. Some of the writers of my generation, such as Dorin Tudoran and Mircea Dinescu, tried to change things. We tried to speak openly. We thought that, if we could solve those things that could not be solved by the press, justice or specialized institutions by means of literature, we would use literature to replace them. I am not sure that such poems will endure in time. Now, they might be understood only by referring to a dictionary of the symbols used at that time. Just looking back on what was taking place then.

**L. V.** I assume you mean a dictionary of interdictions?

**D. C.** Poems that need explanations are not poetry. We used understatement. Anyway, we were lucky not to have become the prey of social descriptivism. I avoided writing poems about lines, cold rooms or bulldozers. This would not seem to have much meaning today. For a foreign reader, these words are not subversive in the least. They are everyday words; that's all. A few years ago, in a cold theater, when a character said, "How cold it is!", I remember that the people started clapping frantically. But their gesture belonged only to that moment. They had nothing to do with the Shakespearian text which itself had nothing to do with the worries of that audience.

Our present drama is that of recuperating our freedom. Before, we knew that certain things would not be accepted, and we waged a war of synonyms. We sent our books to publishing houses where our fellow writers worked. I usually sent my books only to friends. But even friends could not help a lot. The unseen came after them. Both author and editor elaborated a strategy for pushing the original text through. The original text almost never returned as it was when they received it. Except for a few obvious things, which everyone knew were forbidden, the others were aleatory. It all depended on the situation, which changed daily. When they forbade balconies to be enclosed with window panes, you were not allowed to use the word "balcony." For someone living outside Romania this may seem like an aberration. It was an aberration for us too, but we knew from the very beginning that we should avoid the word "balcony." So we started an unseen fight. I never worked with editors who were censors themselves. So we devised a strategy which would either succeed or fail. We waited until the strictest censors went on leave. Or there was another technique, invented by Mircea Ciobanu. He arranged the poems in such a way that he angered the censors from the very beginning with the toughest poems, which were sure to be rejected. But afterwards, the others were accepted. This was a great loss of time and energy. Instead of using all my energy for writing, I spent 40 percent of it devising publication tactics and strategies.

**L. V.** Did you have writer's block after fighting censorship?

**D. C.** It made me more obstinate. I like fighting; I'm an Aries. I also had the satisfaction, however small, of someone who fights a whole, well-ordered system. It was my small contribution to the general fight. It gave me the feeling that I played a role in reality. There was no block for me. It only irritated me. Especially the almost absurd remarks. A love poem, for instance, ended with the line "I haven't and you haven't access to the sea." This reference to lack of access to the sea was fiercely accused. I was told that that was a geopolitical matter and that I thus denied Romania's access to the sea. What could I say? It was unreasonable. It was more than just ill will. You could not help but think that they wanted to destroy you poem by poem, because in every poem, they could find something unacceptable. In fact, they did not want to publish your book at all. A fight with the windmills ensued: you tried explaining to them that you had not meant what they thought you had meant. More often than not, there was no one to whom you could explain this because we did not, in fact, see them.

**L. V.** You didn't get to meet your censors?

**D. C.** No, and neither did the editors. The censors made notes on the manuscripts and spoke to the manager. In 1973, when I graduated and received a job at a publishing house, censorship still existed officially. At least we knew that. Words like angel, church or God were not allowed to be published. Strangely enough, devils were not forbidden. This is probably quite significant. There were some lists, and there were notes for every line. But you could discuss them. I had a strange experience, this time as an editor. A book by Petre Sălcudeanu, which, from my point of view, both as an editor and a writer, did not cause any sort of problems. It took ages to return from the censorship department, so I went to the floor where I knew the censors worked. I went from office to office, which was not allowed. It was a detective novel, so I played the detective. I met the censor for our publishing house, a very nice lady.

**L. V.** Were the censors philologists? Did they graduate from any special school?

**D. C.** Yes, an army of philologists. No special school. The most robust, so to say, were promoted there. Good files, no relatives abroad, high protection. They were advisers. Their salaries were substantial. It was a director's salary, not an editor's. An army of them.

**L. V.** Do you still see them?

**D. C.** I met some of them before, too. If they were stupid enough to get divorced, or if one of their relatives defected, they were fired from that job and transferred to a publishing house. They came to work with us. They were first proofreaders, as punishment, and later editors.

**L. V.** What do they do now? Do they feel guilty at all?

**D. C.** No. Those who were transferred to publishing houses still work there. They might even consider themselves dissidents because they were punished by the former regime. But they were not punished monetarily. They came and stayed with high salaries. It was the law. But let me come back to Sălcudeanu's book. I asked that nice woman what was the matter with it. She said, "The problem is that this book . . . has no problem at all, and I have to write a four- or five-page report indicating what is wrong. That's how I earn my salary." I felt sorry for her, so I did something strange. I cut sentences from the manuscript at various places and rewrote them exactly as they had been. Then I told her, "Well, now you can say that there was something terrible there, that you have worked on the manuscript and now it looks good." She thanked me. It was tragi-comic, you know. But we paid for this tragi-comedy with our lives, our time, our nerves. That is how I saved that book. Around that time, Mr. Sălcudeanu had a heart attack because he could not understand what was going on. Nobody knew that a certain lady had to write a four-page report, and she did not know how to write it because she could find nothing wrong with the book.

**L. V.** Was this a trying apprenticeship, learning how to write books with which there was nothing wrong?

**D. C.** You could never learn how to do that because their point of view was never the same. On any given day you never knew exactly what was not allowed. There were so many party conferences, directions, events, some of which were not even made known. If a book happened to touch upon something that had happened at the top, it was censored, but you never realized what it was all about.

**L. V.** Did the censors know about all these things?

**D. C.** There were stages. The greatest honor was to be censored by comrade Dulea himself. Comrade Dulea was their friend. He was always in direct connection with those at the top, with cabinets 1 and 2. It is very strange that comrade Dulea was not present at any of the trials for the *nomenklatura*. He had been in charge of literature and films. If you melted a book, you lost a few hundred thousand lei. But films were so expensive that the ideological whims of comrade Dulea cost millions of lei. He visited the set when the film was almost finished, and he started changing things. Every "No!" he uttered was worth millions. If someone had amassed all the money spent in vain as a result of comrade Dulea's orders, he could be more concretely sued than many others.

**L. V.** What has become of him? Do you know him personally?

**D. C.** I did fight him on two occasions. He tried to persuade me that I was wrong in what I was doing, and he urged me to write about villages. He had a peculiar gift for intimidating people which he had practised for many years. He had the brusque manner of the comrades, those who make you stand and dominate you from their armchairs.

Many former activists have penetrated the parties, both for and against the government. At first it was mostly amateurs who took part in politics. A few months later, everyone, from the right to the center-left, since the true left never let them go for a minute, realized that they needed pros. But our only pros during the last five decades were these comrades themselves. Every party in the world has an inner discipline, but we were so eager to establish democracy that we completely forgot that we still needed documents and discipline. Well, the comrades mentioned above knew this from the inside, so to say. Only a few months passed, and they were being used in all parties. Most of them are used, however, to doing the inside administrative jobs. With their wooden language, which has been only slightly adapted, they attack their own comrades from another party. It is a very interesting backstage fight. Who knows. They may be necessary after all. I have forgotten the feeling of fury when my books were checked and stopped. I feel somehow detached from it now. They have all passed: the sleepless nights and the fights with the windmills.

**L. V.** If censorship had never existed, would you have written differently?

**D. C.** I never accepted changes. I preferred sacrificing whole poems. What was published has nothing to do with censorship. The books I have written are mine; good or bad, they are mine. And any fault is mine too. Some people were not able to recognize their books when they were published. They gave their friends copies with the pages covered with corrections.

**L. V.** Do you think censorship had any positive effects, considering that discontent could not be expressed directly and had to be concealed, be driven toward the aesthetic?

**D. C.** I never dreamed that censorship could have positive effects. Or that it could compel you to use metaphors if you were unable to do that, or to find symbols, to drag you toward a different kind of language.

**L. V.** Do you think that a writer's block exists now? Has censorship disappeared?

**D. C.** Well, yes. This is a drama. The last five years were unbelievably hard. What censorship had accepted a few years earlier was no longer accepted. We had to break away from two things at once: censorship and the former reality. A book which spent five months with the censor, instead of three, was more favorably commented upon. A book which included more of the so-called lizards" (bulldozers . . .) implicitly became better. It was more appreciated by readers, who saw images of the dictator in certain characters. The book would become a bestseller overnight. The authors of such books, all honorable men and good writers of course, acquired a halo, and started taking it for granted that they were very good. Some writers became symbols, and this was in direct connection with the amount of reality included in their works. Some were good; some were very good. Only their glory was not real. Now that we are allowed to write anything that crosses our minds, they experience true tragedy. They have lost the forbidden zone which made them more gifted than they really were. They find themselves free to speak out. The thing which made these authors seem better than those who were, in fact, as good as they were, but who had chosen to deal with fundamental aesthetic topics as opposed to reality and had not acquired that halo, well, that kind of courage which had made them look different was no longer enough. Some writers need glory; they need to be admired by the public, and they ignore the fact that the public admired them for the least important part of their literature: for insignificant arrows slung at reality. Here come suffering and tragedy.

**L. V.** How do you write, now that the obstacles and nerve-consuming censorship have disappeared? Is your writing better now? Do you still write?

**D. C.** I have written some poems since December 1989. They are probably no different from what I have always written. I reread parts of my books, afraid that I might find them obsolete or too much connected with past history. My fears have abated. I do not know how good they are, but they can still be read without explanation.

**L. V.** But you did write poems with lizards, didn't you?

**D. C.** Yes, especially in the winters of 1984 and 1985, when we had to keep our winter coats on all the time and our fur caps, too. It was the first time when external pressure overwhelmed my inner pressure. What used to come first was my inner demon; outside things seemed pale and inefficient to me. Faced with literary history, material hardships will save no one. A tragic or serene life story hardly matters at all. We are all equal in the face of time. From my point of view, only what you leave behind really matters. No one will forgive you for writing badly just because you had no bread at that time. There was a time when I even thought that pressure and suffering helped you to be more sensitive. The literature of Eastern Europe, although it is not very well known outside the region, is much more profound and full of life than the literature of consumer societies. After the revolution, my friend Fleur Adcock, the translator of a book of my poems (to be published at Oxford), said to me, "How lucky you are to have had such a life story. A revolution. . . . Nothing ever happens here." So I imagine we should beware of a general welfare.

**L. V.** Do you think literature might die?

**D. C.** No. At least not for those whose engine was inside and not outside themselves. My dramas were interior, not external. I feel positive that the true material for literature is not life mirrored by art, but life which squeezes inside and is filtered by one's own suffering, one's own laboratory.

**L. V.** Does the present economic censorship require a new arrangement of genres?

**D. C.** We still think communistically. We want a market economy, but books are also goods. As in the West, they will be part of the game of the market-oriented economy. I guess that less poetry will be published, like everywhere else. Unfortunately. It will be hard for novels which lack sex, politics, adventure, suspense. Literary criticism will have the same audience as before: authors and philologists. Before, sometimes one of my books was known only through criticism because the readers could not find it to buy it. To me it seems natural that criticism should be important. It is important if it teaches people how to read. It has the function of deciphering a book, of making readers see various aims and levels in a book. Taking into consideration the money we now have, which is indeed very little, I wonder how many readers will buy both a book of criticism and the book it deals with. That would be the ideal situation, I think.

**L. V.** How would you explain censorship and its disappearance to a person who has no idea what censorship means?

**D. C.** They are ignorant of quite a lot of things in America; they cannot even locate Romania on the map. I find it natural that great democratic countries should teach us, but first they should at least know who they are teaching.

Two months ago, I was in Greece, for a women's conference. There were thirty women from Romania. All of us acted more like men because that was what we had had to be all this time in Romania. I say this with pride rather than regret, because the equality of women and men had its advantages, too. From the moment we arrived at a particular restaurant, we heard Russian music. There was an American senator there who knew that the Romanians and Bulgarians would arrive soon. Trying to please us, he asked the sirtaki players to play "our" Russian tunes. At first I thought it was part of the program, but soon I was told that the senator was so happy that he could please us, since the players could play *Ochi Chorniye* and *Kalinka* and all the rest just for us. His eyes simply sparkled with joy. I stood up from the table, and the others did the same. We left because that was more than a misunderstanding. If this misunderstanding is transferred to another level, it will cost us another lifetime.

Because the senator was irritated, I explained to him that we were a Latin country, that we had nothing in common with the Russians, and we actually begged him to refrain from making us share anything with the Russians again. Yalta was just about enough. We did not want to be delivered to the Russians once more, because we had had enough of it. His certainty that the Russian songs were ours made my blood boil, and I would be curious to know how far and how widespread this misconception is.

How can they send rockets to outer-space when they do not know exactly what is going on on earth? Or maybe they do not want to know.

*

Irony was what angered them most. At the last national writers' conference, I was asked by the Communist Youth Union to take the floor and speak about the wonderful lives of young writers so I read the following:

"The fact that we are here, trying to solve the numberless, hazy matters with which we are confronted more and more often, by means of mere words again, makes me feel that we are champions of hope. We are optimists who stubbornly believe that a monologue is a dialogue, that words—our words—are not lost in the desert of this present moment, that all our lives—their very essence—what we write, is considered, valued, protected. Champions of hope, that is what we are, as long as we know that the list of all fields of activity ends in 'water, garbage, sewage, education, health, culture.'

Since it would not suit us, the young writers, to give up at least the convention of hope, I will say the following: Suppose that we were to be granted larger publishing plans at this conference, during which important political persons are taking part, especially since we all know that these plans are being cut right now, in another room, here, in Bucharest. Suppose we could have enough paper, publishing space, royalties, which have all remained the same since before we were born. Suppose we could believe that the scholarships which arrive at the

Culture Council will be given to us, and we will at least get to see Bulgaria. Unless, of course, someone stamps "No!" on an invitation, somewhere here again, in some room in Bucharest.

Suppose I were to believe, with unlimited optimism, that writers still meant something in this country. In spite of the fact that I myself witnessed an embarrassing scene when thirty-five writers, headed by the President of the Union, waited for more than one hour, accompanied by people from state television, at the plant "23rd of August," where there were fifteen people in a room, who knew all the small, unpleasant details about us, details that were fatally connected with a handful of dust, but willingly disregarded the fact that they had studied many of us in school.

We work for years to write a book. Books are the concrete form of our work. Paradoxically, our field of activity is the only one in which you are fined if you produce too much. You are not allowed to publish more than a book a year, that is, you are not allowed to produce more than what fits into one book. How very careful!

I now address the comrades of the presidium, those whose salaries end with many zeros. My question is: Do you think getting 10,000 lei for a book which contains three or four years' work is so much? The 10,000 lei are not for one month, dear comrades in the presidium, but appear once every five years. Which means 2,000 per year, 136 lei per month, 5.5 lei per day. Is it really unforgivable if we work for five years and then print two books during the same year? Two books that yield 10,000 lei each? Lots of people who belong to our category of optimists say in such cases, "HE does not help because HE does not know. It's not his fault, poor man. HE knows nothing at all about it. But if HE found out, everything would be different." Consequently, here I stand, telling you the truth. Lest anyone should say, 'I had no idea.'

A young writer has a social standing which is worse than precarious. He does not live in a villa, but in a studio or apartment which is not provided by the state and which he is compelled to buy. He works in an institution for 2,500 lei per month, and once every few years he can earn 10,000 lei. So this is the origin of his enthusiasm.

A year ago, the Communist Youth Union, the Youth Tourism Office, the Council of Culture and other leading organisms who are bent on making us feel comfortable, promised a group of thirty-five young writers that they would be allowed to travel abroad, paying for it, of course. For two months we hoped and were happy. In the end, all we managed to do was ruin our holidays, to feel embittered and pour some more enthusiasm in our writings, of course, because we understood how well we were being taken care of.

I wonder, if I say today what I am saying now, is anyone willing to hear me? Will anyone be willing to understand that if you do not have enough of something, if there is no material or moral token, no matter how little, that your work is valued, you just hate falsifying this reality and saying that it is pink? The color pink, so dear to some, can't possibly originate in police grey, whatever we do. I wish to say that in the end, everything we said here was properly understood. This ending contains the same despairing hope which a dictionary of synonyms ought to equate to willing naiveté."

**L. V.** And what was the reaction of the audience?

**D. C.** It was pretty tough. For about two years, I was not allowed to publish. I could not even go on a trip with other young writers.

**L. V.** Who forbade it?

**D. C.** I did not even try very hard. The hostility was obvious. One night my poems were expelled from *Literary Romania.* I was told that it was no use trying again. I was resigned, even afraid. They reduced the number of people in the publishing house. My income was at stake. I would have been the first one fired. I was not going to make any more trouble because I had no income other than my salary. It would have been thoughtless of me to keep irritating them.

**L. V.** When you did that, didn't you think that you might get into trouble?

**D. C.** At that moment, I was under a kind of anaesthesia. I was angry, because the people from the Communist Youth Organization came to us in the corridor and asked us to speak about how happy we were. Because this conference was a fiasco from the point of view of the political leaders, no other conference was approved after that. It might not have happened if they had not provoked Dinescu and me, if they had not signed us up on the speakers' list. They told us that we had to say that we had received material help, houses, trips abroad. . . . It seemed like sheer impudence to me. I lived in a rented flat, and they wanted me to say that I had been given a house of my own. But even if I had lived in a villa, knowing what my colleagues went through, I think I would have acted in the same way.

It was their doing, I would say, as Ceaușescu did it to himself at that last assembly. They knew that they were in control and would refrain from nothing. They ordered you to do absurd things.

Well, with writers they had a hard time doing that. They did not realize exactly how far they could go. I would like to know if those writers who praised them and wrote scripts for huge manifestations ever got anything. Except for the fact that they were not in danger of being fired, which was an important point, I am very curious about what kinds of advantages they enjoyed. They could not have enjoyed the advantages of the fifties, when, if you praised the party a lot, you could get a villa, a black car, and driver, and you were included in school textbooks. Because it did pay initially. But that changed as time passed. I think the writers who did it later, did so out of a kind of obedience which frightens me. No spine at all. They liked lowering themselves. I have the feeling the high-ranking political persons did not like them too much, they did not really appreciate them; I think they despised them. They took it for granted. All writers should be like that. That's how they thought. This is what servants or court fools were supposed to do. But they were angry when the others did not do it, even though they had no compassion for the others. A writer was a dubious person: a citizen who does not work and lives off other peoples' backs.

**L. V.** How did one go about publishing a book in Romania?

**D. C.** All publishing houses in the former socialist system operated according to the same procedure: the writer went to the publishing house and left his book there. The publishing plan was made on a yearly basis, according to the allocated sum. So many books of poetry, fiction, criticism, but only in the case of a large publishing house. For several hundred places, there were many books already there, hoping to be published. It was a kind of competition. You could not publish a book when you wanted it, pay to have it printed, as it happens in the West. A selection had to be made. If you were not ideologically correct, you did not stand much of a chance. The chosen books were those which praised the party and the homeland.

**L. V.** You mean the "waste paper"?

**D. C.** Exactly. They were the privileged books, which amounted to nearly half the room. For the rest of the places, which were allotted to the aesthetic, so to say, the competition was based on value. When a writer managed to be included in the plan, it meant that he had a good book. Of course, that "good" book would be changed to varying degrees by the censors. But the censors could not make you add twenty patriotic poems. They would have liked to do that, but serious people never accepted.

Well, anyway, a book had to pass many tests before it was published. A writer who did not praise the party, and who managed to have two or three books, could be considered a serious writer. That's how it was.

July 1992

# Poetry

## The Tunnel

The rotten rails, the dark iron.
Metal taste on your palate.
Not even fear.
At a few kilometres' distance, a few pages alter
the mouth of the tunnel.
A while later.
It will come, it is bound to come.
Like a dark cat springing
from the landscape beyond.
From this point on the rails
From the zero level of chance
sniffing the smell of smoke, of red-hot iron.
The mouth of the tunnel,
in which a few friends are cramming
the gag of luxuriant grass, illusion, cheering up words.
A huge green eye staring at you.
Behind it, the tunnel, the optic nerve which enlivens
the other landscape.
And you here, at the zero level of chance
on all fours, polishing the rails, warming them up with your breath
with your wing.
Worker by the day. By the hour.
By the moment.

## The Monster

I have no memory. I have worked hard
to reach this state.
I clutched with my claws and teeth
at the corpse still throbbing with blood
of each past moment.
I have no incidents.
All my incidents are now
the property of other people.
I survive. I look back
and my stare gives birth behind me
to salt columns and mountains of tears
all turned to stone.

## Distance

I was told it was somewhere very far away.
Well, I said, used as I was to huge icy distances
of memory, behind which, during another age,
even the distance between two hugs
seemed a misfortune to me.
Well, how far away?
A few hundred kilometres, maybe even a few thousand,
they answered. Beyond a few mountain chains,
beyond a sea. Is this far away to you?—I shouted
weeping with joy.
It's wonderful, wonderful,
if it can be still measured in common nouns
in terrestrial units of measure.
I am only afraid of the distance
smelling of the sky, crushed down on earth
impossible to be squeezed in any words.

## The Vampiriad

What are you doing there, far away?

In order to write this, I had to take from you
a few moments of breathing in and out.
My words no longer remember you.
They do not miss you.
They have hardly learnt how to forget you.
A flight of ravens and a pack of wolves.
They only sniff
at your body smelling of the end.
Like this, with each of my lines,
your life grows smaller. Night is morning
and morning is noon.
Good God, how I loved you and cannot protect you!
I have shed a sea of tears and, look,
this starving pack has drunk it all.
Look how we lie in ambush together.
See how all verbs go by
like dusty soldiers,
towards the past tense of the narrative.
While I am compelled to write this story
in which there is nothing any more.
I am writing it with the hand that caresses you,

my murderous hand
my hand on which the blood of your soul
flows down, still fresh and alive.

## The Mole below the Temple

As if nothing were happening to me
I am waiting for the morning.
The juggler's circle falls—bump—exactly
at my feet.
Very well, thank you. And you?
My eviscerated words
polish adverbials: of place and of time.
At fixed hours,
more neuter than Switzerland
the gestures, the pulse, the stare.

But the cold mole takes me to its underground tunnels
night after night.

What do you see there, say sooner,
what do you see, it urges  pushing me
deeper and deeper, digging new tunnels
with the cut tongue of my words
with my shout in whose placenta
memory lives.

## Slope

The mountain, the frozen peal of laughter, the salty stalactite
image up which I scramble with my claws and teeth
redeeming—precious analysis of the tear
my illegal copy—this poem.
Craggy and steep memory climbed up again and again
you will fall down I shall fall down
alpinistka maia daragaia maia

## The Raft of the Medusa Raft

I took a lot of years to find out
that nobody was waiting for me outside.
Year by year I toiled
for this floating triangle.
Year by year

I kept feeding Imagination
this beast which gulps me down
whenever I am afraid.

## Breath

My hand which is writing
penetrating the white of the paper, its flesh
cold and neuter, sinking to the shoulder, to the last
wink of the eyelid. A suicide
which is elegant
almost perfect.

## Ground

I thought  I was
a word
turned upside down in his huge pupil
which forgives
all my sins
in his pupil which bears with me and keeps me
under the Ray
in his pupil which is always awake.
And so it was
when I still thought I was deciphered
by his great bounty
until I felt my
a-ni-mal smell
until I saw rotting in the ground
the stone claw
of the sad tiger that's me.

# Denisa Comănescu

born 1954

*Poet, translator: she is editor in chief of the Univers publishing house, Bucharest*

## Our Father Only at Home

**Lidia Vianu:** You were an editor of the English department for the Univers publishing house between 1978–1993, when you became the editor in chief. What was your experience of censorship?

**Denisa Comănescu:** Censorship was an institution which affected Romanian culture in various ways, on various levels of intensity, applied to all fields, particularly literature. The paradox was that it kept a milder eye on foreign literature translated into Romanian than on Romanian literature itself. Univers used to be the major publishing house which brought out foreign literature, criticism, philosophy, culture. It actually was the only one with such status, the other publishers including very few foreign books in their catalogues. There were, of course, strict rules and restrictions for publication. They aimed at ideology, ideas, religion, sex, and reached down to small details, when mere words were forbidden. Books and authors were banned, black listed, such as black utopias (*1984* and *Animal Farm* by George Orwell, *Brave New World* by A. Huxley). It was quite funny when we published *Sons and Lovers* by D. H. Lawrence, and the censor from the Ministry of Culture actually provided his own makeup for the love scenes, cutting off intimate details, replacing two male characters by a male and a female.

From an official point of view, censorship worked on four levels. The editor himself was supposed to be the first censor, yet he actually fought censorship the most in order to see the book out. He was sometimes sacked or reassigned to a menial job for doing it, which was a radical price to pay.

The next step was censorship proper. All manuscripts were directed to the inferior level of censorship, known as the Editorial Central House. The latter was founded in 1971, after Ceauşescu's famous visit to China, when the intellectual witch hunt started.

When the manuscript had been approved of by this department of the Ministry of Culture, it went to the superior body of censors of the same Ministry, who were the strictest and the most official. These people working for censorship were all graduates of some university, even remarkably good in their own field, translators and even writers, some of them. They knew all the codes of censorship, what could be allowed to be printed and what was definitely forbidden, but they were human, after all: some would negotiate, others could even close an eye, but most of them were actually afraid of losing their jobs. Once in the game, they had to stick to the rules.

As far as translations were concerned, Univers was privileged with flexible censors. Consequently, even before 1989, we could publish updated criticism, theory, and philosophy or culture.

It so happened that a few days before the end of 1989 Univers published *The Last Days of Pompeii*. The book had been prevented from appearing by censorship for years on end. The idea was that the readers should not be panicked by the book, which might remind them of the 1977 earthquake in Romania, and they should be protected from any contact with the luxury and deprivation of the Roman aristocracy.

In 1970 we published De Quincey's *Confessions of an Opium-Eater*. In 1971, at the bedside of a famous serial woman killer the police found this book all underlined. The book was withdrawn from the market as well as from all libraries. Although I tried hard to republish the book, I could not do that until 1990.

Publishing Swift's satires in 1985, I myself fought a lot with the censor in order to include *A Modest Proposal*, concerning eating Irish children, which had become subversive here, on account of the meat shortage in Romania. Faced with the alternative of not publishing the book at all or doing it without the famous text, I gave it up.

The supreme level of censorship was a department of the Party Central Committee. It mainly focussed on Romanian literature.

**L. V.** Do you remember your first encounter with censorship?

**D. C.** It was at a very early age. I must have been five or six. My father used to talk to our chickens, making sure in this way that no one could know what he was saying. When he gave them water in his casket, kept from World War II, he told them a little song known by most intellectuals at the time. You could easily go to prison for humming it. The song was about ideological extremes that always meet. It ran like that: "Iron Guard man, do not be sad/ With the Communist Party you go ahead." I enjoyed the rhyme and repeated it during a party. The grownups were all scared stiff. Later on that day, my father explained to me that certain things could be uttered only at home, while others could be shouted anywhere: he listened to Radio Free Europe—which I always did, years later, as it was one of our few contacts with reality in the 1980's—but I was not supposed to tell anyone. It was the beginning of the schizophrenic way of thinking: I had to live in two worlds at once.

When I was in second grade, our school mistress questioned us whether we went to church or not, and told us God did not exist. I remember a short poem I published in my third book of poems in 1987, about what happened then. It was entitled *My Father:* "School in the rain like a boat adrift./ Second grade kids write faster/ they like the composition this time/ they will fight during the break:/ my father is stronger, no, mine is./ A little girl watching the rain/ the school mistress tells her to write/ she watches the rain/ the mistress is annoyed and menaces her./ Will she punish her?/ A lightning cuts off the kids' heads/ a few scream all scared./ The little girl starts writing:/ "Grandma taught me Our Father/ to be said only at home."

# Poetry

### Provocation

Somebody has reckoned right.
On such a real morning
and fresh,
the eye might have rent it
in a jiffy
if it could,
I met an armour.
People passed by and did not see it,
it turned up for my imagination on purpose.
Spider caught in another kind of web
than his,
ship wrecked on the beam of a lighthouse
in mid sea,
my soul did not want it.
Do come on
dress me
I am the perfect manager
for you
no dominion shall have
love, hate
I am etherreality.
As if in a nightmare
I am wandering across the city,
in magnetic cuffs
it caught my breath
nobody sees it
I alone feel the dark iron
dipping in the blood
move after move. Sssoo.
And I lack the strength.
Poor country
For every ten pheasants just one hare
like a manger the grey feathers,
with the bloody blade
we peel the fur off the warm body,
almandine statuette
fresh flakes cover stiff eyes
like a halo.

# Florin Bican

born 1956

*Writer of fiction in English, living in Germany.*

## Language behind Gilded Bars

**Lidia Vianu:** What had you been doing till 1989?

**Florin Bican:** Writing under cover. After graduation from the university, in 1980, I was posted as a Russian teacher in a village near Bucharest. I left the job after three years to work as a translator at a Bucharest water research institute, which was closer to my university than my former job. In space and spirit, I mean, since I had written my thesis on the expressive recurrence of water in the works of James Joyce. Since 1990, I have been working for the Writers' Union.

**L. V.** What would you say has changed in your life as a writer?

**F. B.** Internally, nothing. Outwardly, many blind alleys have been opened, but I am still unable to take them. Back in 1982, I found it was impossible to go on writing poetry in Romanian, because the language had been taken away from me by vile propaganda. My own words were sort of mocking at me from the papers, radio, TV, speeches of all kinds, and finally propaganda threatened to seep into private conversations, and ultimately into my stream of consciousness. Perhaps I overreacted. Lots of writers went on writing in Romanian, but I felt I couldn't. I dried up.

For a couple of weeks, after working for two years as a teacher, I was totally at a loss, because writing poetry was my way of reappropriating reality. But the end of expression turned out to be the end of perception, in my case. I couldn't perceive what I couldn't express. So I lingered in this creative limbo for some time, until, one morning, I was struck by a poem in English. It just came into my mind, and in the beginning I thought I was quoting to myself, and, trying to locate the author in the muddled corridors of my memory, I found out the author was myself. From that moment on, I went on writing poetry in English, and it felt like I was breathing again.

Ten years later, and a very eventful ten years, it was, I find I can't switch back to Romanian. The moment I try writing poetry in Romanian, the old propagandistic embarrassment is back again, and I feel like a Pavlovian dog, for which every word in Romanian is a ringing bell.

**L. V.** Has the language changed according to politics? Has our political situation changed much, as compared to what was before 1989 (which I purposely avoid calling a "revolution")?

**F. B.** No, the language hasn't changed at all, because language is, and always will be, the prisoner of thought. As long as thought is a cage, the language will be chirping behind bars. You might argue that sound carries through bars, but the spirit will always be on the wrong side of the bars. Any political changes that might have occurred could only put the language behind gilded bars. One cannot expect instant recovery after almost fifty years of the disease called communism, which is as destructive as AIDS, I daresay, because it aims at the very cell of our physical and spiritual structure.

In 1989, we thought the communist cancer had been scalpeled off. But as I see it now, a bizarre system was grafted on the body of Romania, and now we are confronted with a galloping communisto-capitalistic centaur.

**L. V.** Since you did not try to publish under censorship, can I assume you were not affected by its effects in your English writings?

**F. B.** All the time I thought I was writing for myself. I am aware now I am guilty of an act of hubris. No writer has ever been writing for him or herself. The writer is constantly shadowed by a readership. By writing for myself, I willingly put myself in prison, considering myself, as Hamlet did, king of infinite space.

**L. V.** Do you feel censorship has disappeared, for you?

**F. B.** A strange phrase from the *Book of Mormon* comes to mind: "Where there is no law, there is no punishment." I could paraphrase this to: where there is no writing, there is no censorship. Censorship is an ongoing condition of writing, but the nature of censorship makes the hell of a difference. It's not hard to choose between the communist type of censorship and its capitalistic version. I'd have the latter any time, although some writers find the former more stimulating.

December 1992

# Simona Popescu

**born 1965**

*Poet, lecturer of Romanian literature*

## The Black Holes

**Lidia Vianu:** How did you react to censorship as a very young poet? What did it mean to you? What do you think is going to happen now that the old censorship is said to have disappeared?

**Simona Popescu:** Until December 22, 1989, censorship in Romania possessed all the mystery of the black holes in outer space. The deep, troubled waters of cultural bureaucracy could swallow any book, leaving no trace of it at all, no hope that it might be printed. Ever. We all knew that it was exerted by people alien to culture, who acted randomly, not governed by criteria, but whimsically and out of instinct. Censorship was a kind of inhibition at all levels, not just the official level. There was the self-censorship of authors who conceived their books thinking of it all the time.

Then there was the inhibition (form of violent self-defense) of the editors who prepared the book; they took into account possible further reactions. In fact, only some of the editors were sympathetic; the others were worse than the censors themselves. Whether that was out of opportunism, stupidity or evil nature, I wouldn't know. To the normal mind, that mechanism was impossible to understand. Some very benign books were rejected, while others, which were really aggressive and inflaming, were accepted. Some authors (not necessarily the most dangerous) were rejected *de plano*, while others were published fairly regularly, although they had not really compromised. What I mean is that there was an absurd and confusing net of privileges, even as far as offensive texts were concerned. A poem containing "lizards," which was written by some well known poet, could be printed. But the dissenting poems of someone who had hardly ever published were constantly rejected. In a paradoxical way, the more integrated into the system you appeared to be, the better you could flirt with the idea of revolt. Censorship was the most whimsical of all activities. It was down-right frivolous, I would say. Even now, I fail to understand the mixture of con-tradictory things, of shrewdness, of bargaining, privileges, compromises, which characterized both the officials and the writers themselves.

A very special situation was that of young authors who, about the end of the '80s, had lost all hope of ever publishing a book. Being young was a grievous fault. The power had its perfect system. You begin to refuse to continue doing it until they give in, lose all confidence in themselves and their personality is extinct; you can turn them into unimportant writers, who are satisfied with any-thing they can get. Beginning in 1983, the collective debut (collectivization of culture) was imposed as a kind of "communist test" which could lead you fur-ther, to the heaven of publication. . . . The collective debut (anthologies includ-ing between three and thirty writers) became a form of fulfilling the plan of cul-tural production, and also a way of levelling values, amalgamating them, and disarming the few good ones who managed to make it through. I am not speak-ing about those who were rejected, left to ripen until they were ready to give in. Like lately, even though the humiliating debut contests of the publishing hous-es were abolished, chances to publish simply vanished.

Cultural magazines, on the other hand, discouraged and did not accept young writers. As in other fields, young writers had to undergo long probation periods in order to be noticed by some writers. From this point of view, grey hair was an advantage. For these years, youth was a kind of concentration camp: after surviving it, if you behaved yourself, you might be accepted as a writer.

The only way of acting like a writer was in the literary circles, led by the best critics, where the atmosphere and the circulation of ideas were really stim-ulating. This "oral" form of culture, shared by young authors and a few of the best-known writers, proved ultimately to have been useful. It was a circle within which the cultural act had an intensity and spontaneity which was more alive than in other places, perhaps also because of the fact that everything took place *à chaud*. At the same time, the circle was a place of normality, where commu-nist behavior (based on humility, extraliterary precautions, privileges, dissimu-lation, etc.) was not required.

We were confronted with several strategies for existing in a culture which bordered on abnormality: the way of those who make political compromises, thus helping their careers, the way of those who make aesthetic concessions, the way of those who did what they thought they should do and found them-selves isolated to the furthest limit and the way of those who waited twenty years for their debut. . . . The sociopolitical context offered two alternatives: try-ing somehow to become integrated, to adjust and endure while trying to find your way, or trying to ignore it, to defy it, escape from all cultural fields, trying to be absolutely free while writing, yet aware that publication was impossible and that this was, after all, not the most important thing.

The latter idea could even be stimulating. It is true that we could afford thinking (with a special satisfaction which some people could not understand) that we would stand aside five or ten years (we never thought that Ceauşescu would last longer than that), because it is an easier thing to do when you are nineteen or twenty (I mean the writers who were my age).

Many writers tried to do both, to make it through censorship and win the admiration of the audience with small acts of shrewdly hidden courage. I found this shrewdness somehow disgusting, although it did cheat the censors who were very careful. These strategies which put the censors to sleep were numerous: from codes to hermetic language, general parable, and Aesopic texts. Some methods were invented (and promptly accepted by our comrades, the censors) by the editors themselves. The more pessimistic texts would be accepted if they were written about some town in the rotten capitalist world, even if the authors had never seen that town. They just had to mention it at the end of the poem. Other manuscripts had to accept political additions which would keep the cultural activists busy cleaning them and make them content they had done their duty by expelling what was ideologically wrong.

After 1989, the papers actually wrote about a kind of literature created under the compulsion of censorship, a literature of refinement, hints, ambiguity, plays upon words, artistic intelligence where the readers learned to decode the messages. These textual strategies, created by a regiment of activists who checked everything, consequently led to perfecting the complicity between reader and writer, which is pleasing even today, but it also caused alienation and deep lack of authenticity.

Those who chose to ignore the context, thus refusing to integrate, had the advantage of total freedom. Their only audience was the literary circles mentioned above. At their best, they sometimes brought together fifty to sixty people, mainly writers or students. You were presented with a genuine and also professional audience who knew world literature very well, in spite of hard conditions. Even the idea that there might be security agents among them was stimulating. This freedom did not prompt us to write primitive protest texts. We all knew what resistance literature had meant within the context of universal culture: it was so boring and empty! "Tough" texts (some written with the permission of the officials) existed of course. But what interested me personally was the description of a more complicated reality, of human inner life, besieged by obstacles and interdictions. I was not interested in compromising my literature with officialities or in small revolt. I was interested in the vehemence of the artist who doubts everything, who is ill with discontent. The evil was not necessarily inherent in the system. It was a general Evil—everyone's evil—pertaining to human nature, and therefore incurable.

What has amazed me since December 1989, was the desire for texts that were up to date, incisive, strong, tough, political, not only for Romanian journals, but for foreign ones as well. I saw with my own eyes how revolt and misery were used as goods, converted into consumer goods. I partially understood this reaction, but it also made me indignant. It was a new kind of restriction: "Give us something very short and tough," "Give us something very political," etc. I found this trade with suffering disgusting. These were frustration and other expensive merchandise "made in Eastern Europe." This seems to have subsided in the meantime. The West has had enough of cultural news from totalitarianism. Their appetite for daily horror has been appeased. The word, however sharp, has no more power or value here.

We have entered a new stage of political strategy: indifference. How can we oppose it? This is a reality which finds us unprepared. It is an area which the Romanian writer is only now discovering. . . .

June 1991

# Index